Trinity and History

Princeton Theological Monograph Series

K. C. Hanson, Charles M. Collier, D. Christopher Spinks,
and Robin A. Parry, Series Editors

Trinity and History

The God-World Relation in the Theology
of Dorner, Barth, Pannenberg, and Jenson

Scott P. Rice

☞PICKWICK *Publications* · Eugene, Oregon

TRINITY AND HISTORY
The God-World Relation in the Theology of Dorner, Barth, Pannenberg,
and Jenson

Princeton Theological Monograph Series 246

Pickwick Publications
An Imprint of Wipf and Stock Publishers
199 W. 8th Ave., Suite 3
Eugene, OR 97401

www.wipfandstock.com

PAPERBACK ISBN: 978-1-5326-6812-8
HARDCOVER ISBN: 978-1-5326-6813-5
EBOOK ISBN: 978-1-5326-6814-2

Cataloguing-in-Publication data:

Names: Rice, Scott P., author.

Title: Trinity and history : the God-world relation in the theology of Dorner,
Barth, Pannenberg, and Jenson / by Scott P. Rice.

Description: Eugene, OR : Pickwick Publications, 2022 | Princeton Theological
Monograph Series 246 | Includes bibliographical references.

Identifiers: ISBN 978-1-5326-6812-8 (paperback) | ISBN 978-1-5326-6813-5
(hardcover) | ISBN 978-1-5326-6814-2 (ebook)

Subjects: LCSH: Trinity—History of doctrines. | Dorner, I. A. (Isaak August),
1809–1884. | Barth, Karl, 1886–1968—Contributions in doctrine of the Trin-
ity. | Pannenberg, Wolfhart, 1928– —Contributions in concept of the Trinity. |
Jenson, Robert W—Criticism and interpretation.

Classification: BT111.2 .R53 2022 (print) | BT111.2 .R53 (ebook)

04/08/22

Select, slightly modified paragraphs from the following essay by the author of this work appear in chapter 2. Scott P. Rice. "'Unchangeably Alive': Karl Barth's Trinitarian Doctrine of the Divine Constancy." *Canadian Theological Review* 4.2 (2015): 1-10. Used by permission.

Select, slightly modified paragraphs from the following essay by the author of this work appear in chapter 4. Scott P. Rice. "Timely, Transcendent, and Alive: Trinity in Robert W. Jenson's Understanding of the God-World Relation." *Pro Ecclesia* 28.3: 253-66. Used by permission (SAGE publications).

For Abigail Rice, in loving gratitude for your support

Contents

Acknowledgments

THIS BOOK IS A substantially revised form of my dissertation from the ThD program in Theology at Harvard Divinity School. I wish to express my gratitude to those who assisted me in this project. First of all I am thankful to the members who served on my committee: Francis Schüssler Fiorenza, David Lamberth, and Michelle Sanchez. I am thankful for the wisdom, guidance, and encouragement given to me by my adviser, Professor Schüssler Fiorenza. His support and patient assistance in helping me shape my own theological voice has been invaluable. Professor Lamberth helped me in crafting this project through his guidance during coursework, general exams, and preparing the prospectus, and the way that he challenges students to craft an argument has been a great benefit to me. I am grateful to Professor Sanchez for processing the theological arguments of this work with me and her willingness to examine how theology bears on the life and practices of the church community and her exemplary approach to teaching. Beyond the members of my committee, I note the fond memory I have of reading the *Church Dogmatics* with my first advisor, Professor Ronald Thiemann, alongside a small group of students at his home in Concord, Massachusetts before his sudden and regrettable passing in the fall of 2012.

I am the sort of theologian that takes theology to be in service of the church. Over the past nine years, however, there has been a specific church community that has shown me and my family great hospitality. I am grateful to the pastoral staff and community at Highrock Covenant Church in Boston, Massachusetts for the many ways they have supported my work. Several others have been exceedingly helpful in seeing this work come to fruition. I owe thanks to Catherine Barsotti (Fuller Theological Seminary), F. Dale Bruner (Whitworth College), Harvey Cox Jr. (Harvard Divinity School), Darrell Guder (Princeton Theological Seminary), George Hunsinger (Princeton Seminary), Robert K. Johnston (Fuller Seminary), and Bruce L. McCormack (Princeton Seminary). Each has played a formative role in my theological development. Robert W. Jenson was kind enough to meet with me in the early stages of my doctoral program and while writing the dissertation form of this work. His passing in 2017 was a great loss to the church and theological studies. I am thankful to both him and his spouse, Blanche, for welcoming me into their home. I am also thankful to friends and colleagues who have been encouraging dialogue partners along the way, especially Matthew Aragon-Bruce, William Barnett, David Chao, Meghan DeJong, John Drury, Ryan Gregg, Aaron Griffith, Joel Guerra, Logan Hoffman, David Kim, and Justina Torrance.

Above all, I must thank my family for their encouragement and care. I have been able to undertake this project because of the values and work ethic instilled in me by my parents, Bill and Karen. My mother-in-law, Marcia, has been a continual source of encouragement, also freeing me to read and write with the childcare that she has provided for our family. My wife and I welcomed our first child into the world just before I began the dissertation form of this work. Our second child was born while revising it. They are a great source of joy to me. To go from writing on trinitarian metaphysics to a Daniel Tiger teatime with a toddler, and then back to the metaphysics, is a wonderfully bewildering experience that has helped me better appreciate the precious nature of life in sometimes quite different ways. Most importantly, I thank my spouse, Abby. Her capacity to empathize when the challenges of this work weighed down on me, and her encouragement and wisdom have sustained me throughout this process. I cannot adequately say just how grateful I am to her and just how much I appreciate her love, care, and support; but I am and I do. I dedicate this work to her.

Introduction

How does God relate to the world? What difference does our understanding of God's being make for conceiving of God's relation to us? If God has become incarnate in Christ, if God somehow shares created history with us, how should we think about eternity? How should we think about divine transcendence? This book addresses these questions by way of a theological inquiry into Christianity's foundational concept for God: Trinity. More specifically, this work reflects on how the doctrine of the Trinity provides a solution to the problem of understanding the relation between divine and created reality. The Christian theological tradition has historically understood the eternal reality of God in a timeless way. As Augustine writes, "in eternity nothing moves into the past: all is present."[1] And as Boethius famously states, eternity is the totally simultaneous and perfect possession of unending life.[2] In his adaptation of Boethius' idea of eternity, Thomas Aquinas claims that God "is present to all time," and "his glance is carried from eternity over all things as they are in their presentiality."[3] However, the timeless conception of eternity raises some obvious and difficult questions. Above all, how does a timeless God become incarnate? How does a timeless God live out a history with others? This study enters into a conversation on the way that the doctrine of the Trinity can inform our understanding of the God-world relation. Tweaking the second question above, this study asks: What difference does Trinity make in a theological attempt to square the eternal life of God with the vitality of God revealed among us?

Two points illuminate the basic background from which the study proceeds. First, the thesis of this work is set within the context of the revitalization of the classical doctrine of the Trinity in contemporary theology. Immanuel Kant once remarked that the "doctrine of the Trinity, taken

1. Augustine, *Confessions*, XI.11. Cf. Augustine, *De Trinitate*, IV.47.

2. Boethius, *Consolation of Philosophy*, V.VI.10. While Boethius makes the novel move of identifying eternity with the divine life itself, his definition has been received in the tradition mainly as the absence of time. See the example from Thomas Aquinas that follows, as well as *Summa Theologica*, 1.10.1. See also Peters, *God as Trinity*, 148.

3. Aquinas, *Summa Theologica*, 1.14.13; 1.57.3.

literally, has no practical relevance at all."[4] And as recent as the middle of the twentieth century, Claude Welch could still lament Trinity's place in prominent strands of modern theology as a "doctrine of the second rank."[5] This all changed, however, in the final third of the twentieth century. It is now widely acknowledged that the doctrine of the Trinity has come to fully occupy a central place in constructive theological reflection. One can readily find Trinity being put to use in the theological interpretation of Scripture, debates on personhood and subjectivity, gender studies, inter-religious dialogue, and much more.[6]

The second is a practical concern. This is a work in theology that follows the Augustinian-Anselmian dictum of *faith seeking understanding*. The use of Trinity in reflecting on the God-world relation in this study is meant to aid in understanding already existing beliefs in realities like divine presence and the sovereignty of God. I show how a trinitarian idea of God can resource a theological account of God's relation to history that builds on these and other basic beliefs of the Christian faith. Relatedly, this work upholds the sentiment behind the slogan with which Karl Barth begins his *Church Dogmatics*: theology serves *church* proclamation. One of the central tasks of this study is to put forward an understanding of divine presence and the transcendence of God as simultaneously true, that is, to hold at the same time. To underscore the full presence of God in Jesus as the incarnate Son neither nullifies nor competes with the sovereignty and (omni)presence of God in and over all creation. To be able to wholeheartedly affirm the truth of God's presence, to say to others, to the suffering and the dying, God is *with us*—God is with *you*—is a statement of immense pastoral significance. Equally important, though more conceptual, is to be able to say this without a divided perception of God's being: of God with us or God below, present in the contingencies of creaturely reality, and God above, utterly transcendent in the absolute character of the divine nature; in short, two Gods. The solution to a problem like this lies in a trinitarian idea of God. I argue that Trinity affords an understanding of divine presence and transcendence to hold at once—one Trinity, with us by means of the transcendent liveliness of God's own being.

Utilizing the doctrine of the Trinity, this work addresses the relationship between God and history in four theological figures: Isaak A. Dorner, Karl Barth, Wolfhart Pannenberg, and Robert W. Jenson. Each of these

---

4. Kant, *The Conflict of the Faculties*, 65–67.

5. Welch, *In This Name*, 3–9.

6. For a sample overview of different applications of trinitarian theology, see Green et al., *The Trinity among the Nations*; Adiprasetya, *An Imaginative Glimpse*; Johnson, *Quest for the Living God*, 202–26; LaCugna, *God for Us*.

figures attends to the way that God's revelatory activity in history proceeds from the Trinity of God's being. In this way they take part in a tradition that includes Athanasius, Aquinas, Luther, Edwards, Hegel, and a host of contemporary theologians, such as Hans Urs von Balthasar, Leonardo Boff, Catherine Mowry LaCugna, Kathryn Tanner, and Miroslav Volf. More specifically and in highlighting the contextual nature of all theology, the central questions of this study derive from and are situated mostly explicitly within the German theological tradition as extended into English-language scholarship of the North Atlantic region. As I show, the historical and contextual connections which link together the four central figures of this study provide a rich supply of material that I build into the constructive analyses of this work. This often takes shape through the reception of theological ideas and their redeployment. For example, as I explore in chapter 2, Barth takes over Dorner's doctrine of divine immutability in his treatment of divine constancy in *Church Dogmatics* II/1. However, Dorner's idea of immutability can be seen to undergo a subtle but significant modification by Barth in *Church Dogmatics* II/2 in order to bring the vibrancy of God's history with us into closer alignment with God's unchanging being. Furthermore, while I treat each theological figure separately, increasingly bringing the relevant connections between them to bear as the work unfolds, the individual chapters of this book work together in order to provide a general outline of God's relation to history. After clarifying the main problem of reconciling the eternal being of God with the vitality of God in history, I turn to the use of Trinity for an understanding of God's living relation to history that takes into account three essential dynamics: the link between God's *pre-temporal* eternity and God's revealed history; the *inner-historical* vitality of God; and God's *transcendent-eschatological* relation to history.

The subject of God's living or real relation to history is contested. Thomas Aquinas famously states, since "God is outside the whole order of creation, and all creatures are ordered to Him, and not conversely, it is manifest that creatures are really related to God Himself; whereas in God there is no real relation to creatures, but a relation only in idea."[7] By rejecting a real relation to the world, according to William J. Hill, Thomas does not mean the absence of an actual relation with created reality, but the absence of one that designates "an ontic determination of deity, a passive dependence upon creatures."[8] The efforts I make in this study to speak of God's living or real relation to history do not mean that God is at the whim of creatures or creaturely reality. In relating to the world God remains

---

7. Aquinas, *Summa Theologica*, 1.13.7.

8. Hill, *The Three-Personed God*, 213.

sovereign Lord over and in all of the various parts of God's creation. My aim in this study rather is to explore and tease out the possibilities for understanding some of the particularities of God's living relation to the world through Trinity as a theological resource. This study is thus similar in intention to the claim of Thomistic scholar W. Norris Clarke when he writes, in God's triune being receptivity is "present in the Son and the Spirit . . . as a pure perfection of existence at its highest."[9] Receptivity, in other words, is not alien to God but characteristic of God's being insofar as God is triune. How does such a conception of God's being, specifically as a perfection of God's triunity, open up new possibilities for understanding God as not only active but also receptive in relation to us, in hearing and responding to the prayers of the faithful and so on? My concern in this work is not divine receptivity per se, though I do treat the question of whether history somehow determines God's being. Rather, my central concern is how the idea of God as triune can help to inform an understanding of the transcendent movement and presence of God in time and the process of history. How does the triune God act and move among us based on the internal movements of God as Father, Son, and Spirit?[10]

The topic of God's relation to the world involves the divine attributes. I treat several of them over the course of this study that bear on God's living relation to history, specifically those that touch on divine transcendence and the reality of God's presence with us. The question above on whether history determines God's being points ahead to an engagement with the doctrine of divine immutability. Does God change? How does a trinitarian idea of God impact our understanding of whether (or how) God changes in God's living relation to history? Also important are the doctrines of divine infinity and eternity. I largely leave aside two closely related themes: im/passability and divine foreknowledge. I attend to questions of God and the (self-)constitution of God's being in the events of Christ's life, death, and resurrection, but a definitive position on the question of im/passability goes beyond the scope of this study. The im/passability question is both deeply significant and highly divisive in contemporary theology.[11] Likewise, the theme of divine foreknowledge could be addressed at different points in this work. Because of the central place of matters of divine ontology in this study, I focus rather on the question of the presence of the future to God, or, put somewhat crassly, God's physical presence to the future.

9. Clarke, *Person and Being*, 20–21, 82–87.

10. For a similar expression that anticipates many of the arguments in this work, see Balthasar, *Mysterium Paschale*, 28.

11. For a helpful discussion on im/passability, see Keating and White, *Divine Impassability and the Mystery of Human Suffering*.

Outline of Work

The chapter outline of this book is as follows: I make use of the work of the mediating theologian Isaak A. Dorner in chapter 1 in lieu of a longer introduction here to the theme of God's relation to history. The engagement with Dorner's important essay on divine immutability further specifies the problem of this study and shows how it takes shape within the context of the second half of the nineteenth century. The essential contribution of Dorner for the purposes of this work lies in the clarity with which he poses and responds to the question of how to reconcile a notion of divine immutability with the revealed vitality of God in history. Immutability, as noted above, is a secondary theme to be addressed in this study. The larger point here lies in the way that Dorner makes recourse to an ethical concept of God, construed along trinitarian lines, as the solution to the problem of reconciling immutability and the livingness of God. I show how Dorner's approach, with a slight modification, can be adapted to form the basic question of this study in terms of how the doctrine of the Trinity works to establish a notion of God's living relation to history.

The more constructive argument of this work begins in chapter 2 and the engagement with the trinitarian theology of Karl Barth. This chapter consists of two parts. In part 1, I assess how Barth incorporates his trinitarian idea of God into his doctrines of revelation in *Church Dogmatics* I/1 and divine constancy in *Church Dogmatics* II/1 in order to show how God's activity in history proceeds from the eternal (or antecedent) Trinity. Barth's theology demonstrates the way that trinitarian reflection animates the theological approach of faith seeking understanding. More critically, I utilize Pannenberg's argument concerning divine subjectivity and a key claim from Kathryn Tanner's theology on the way that history impacts God's identity in order to assess limitations in Barth's trinitarian theology around both divine presence and how God is understood to abide and move in history. In the material treated up to *Church Dogmatics* II/1, I show how Barth makes only little of an advance on Dorner's immutability essay. In part 2 of this chapter, I follow through on a point of doctrinal development in Barth's theology and his use of Christology in the doctrine of election from *Church Dogmatics* II/2. This solves several dilemmas from part 1. I argue that Barth's concept of the Son's obedience, grounded in the concrete history of Jesus, provides a sense of continuity between God's pre-temporal eternity and revelatory history and also precludes the problematic notion of a two-fold history of God. I also consider how Barth's doctrine of election enables a view of divine immutability that more coherently integrates God's eternal reality and living history than Dorner's immutability essay.

In chapter 3, I consider Wolfhart Pannenberg on the trinitarian mediated history of God. I return to Pannenberg's criticism of Barth on the divine subjectivity, bringing it into shaper focus through a similar assessment of Barth's theology by Jürgen Moltmann, in order to highlight the central themes of Pannenberg's theology for understanding the God-world relation: eschatology and the reciprocity of the divine persons. I then lay out Pannenberg's early views of God, revelation, and futurity before turning to his mature doctrine of the Trinity and trinitarian concept of eternity. This chapter also introduces a common way to conceive of God's being and God's activity *ad extra* in later twentieth century theology as the relationship between the immanent and the economic Trinity, which I employ in subsequent parts of this study. In the critical analysis of this chapter I show how Pannenberg sets forth a trinitarian concept of God compatible with God's revealed history. More constructively, I utilize Pannenberg's concept of the dependent monarchy of the Father to make the case for an understanding of the movement of God in time and the process of history. The key to this conception is an eschatological interpretation of the relations of origin from the classical doctrine of the Trinity. I pair this conception with a reflection on the immutability of God's being in the midst of a changing history. My argument is that the unchanging God moves in history based on the (trinitarian) unity-in-distinctions of God's being. In the final section of this chapter I highlight some ambiguities in Pannenberg's doctrine of eternity that result in a timeless notion of divine reality. I argue that this stems from an inadequate application of Pannenberg's trinitarian theology to his concept of eternity and show how this points up the need for an understanding of how God simultaneously transcends and indwells temporal reality.

In chapter 4, I consider a temporally structured idea of transcendence based on Robert W. Jenson's trinitarian theology. This chapter brings together Jenson's early proposal for a temporal (futuristic) concept of transcendence with the trinitarian theology of his later work. Drawing from both my evaluation of Pannenberg's doctrine of eternity in chapter 3 as well as Jenson's critical assessment of Barth's doctrine of election, I demonstrate the need for a more historical understanding of divine freedom. The concept of transcendence in this chapter rests on Jenson's temporal ontology of the Trinity, which I unpack through his notions of narrative identity, divine envelopment, and his articulation of eternity through the events of Christ's passion and resurrection. I argue that Jenson's divine ontology, with key emphases on the governing role of the trinitarian unity-in-distinctions and the Spirit's identity in God, opens up a way to conceive of God as present in history and transcendent being at once. I make this argument by drawing from both previous claims of this work, such as Tanner's understanding of history's meaning for God's being, and distinct elements in Jenson's trinitarian theology. I conclude by building on chapter 3's claim on God's movement in time and the process of history with a view of the Trinity as the transcendent source of time's movement.

The final chapter recaps the arguments of this study and highlights an intention that underlies the work as a whole: to demonstrate just how fruitful the doctrine of the Trinity is for conceiving of God's relation to the creaturely reality God loves. I conclude the work with two constructive proposals that build on the arguments from chapters 1–4. The first is methodological. I make the case for a theological formulation of God's being as Father, Son, and Spirit that includes the historical telos of their relations as a (self-)determinative fact of God's being. I connect this proposal to Thomas Aquinas' view of the eternal relations or processions of the divine persons as containing the temporal missions. In the second proposal I fill out a lacuna in Pannenberg's and Jenson's assertion that the immanent Trinity is the eschatological Trinity. I propose an eschatological understanding of the immanent Trinity based on the revealed being of God that utilizes both the concept of the Father's realized monarchy and the Augustinian view of the Spirit as divine love. I show how these concepts serve as bookends of sorts, pointing to the animating source and the triumphant power of God's self-enabled and living relation to history.

An Acknowledgement and a Note on Gendered Language for God

Before proceeding to the main body chapters of this work, two notes are in order. As mentioned before, this work is situated within the German theological tradition as it extends into areas of English language scholarship. Over the past few decades trinitarian theology has undergone a flourishing of activity in different theological domains and geographical areas. Moreover, this book reflects on the work of four theologians, all of whom are white males. I acknowledge at the forefront of this study that these factors place a significant limitation on the scope and perspective of this work. This study therefore makes no claim to be a comprehensive statement on the topic of the triune God's relation to the world. Rather, while I believe these figures offer helpful contributions to the central theme of this essay, a fuller understanding of the triune God's relation to the world will come by way of attending to a geographical, cultural, and social diversity beyond the focus of this study, especially to the essential contributions of women, persons of color, and LGBTQ+ people. In my own growing realization of the significance of these points, an important function of this work for me is to serve as an entry point into a vital and broader conversation that is giving shape to Christian theological studies and the church today.

And second, I use the traditional nomenclature of Father, Son, and Spirit in this study. I realize that no simple equivalency in meaning can or should be made between these terms, especially of Father and Son, as they apply to God and their creaturely counterparts. I use this nomenclature in keeping with the teachings of the New Testament Gospels, specifically Jesus' instructions on prayer in Matthew 6:5–15 and Luke 7:1–4 and the baptismal formula in Matthew 28:19. I also employ it based on the conviction that it holds a place of theological and liturgical primacy—though by no means, of course, exclusivity—insofar as it captures both the specific coordinates of the gospel's storyline and the particular identities (persons) of the Trinity in a way that proposed substitutes do not, such as Creator, Reconciler, and Redeemer. I use the masculine pronoun when referencing Father, Son, or Spirit individually, but not in reference to the word God. I recognize the pastoral sensitivities that need to be considered here. I also acknowledge the important place of many feminist and womanist theological criticisms around divine naming, which rightly call attention to discerning forms of patriarchy and male sexism that accompany theological speech, and the need to root them out. Finally, I note my commitment here to regularly reevaluate the reasoning, significance, and broader impact of the language that I use to describe and name God. Theology is a living conversation, and for that to work I must leave open the possibility of changing my mind. I am deeply appreciative of those at Highrock Covenant Church (Boston, MA), where I currently serve as a Resident Theologian, and particularly to the members of the Theology Lab community whose persistent and thoughtful engagement on this subject helps to provide both accountability and a constructive context for theological dialogue.

I

The "Living Immutability" of God

*Trinity and History in the Theology
of Isaak A. Dorner*

HOW DOES THE DOCTRINE of divine immutability square with the revealed vitality of God? This is the question that Lutheran mediating theologian, Isaak A. Dorner, put forth in his three-part essay for the *Jahrbücher für deutsche Theologie*, "On the Proper Conception of the Doctrine of God's Immutability, with Special Reference to the Reciprocal Relation between God's Suprahistorical and Historical Life" (1856–58).[1] I begin with Dorner's immutability essay as a way to frame the central problem of this study. The problem derives from a modified version of the question above on bridging divine immutability with God's revealed vitality as well as, *mutatis mutandis*, reconciling God's unchangeability with the living character of God's being. I ask: How does the eternal nature of the Trinity square with the revealed vitality of God? Specifically, how does the triunity of God's being ground and enable God's living relation to history? The scope of these questions will include treatments of Trinity's significance for examining divine presence, the movement of God in time, the relation between divine transcendence and immanence, and the formulation (and reformulation) of divine attributes, such as divine immutability.

This chapter, however, presents more than a mere overview of Dorner's immutability essay that frames the basic problem of this study. My way to this problem comes through a critical engagement with the role of Trinity in Dorner's immutability essay. I argue that Dorner applies the trinitarian understanding of God more consistently to the latter of the two problems posed above; that is, he constructively applies Trinity to the problem of reconciling immutability and the vitality of God's *being*. This opens up a dynamic

---

1. Dorner, "Über die richtige Fassung des dogmatischen Begriffs Der Unveränderlichkeit Gottes, mit besonderer Beziehung auf das gegenseitige Verhältniss zwischen Gottes übergeschichtlichem und geschichtlichem Leben." Hereafter cited as *Der Unveränderlichkeit Gottes*.

9

ontology for understanding how God relates to history through God's tri-unity. But Dorner does not similarly employ Trinity for the other problem of reconciling immutability with the revealed being of God in history. The meaning of Trinity for the history that God lives with others is largely left unsaid. This lacuna in Dorner's application of a trinitarian ontology to the God-world relation marks a gap that I attempt to fill out in subsequent chapters through engagements with the other central figures of this work. Furthermore, Dorner's essay plays a significant role when we turn to Karl Barth's trinitarian theology in chapter 2. While the immutability essay garnered little attention in the theological scene of Dorner's time, it was given something of a historical lifeline shortly before the middle of the twentieth century when Barth noted his indebtedness to the work in his doctrine of God from *Church Dogmatics* II/1.[2] In chapter 2 I use Dorner's essay for two purposes: first, as a key point of comparison in the critical assessment of how Barth's trinitarian theology construes God's living relation to history; and second, to demonstrate the importance of election for a concept of immutability that includes both God's eternal vitality and being in time.

Dorner's constructive proposal centers on his concept of God's ethical being in part III of the essay. In order to understand both how Dorner arrives at this notion as well as the underlying problems he identifies in the doctrine of immutability, and the role Trinity plays in fixing them, it is important to consider the immutability essay more broadly. In section 1 of this chapter I lay out Dorner's objection to the classical understanding of immutability. Next I unpack Dorner's initial use of trinitarian doctrine to conceive of the liveliness that underlies God's immutability, giving specific attention to the way Dorner relates this concept to God's involvement in creation. I then turn to Dorner's trinitarian understanding of God's ethical immutability. Section 2 of this chapter concludes with a critical analysis of Dorner's account that derives the central problem of this study by recasting Dorner's task in the immutability essay along more robustly trinitarian lines.

---

2. Barth, *CD* II/1:493. Although Dorner was perhaps the most prominent figure of the mediation theology (*Vermittlungstheologie*), Jörg Rothermundt (writing in 1968) claims that the references which Karl Barth makes to Dorner in his *Church Dogmatics* are the only explicit points of influence of Dorner on twentieth century theology. Rothermundt, *Personale Synthese*, 45–46. Increased attention has been given to Dorner's theology over the past few decades within English language scholarship due to Claude Welch's translation of part III of the immutability essay in the 1965 volume, *God and Incarnation*, followed by Robert W. Williams' translation of parts I and II in 1994 (Dorner, *Divine Immutability*). See Sherman, "Isaak August Dorner on Divine Immutability"; Gockel, "On the Way from Schleiermacher to Barth"; Drewer, "Dorner's Critique of Divine Immutability"; Norgate, *Isaak A. Dorner*. In German language scholarship, see esp. Lee, *Karl Barth und Isaak August Dorner*.

1: Immutability, Trinity, and the Vitality of God

1.1: The Context of the Immutability Essay

Dorner's immutability essay is occasioned by the kenotic controversy of the mid-nineteenth century. In part I of the essay Dorner assesses this controversy. The debate, mainly between Lutheran and Reformed theologians, laid claim to the concept of the *communicatio idiomatum* or the communication of properties that belong to the distinct natures (human and divine) of Christ's person. A key Lutheran figure in the debate, Gottfried Thomasius, advanced the idea that the incarnation of the *Logos* entails not only the non-use but the actual divestment of certain divine attributes. The *Logos* surrenders the relative divine attributes, or those that pertain to the divine essence in the being and activity of God *ad extra* (e.g., omnipotence, omnipresence) and not the necessary attributes of God such as divine love and wisdom.[3]

Dorner is severely critical of Thomasius' Christology. Thomasius wants a conceivable account of the unity of divinity and humanity in Christ's person. But to achieve this by way of a self-divestment of the *Logos*' divine attributes, Dorner argues, comes at the expense of one of the very things that Thomasius wishes to uphold within the unity of Christ's person: his deity or divine nature. Consequently, "it is not the immanent eternal Son of God, but only another, naturally subordinate 'great man' that becomes incarnate."[4] Moreover, Dorner takes issue with a problem that he finds endemic to the kenotic project of his contemporaries as a whole. On one hand, they dwell on a "fixed unity" between the *Logos* and humanity that begins at the outset of the Son's incarnation; on the other, this unity is conceived as a goal to be attained over the course of Christ's life. The kenoticists therefore assume an idea of divine immutability, in this case, one that dictates the terms of Christ's personal development in time, which they otherwise oppose.[5] Dorner's dissatisfaction with the kenotic project is, however, only mildly telling of his larger aims. His constructive proposal

---

3. Dorner, *Divine Immutability*, 68–69. Thomasius writes: "The immanent attributes God cannot give up because he would thereby give himself up; the relative attributes he can renounce because the world, and thus also the relation to it, is not necessary for him. In renouncing them he surrenders nothing that makes him to be God; his essence thereby suffers no diminution. But he renounces them in holy love, in order to be able to experience in truth a humanly natural life, a life in the flesh, and to redeem us. During this stage he is thus no *all*-mighty, *all*-present, *all*-knowing man." Thomasius, "Christ's Person and Work," 94.

4. Dorner, *Divine Immutability*, 72.

5. Dorner, *Divine Immutability*, 74.

around divine immutability becomes more clear through his foray into the doctrine of God in part II of the essay.

He begins part II with an overview of Augustine's idea of God and his understanding of immutability. God, according to Augustine, is the highest good and does not change. All that comes into being through God's creative power is distinct from God and subject to change. As Augustine puts this in his *Confessions*, "all mutable things have in you their immutable origins. In you all irrational and temporal things have the everlasting causes of their life."[6] Augustine's concept of immutability is bound up with his doctrine of divine simplicity, captured in the succinct expression that "all that God has, God is."[7] Therefore God is identical to God's attributes; God does not merely have power, but *is* omnipotent. For created entities, in contrast, an underlying distinction applies between being itself and the more fundamental parts upon which creatures depend for actualization. In terms of divine immutability, divine simplicity means not only that God does not change—as perfectly good, change in God could only be change for the worse—but God cannot change.[8] Dorner also considers Thomas Aquinas' concept of God as pure act (*actus purus*). Key here is Thomas' rejection of potentiality in God. Potentiality belongs to the world that God creates, the world of change. God, however, does not change. Because God is purely actual no potentiality belongs to God's being. Moreover, although the distinctions of the divine attributes have subjective significance for the perceiver, they entail no corresponding and objective distinction in God's simple essence.[9] As simple and unchanging being, God is free from the determinations of the created world.

Dorner is concerned with the compatibility of historical reality and the classical conception of God's being. He identifies at least two related problems. First, he asserts that the contrast between the characterization of God's being in terms of absolute simplicity, on one hand, and historical and determinate reality, on the other, creates a conceptual barrier for understanding how the world has its origin in God. "The riddle remains, where does such a pluralistic world come from, if all plurality and change are excluded from God?" The world is grounded in God, the highest good (Augustine), but nothing in God "explains the world in its concrete and determinate existence and particularity."[10] And second, the total exclusion

---

6. Augustine, *Confessions*, I.6.

7. Dorner, *Divine Immutability*, 91.

8. Dorner, *Divine Immutability*, 91.

9. Dorner, *Divine Immutability*, 94–97.

10. Dorner, *Divine Immutability*, 96.

of change and potentiality in God's simple essence leads to a distinction between God and creation that subtly, though ultimately devastatingly, undermines the world's objective reality. Dorner's argument runs like this: God is ultimate life, the truest form of reality. Before the absolute actuality of this life, conveyed through the "refined [classical] concept of God," the ever-changing and composite world appears as an illusion.[11] What the world lacks on this view is a sense of its own distinct, albeit created, existence in relation to God. The gap between the classical concept of God's being and the determinate world is so great, Dorner contends, as to reduce the latter to an idea in the mind of God. "In the doctrine of God, especially divine immutability, there is a conception of God's idea of the world that has too great a similarity with the Platonic realms of Ideas—a realm that is unhistorical, unfree, in no way conditioned by God's will or doing."[12] Pushed to an extreme, the stark contrast of divine and worldly realities entails that when God finally reclaims creation in the consummation of all things, the world will return to the indeterminate reality of God, which Dorner describes as a different (inverted) form of pantheism.[13]

However, the solution is not to do away with a concept of immutability or the classical attributes of divine perfection. Why not? Dorner affirms a notion of immutability as essential to the biblical idea of God. The revelation of God in Exodus 3:14 as "I am who I am" presents God not only as living person, but also as "the unconditional self-identical being that is free from contradictions."[14] Likewise, God is without beginning or end: "from everlasting to everlasting you are God" (Ps 90:2). Unlike the fleeting nature of created things, God does not change insofar as God perfectly abides. This point has foundational significance for faith. Dorner states, "only when God is discovered to be immutable has an absolutely trustworthy object been found."[15] The point is echoed by Christoph Schwöbel: "God's everlasting being posits God as the only true object of ultimate trust," for "God's relationship to creatures has a trustworthiness and validity that transcends the trustworthiness of created beings."[16] The Psalmists' repeated use of the metaphor of God as the rock which provides

---

11. Dorner, *Divine Immutability*, 96.

12. Dorner, *Divine Immutability*, 106. See also 270.

13. Dorner later identifies this as substance pantheism. "Substance pantheism never achieves a world that is actual, but, insofar as it attributes being (reality) to the world, the latter is essentially identified with God." *Divine Immutability*, 110.

14. Dorner, *Divine Immutability*, 85.

15. Dorner, *Divine Immutability*, 87.

16. Schwöbel, "The Eternity of the Triune God," 346.

stability and strength points to this basic function (e.g., Ps 18:2; 78:35).[17]
The same point applies to the ethical nature of God, which proves particularly important for Dorner's argument in part III of the immutability
essay. Every good thing comes from "the Father of lights, with whom there
is no variation or shadow due to change" (Jas 1:17). God, Dorner writes,
is "intrinsically righteous," and so the being of God, "the primal good in
itself, is self-identical and thus unchangeable."[18]

Dorner holds onto a concept of divine immutability. His concern,
however, is the "one-sided development" of this doctrine.[19] For Dorner the
doctrine of immutability must not be conceived apart from God's intimate
involvement with the semi-independent and determinate reality of creation.
In the following parts of the essay Dorner takes up the task of reconciling
immutability with the revealed vitality of God. He asks, how does a notion of
immutability align with the activity of God in both creating the world and becoming incarnate? Dorner approaches this question through the conceptual
resources available within the doctrine of God, to which I now turn.

1.2: The Vitality of God and Creation

In part III of the immutability essay Dorner introduces his idea of ethical immutability. With this notion Dorner attempts to reconcile divine immutability
with the revealed livingness of God in the "higher principle" of God's ethical
being.[20] Dorner draws on other doctrinal loci that support a dynamic notion
of immutability, above all the trinitarian understanding of God. In what follows I outline how Dorner incorporates Trinity into his developing concept of
immutability (which culminates in the ethical idea of God). I then consider
how Dorner applies this to the reconciliation of immutability and God's revealed vitality in his treatment of God's creative activity.

Dorner views the task of reconciling immutability with God's revealed
activity in relation to the Reformation's insight into the personal nature
of God. The Reformation's great discovery lies in the boldness by which it
articulates the reality of faith in its doctrine of salvation. Implicit in the doctrine of salvation is both the proximity of God in the gift of faith as well as
the transcendence of God in the sovereign act of justification. The doctrine
of God, however, went largely untouched during the Reformation period.
Nor did the later Protestant scholastics apply the insight into the personality

---

17. Dorner, *Divine Immutability*, 87–88.
18. Dorner, *Divine Immutability*, 87.
19. Dorner, *Divine Immutability*, 89.
20. Dorner, *Divine Immutability*, 131.

of God to the attribute of immutability or the absolute character of God's being. Dorner thus interprets the theological task of reconciling immutability with the revealed vitality of God as an extension of the central principle of the Reformation into the doctrine of God.[21]

As noted in the previous sub-section, Dorner's criticism of the traditional conception of immutability has to do with its incompatibility with God's relationship to created reality. Dorner's solution to this problem consists in adapting another central doctrine into the understanding of divine immutability: the doctrine of the Trinity. By bringing Trinity into the purview of immutability, Dorner, to borrow a line from John Webster, works against a tendency to "overinvest in whatever generic sense may be attached to the concept of [immutability]."[22] Furthermore, with recourse to the doctrine of the Trinity, Dorner's attempt to square the notion of divine immutability with the revealed vitality of God begins with an analogous form of the same problem: squaring the unchangeable nature of God and the living character of God's being. In short, Trinity is the means for understanding the vitality of God's immutable being. This opens up a concept of God's living immutability suitable for understanding God's relation to a world marked by flux and change.

Within the realm of classical trinitarian doctrine, Dorner relies on the notion that the relations of the divine persons—Father, Son, and Spirit—belong to the essence of God.[23] Dorner has Protestant scholastic theology in view when he asserts that this idea contradicts the notion of simplicity as the "objective absence of distinction" in God.[24] This idea of simplicity is at odds with the plurality and distinctions of the eternal persons of the Trinity, "especially when the generation of the Son and the procession of the Holy Spirit are conceived (with the orthodox early church) as perennial (*perennirend*) and not as complete by a once-for-all act."[25] In the divine being, Dorner asserts, there is both "positing and posited life."[26] The Father posits the Son and Spirit; the Son and Spirit are posited therein. In paternity (the Father), filiation (the Son), and spiration (the Spirit), God is the living God: God is "absolute life . . . constituting itself out of the trinitarian distinctions

21. Dorner, *Divine Immutability*, 135.

22. Webster, "Life in and of Himself," 108. Webster is addressing the notion of aseity, but admits that this reflection belongs to "any of the other divine attributes."

23. E.g., Aquinas, *Summa Theologica*, 1.28.1.2.

24. Dorner, *Divine Immutability*, 136.

25. Dorner, *Divine Immutability*, 136; Dorner, *Der Unveränderlichkeit Gottes*, 305.

26. Dorner, *Divine Immutability*, 137.

and [having] its existence only in them."[27] This understanding of God as life itself, specifically in terms of the inner-trinitarian relations, works to overcome "a static conception of God as subsistent being and so to draw attention to God's eternal self-activation."[28] The unmoved or motionless God, Dorner claims, "could only be rigid dead substance or equally lifeless law."[29] In contrast, the triune God is eternally self-generating life.

For Dorner the perennial nature of the trinitarian relations underlies a notion of divine immutability. The self-posting and self-posited being of the triune God contains a "multiplicity of moments," such as the begetting of the Son and the Spirit's procession. However, these moments in God are not strictly sequential. Rather, they cohere in "indissoluble unity." Dorner articulates these movements in terms of a life-giving process in God that consists of "an eternal going out from itself and an eternal return."[30] In God divine externalization and return are identical to God's essence; the movements in God are one, a unity, because of their simultaneity and the fact that they are internal to the being of the one God. Figuratively speaking, Dorner claims, divine being is a "cycle of life (*Kreislauf des Lebens*)."[31] Underlying the diversity and change that characterizes God's being is a fundamental stability, the immutable nature of God in these divine, self-constituting relations. Moreover, in view of the "self-rejuvenating divine life-process," Dorner conceives of God as not only "absolute actuality (*absolute Verwirklichung*)" but also "absolute potentiality (*absolute Potenz*)."[32] As *absolute* potentiality this notion is stripped of any association with a sense of lack or incompleteness regarding God's sovereign perfection. Positively, the potentiality-actuality dialectic points to the unique nature of God's self-establishment. This does not indicate a beginning in God, but rather the ongoing, life-giving actuality of the divine persons in relation to one another: divine aseity. What makes God immutable being is the unchanging nature of God's inner-trinitarian vitality.

The significance of this trinitarian based idea of immutability does more than overcome a motionless concept of God. The rest of Dorner's argument hinges on the positive side of God's aseity: "God's *particularity*, his characteristic essence, is his aseity, through which he can be the *universal*

---

27. Dorner, *Divine Immutability*, 137.

28. Webster, "Life in and of Himself," 117.

29. Dorner, *Divine Immutability*, 136–37.

30. Dorner, *Divine Immutability*, 137.

31. Dorner, *Divine Immutability*, 136–37; Dorner, *Der Unveränderlichkeit Gottes*, 307.

32. Dorner, *Divine Immutability*, 137; Dorner, *Der Unveränderlichkeit Gottes*, 307.

ground of all being."[33] In part II of the immutability essay Dorner criticized related notions of simplicity and immutability that result in an idea of God and the created order as mutually incompatible. In response, Dorner has formulated a doctrine of God with two key elements. First, Dorner upholds the absolute character of God that distinguishes God from the world. Even the potentiality of God is *absolute* potentiality, and so unique to God's being. Second, and to borrow from the same example, the inclusion of a concept like potentiality, however diversely qualified, intends to demonstrate the simultaneous relatability of God's being with the complex world that God indwells. I will have more to say about this below and in subsequent chapters of this work. The key point to note here is Dorner's metaphysical starting point in Trinity. The Trinity concept includes both points of identity and difference from the created world, grounded in the unity-in-distinctions of God's being. With the idea of God's living immutability in place, Dorner takes up the relationship between God's vitality *ad intra* and the divine relationality *ad extra*. Next I consider the central place that Dorner gives to the doctrine of creation and creaturely freedom in the relation between God's being *ad intra* and God's being *ad extra*.

Dorner outlines a doctrine of creation in light of a revised notion of the grounds for God's eternal decree. According to the divine decree, "God thinks and knows himself and the world with one and the same eternal and simple act."[34] This does not mean that creation is coeval with the self-determining decision of God's eternal decree. God has no beginning; creation does. Rather, it means that God thinks and knows Godself so absolutely as to include the self-knowledge and self-grounded willing of a world distinct from God. The older dogmatic formulas understood the eternal decision to entail an internal order distinguishing God's self-constitution and the will of God to create.[35] Dorner thinks this much correct. The problem, he argues, is that the distinction is unfounded in view of God's absolute simplicity. However, a basis for the complexity required for the necessary ordering of the divine decree can be found in the idea of God's self-positing being, Trinity.[36] The trinitarian idea of God, with the diversity it entails as proper to the one God, allows for a logical distinction to be made between God's essential self-willing, the "necessity of the divine essence," on one hand, and God's willing of a world that belongs to the "activity of his perfect being," on the other.[37]

---

33. Dorner, *Divine Immutability*, 139.
34. Dorner, *Divine Immutability*, 141.
35. See Heppe, *Reformed Dogmatics*, 140.
36. Dorner, *Divine Immutability*, 141.
37. Dorner, *Divine Immutability*, 142.

God is not "absorbed into being the world-cause," which Trinity secures against and the unqualified idea of simplicity risks confusing. Rather, God's being is the loving instrument behind God's will to create.[38]

As for God's creative activity, Dorner argues against the prevailing deistic concept of his time in order to maintain a notion of God's immediate relation to the spatial-temporal world. Such a relationship, however, entails a "change in God's living self-exercise."[39] Particularly important here for Dorner is God's way of relating to self-determining creatures. The free creature is the highest created cause, and consequently bears greatest witness to the omnipotent causality of God.[40] Moreover, the relation between God and the free creature is "*mutual and reciprocal*."[41] The creature possesses a divinely endowed sense of autonomy and freedom. And yet, God shares in the creature's historical life, willing to "dwell and move *in them*," as they "live and move and have [their] being" in God (Acts 17:28; 2 Cor 6:16).[42] Dorner asserts, "thus it is undeniable that God, so far as he dwells in man, also leads an historical life in the world."[43] The goal of this relation is a communion of love. The creature, at once free and dependent on the divine being, realizes its ethical end through participation in God, the highest good. In this ethical relation God enters into fellowship with the creature where new forms of the good, new realizations of this love, become possible.[44]

This new realization of the good is, at least in part, what Dorner means by a 'change in God's living self-exercise.' In relation to creatures in time the effective will of God contains good that is yet to be realized. Dorner subtly connects this with the notion of God's inner-trinitarian vitality when he likens the emergence of the good in time through God's communion with free creatures to the potentiality of God's being.[45] For as indicated above, the specific way Dorner pairs potentiality with actuality in God gives the concept of divine actuality the sense of a recurring and yet always realized reality in God. More concretely, it points to the perennial nature of the Son's begetting from the Father and the Spirit's procession; in God there is ongoing reality, eternal novelty. One can see how God relates

38. Dorner, *Divine Immutability*, 142, 179.

39. Dorner, *Divine Immutability*, 143.

40. Dorner, *Divine Immutability*, 144. On the link between the doctrine of God and the natural order in Dorner's theology, see Dorner, *A System of Christian Doctrine*, §§22a–22b.

41. Dorner, *Divine Immutability*, 147–48.

42. Dorner, *Divine Immutability*, 144–46.

43. Dorner, *Divine Immutability*, 145.

44. Dorner, *Divine Immutability*, 147–48.

45. Dorner, *Divine Immutability*, 148.

to creatures in new realizations of the good through the inner-vitality of God's being. Trinity grounds this ongoing and changing fellowship. What is more, the introduction of something new to the God-creature relation does not entail a lack or imperfection on God's part. On the contrary, the tie that Dorner makes between the ongoing good God brings forth and divine (absolute) potentiality means that new goods proceed from the generative nature and abundance of the divine life.

In sum, the trinitarian idea of God allows Dorner to conceive of God's being as eternally alive. The actuality of the trinitarian relations ground the *steadfast* and *dynamic* nature of God's being. Dorner's trinitarian idea of God's living immutability carries over into God's relation with free creatures, serving as the semi-explicit basis for the emergence of the new with God in created reality. The two underlying categories here are clear: divine immutability and the livingness of God—both internally to God and in God's activity *ad extra*. In part III of the essay Dorner puts forward a more specific concept in order to describe how the immutability of God and the vitality of God go hand-in-hand. The task is admittedly speculative. Yet, Dorner asserts, it has Christology as its archetype. For the supposition that God becomes incarnate in Christ without loss to God's deity raises the question of how the eternally unchanging reality of God and the living being of God in history are one.[46] The answer for Dorner lies in the ethical concept of God.

1.3: *The Ethical Concept of Immutability*

According to Dorner, the ethical idea of God is at least in some sense given. The thought of the ethical has "a kind of ontological necessity." To think God good is to think of the "absolute excellence" of the divine nature.[47] But how is the general concept of God's goodness to be refined? The concept of love presents an analogous problem; it is too elusive and indefinite to serve as a conceptual starting point for the purposes of uniting immutability and the vitality of God. To clarify the relationship between God and the good Dorner finds one of the classical philosophical-theological conundrums more helpful. He turns to a version of the Euthypro dilemma. Is the good good because God wills it to be good, or does God will the good because it is good?[48] However, as we will see, this question serves less as an actual

---

46. Dorner, *Divine Immutability*, 160–61.

47. Dorner, *Divine Immutability*, 166.

48. Dorner, *Divine Immutability*, 167.

starting point for Dorner's concept of God and more so as a placeholder for a trinitarian version of the ethical.

As the question was posed by the scholastics, Duns Scotus and the nominalists argued that the ethical is subordinate to the freedom of the divine will. Thomas Aquinas and the intellectualists made the case that God wills the good insofar as it is good. Dorner advocates neither option, though he ends up nearer to the intellectualists. Problematically, according to Dorner, the nominalist view envisions God ultimately as sheer power. This makes the good accidental and thus God's underlying relation to it a matter of indifference. The intellectualist option runs into the same problem. If God wills the good because God knows it as such, then the good would appear to exist in its own right. Again, the good is not essential but rather accidental to God's being.[49] What is needed, argues Dorner, is to understand the good as identical to God. God is the "primal ethical (*Urethische*)," the "ethical in itself."[50] Yet this is only a first step. For the essential goodness of God does not answer how God is ethical. The ethical, identical to God's being, is never simply immediate to God or dormant. Rather, it desires to become actual, to be posited by the will. Divine nature *as* ethical and the *willing* of the ethical are necessary to God. The two are distinct but united in God because of God's "*multiple and yet inwardly coherent mode of existence.*"[51] In other words, because God is triune.

Dorner begins with the necessity of the ethical. The absolute necessity of the good has primacy of place in God. Dorner writes,

> the ethical in the character of the necessary is rather a necessary *mode of being* of God and indeed the primary one. We cannot begin with the divine will as free if God is to be conceived ethically. For had we only the free, without any kind of conditionality and determination by the ethically necessary (*Notwendig*) . . . then we would be left eternally in capriciousness.[52]

The underlying concern here is the same as the paragraph above, voluntarism. The voluntaristic conception of deity is unstable, for it is not certain whether the good that God wills truly encapsulates God in an absolute sense. God could have willed otherwise (and may still). For Dorner God is necessarily good. He equates this goodness with the first person of the Trinity. As ethical necessity, the Father is the "holy and necessary power which

49. Dorner, *Divine Immutability*, 167–68.

50. Dorner, *Divine Immutability*, 168–69; Dorner, *Der Unveränderlichkeit Gottes*, 343–44.

51. Dorner, *Divine Immutability*, 170–71.

52. Dorner, *Divine Immutability*, 171; Dorner, *Der Unveränderlichkeit Gottes*, 346.

neither will nor can renounce itself."[53] The Father is the goodness of God that just is, the root of God's ethical immutability.

Ethical necessity, however, does not exist for itself. Rather, the good is expansive in nature and meant to be enjoyed. It tends toward actualization—it 'ought to be.' As Dorner puts this, ethical necessity desires to actualize the good in freedom (*Freiheit*).[54] Ethical necessity posits an ethical freedom that affirms itself, which in turn confirms the totality of the divine goodness. Dorner equates this principle of willing in God with the second person of the Trinity. The Son's role as ethical freedom is constitutive of the Godhead. As Dorner writes, ethical necessity itself "does not suffice for the ethical in [God]."[55] Without freedom the ethically given goes unrealized; "without freedom there is no love."[56] In other words, the essential goodness of the Father depends for its actualization on the ethical freedom of the Son.[57] On the side of the Son, ethical freedom consists in a specific orientation toward the Father. The Son's freedom is not libertarian, but freedom to bring about the realization of the Father's necessary goodness. "My food is do the will of him who sent me" (John 4:34).

Ethical necessity desires to be for the free and freely actualized. Ethical freedom, on the other hand, knows the truth of its essence in the highest good, its freedom for the ethically necessary. However, freedom in this sense is primarily an orientation or condition. It does not yet will its own actualization of the ethically necessary. "The free in itself and as such," Dorner writes, "is nothing more than the real possibility for the eternal self-generation of the ethical into actuality."[58] Herein lies the Spirit's role in God's ethical being. The Spirit is the power or ethical actualization of God. By the Spirit the Son freely wills the necessary goodness of the Father. The Spirit "mediates these antitheses," necessity and freedom, "into the eternal absolute actuality of the ethical divine personality."[59] The Spirit makes God's

---

53. Dorner, *Divine Immutability*, 171.

54. Dorner, *Der Unveränderlichkeit Gottes*, 347.

55. Dorner, *Divine Immutability*, 173.

56. Dorner, *Divine Immutability*, 172.

57. For this reason Robert W. Brown is misguided in his claim that Dorner's ordering of the Son after the Father in the immutability essay "undercuts his own emphasis on divine will and freedom," concluding his treatise "with a philosophical account of ethical immutability that sounds more like Hegelian necessity than Schellingian voluntarism." Brown, "Schelling and Dorner on Divine Immutability," 247. Dorner prioritizes the Father's ethical being, and he rejects voluntarism more staunchly than other positions, but the actuality of ethical necessity in God (the Father) hinges on divine freedom (the Son).

58. Dorner, *Divine Immutability*, 173.

59. Dorner, *Divine Immutability*, 173.

nature ethical being, and in this way plays the traditionally (Augustinian) articulated role of the bond of love in the Godhead. What is more, the Spirit's divine role removes any sense of arbitrariness in the ethical nature of God's being. For by the mediating power of the Spirit, ethical freedom in God has its "unshakable objective," the ethically necessary goodness of the Father which the Son desires, loves, and freely posits.[60] The essential goodness of God is freely actualized through the Spirit.

As mentioned above, Dorner does not begin his theorization of God's ethical being with a concept of love. He fears this would lead to an abstract understanding of love, apart from the revealed relations of God's being. Having set forth these relations, coded in ethical terms, Dorner uses a notion of love to summarize God's ethical nature. The eternal actualization of God's necessary goodness in freedom is God's loving nature. While this means that God always loves, or is always loving in Godself, it also entails the equally important claim that, *as* ethically immutable, God is love.[61] God is ethical being itself. Furthermore, the shorthand concept for God's ethical immutability, the divine self-love, serves as the basis for God's interactions with created reality.

God's self-love stands behind the will to create. According to Dorner, the world comes into being neither by means of an arbitrary act nor as the necessary completion of God's being. Either scenario would plunge us back into the problem of an essential mutability on God's part. Rather, as Dorner puts it, God creates from the "blessedness and perfection of his love and out of the self-identity of its free being."[62] As the necessary ethical, God is the fullness of goodness itself, whose will and freedom grasp the good that God is as a "self-affirmation of the majesty of the holy and the good generally." The divine loving is "reflected in itself, conscious of itself, having and willing itself."[63] God's self-love, in short, manifests God's perfectly ethical being. At the same time, Dorner locates the underlying rationale for God's willing of a reality distinct from Godself in divine love. Within the "perfection of [God's] love . . . lives the desire of self-impartation."[64] The divine love serves as the internal motivation for God's creative work. Dorner writes,

60. Dorner, *Divine Immutability*, 173.

61. On the former view that identifies Dorner's concept of ethical immutability with God's loving actions, see Ware, "An Evangelical Reformulation," 437. Similarly, Weinandy, *Does God Suffer?*, 61–62.

62. Dorner, *Divine Immutability*, 181.

63. Dorner, *Divine Immutability*, 177.

64. Dorner, *Divine Immutability*, 181.

[The] willing of objects is included in God's self-love because within and for the divine sphere itself the self-impartation of pure love cannot yet, in the proper sense, reach manifestation. It is to be insisted that love, as imparting, does not yet find the proper place of its manifestation in God himself, but only where purely free original giving takes place, only where there is pure want in the recipient.[65]

The divine love extends to the point of a possible self-giving that does not receive back what it gives. For Dorner the creature endowed with freedom is precisely this possibility.

Dorner contends that the ethical idea of God as love allows for an understanding of immutability in God's way of relating to free, self-determining creatures. For the sake of the creature God "determines himself to enter into alteration and change."[66] The change here involves the divine establishment of a new communion of love with the creature. And while the communion is new for God and creature alike, God establishes it through the "constantly self-identical love" of God.[67] That is to say, what God creates is an extension of God's being *ad intra* in the activity of God *ad extra*. God's self-impartation to the creature "is in no way a loss of self, a giving up of self by God; it is rather the power of love to be in the other itself and to be itself in the other."[68] Bringing together both aspects of God's revealed vitality and the immutability of God's being, Dorner states,

> God remains unaltered in self-identity, even as he posits the world as the end-in-itself of his love, for he affirms himself therein as love for the life of love which has its primal reality in him; but he manifests this joy in the life of love by establishing the possibility of the new life of love [i.e., God's relation to free creatures] along with his.[69]

The act of creation, specifically, establishing a new communion of love with free creatures, exhibits what God is in Godself: divine love. God "loves love" in that God, beginning with the divine self-love, wills creation's end as a fellowship of love.[70] The key concept of love, then, captures both the unchanging element of God's being as well as God's living relation to others.

65. Dorner, *Divine Immutability*, 178.
66. Dorner, *Divine Immutability*, 182.
67. Dorner, *Divine Immutability*, 182.
68. Dorner, *Divine Immutability*, 178.
69. Dorner, *Divine Immutability*, 181.
70. Dorner, *Divine Immutability*, 181; Dorner, *Der Unveränderlichkeit Gottes*, 359. English translation slightly altered.

Finally, love as the shorthand expression for God's ethical being underlies the remaining topics Dorner takes up in the immutability essay. In his treatment of God's reciprocal relation with humanity, Dorner picks up on the account of creation above and God's intention to actualize a communion of love with creatures, with additional emphasis on both the "atoning and forgiving love" that "woos" the creature's soul as well as the devotion of creatures to fellowship with God.[71] Likewise, Dorner asserts that the incarnation fulfills the nature of love insofar as being in history is not merely an idea of God fixed to the eternal decree (i.e., a form of docetism). On the contrary, God participates "in a living way in historico-temporal humanity, sharing in it in order to give a share in itself."[72] And lastly, Dorner characterizes reconciliation, the "inner sanctum of the Christian religion," as the "living participation of the whole person of Christ in humanity," such that in his death the "divine-human love . . . affirm[s] itself" in the most extreme of historical realities.[73] Once more the concept of divine love serves a two-fold purpose: on one hand, love indicates the unchanging nature of God's being; God loves through God's love. On the other, by the dynamism of this unchanging love God relates to, enters into fellowship with, and reconciles creatures in time. Thus Dorner can say, the unchanging being of God is not a "fixed" thing but rather a "living immutability (*lebendige Unveränderlichkeit*)."[74]

2: Immutability and the Livingness of God

Dorner's immutability essay highlights some of the critical issues at stake in the treatment of this classical doctrine. Initially driven by the question of whether or how God changes in the incarnation event amongst fellow Lutheran and Reformed theologians, Dorner proceeds to address the need for a concept of immutability consistent with the active expressions of God in revelatory history. Neither divine immutability nor divine vitality is dispensable. They are united under the common denominator of salvation: God's unchangeable nature is the basis for faith's certainty in God as the trustworthy grounds for salvation; through the vitality of God's being God acts in history to achieve the creature's salvation.

71. Dorner, *Divine Immutability*, 184–86. The parallels between Dorner and process thought are perhaps most explicit here. See Drewer, "Dorner's Critique of Divine Immutability," 77–91.

72. Dorner, *Divine Immutability*, 188.

73. Dorner, *Divine Immutability*, 189.

74. Dorner, *Divine Immutability*, 175; Dorner, *Der Unveränderlichkeit Gottes*, 351.

Accordingly, the question which animates Dorner's essay is how immutability and divine vitality are to be reconciled. The question has two sides. On one side, it has to do with the reconciliation of immutability and the livingness of God *ad intra*. This involves Dorner's adaptation of Trinity into his idea of ethical immutability, specifically the Spirit's actualization of the Father's necessary goodness through the freedom of the Son. On the other, it involves reconciling God's essential immutability with the revealed vitality of God in history. The two sides are related. For the need to reconcile immutability with divine livingness in the being of God *ad intra* stems from the two-fold witness to God's unchanging being *and* vitality in revelation; God is the sure grounds of faith, the rock of salvation, as well as the living means of this salvation in the revealed history God lives with others. Furthermore, for Dorner the unchanging vitality of God among us is grounded in God's being; God is prior to all other reality. Hence there must be a uniting principle in God that maintains the diverse yet singular reality manifest in God's self-revelation (i.e., God as immutable *and* living). This uniting principle, of course, is Dorner's idea of ethical immutability.

Dorner makes a significant move in handling the first side of the question here, the reconciliation of immutability and the livingness of God *ad intra*. As we will see, his method sets a kind of precedent in utilizing the doctrine of God for understanding the God-world relation that subsequent figures of this study follow and develop in varying ways. Twice Dorner invokes the doctrine of the Trinity in connection to the inherent vitality of God's being; first, in his more general attempt to reconcile immutability and livingness in God, and, second, in his formulation of God's ethically immutable being. This move, the construal of immutability and the vitality of God through Trinity, is metaphysically decisive. While I think there are legitimate reasons to question the accuracy of Dorner's reception of the traditional notion of simplicity, especially given the findings of scholarship and projects aimed at a return to classical theological sources (ressourcement and retrieval) in recent decades, the point I wish to highlight here is the positive contribution that Dorner's immutability essay makes for conceiving of divine ontology.[75] The governing concept for understanding God's being is not a notion of simplicity gleaned strictly from the idea of God as creator; Trinity is.

---

75. See, e.g., Allen, "Divine Attributes"; Swain, "Divine Trinity"; Flynn and Murray, *Ressourcement*. Tellingly, Dorner would in all likelihood agree with the contemporary interpretation of simplicity, derived from the traditional understanding, stating that it "only proscribes division and composition in the Godhead, not distinction." Dolezal, "Trinity," 85. See also Richards, *The Untamed God*, 228–31.

What differences does the leading role of Trinity make? An example from Dorner's essay is telling. The classical concept of immutability sets God apart from the world. God is unchanging, even unchangeable, due to the actuality of God's being that is without potentiality. This makes for a lucid concept of divine transcendence, but it does not make clear how God relates to the complex world God has made. Dorner muses over the implications of this contrast between God and the world, supposing that it even leads to an inverted form of pantheism upon the world's return to its divine source in the consummation of all things. While Dorner does not put it this way, Trinity provides a solution to problems like this, and makes a vital difference for understanding the God-world relation, by way of maintaining the dialectic of God's identity with and distinction from the world. The trinitarian being of God includes the actualization and unchanging reality of God in the divine persons, Father, Son, and Spirit. This characterizes God as wholly other, utterly unique from the created order. And yet the complexity and change of the created world can be understood to have a basis in God's being. For the actualization of the divine relations is not a one time occurrence; it is eternal, perennial, the always actualized (or actualizing) potentiality of the relations between Father, Son, and Spirit. God is both utterly distinct from and related to the world God has made. God is both at one and the same time because God is triune. For the inner-trinitarian relations of God, in their simultaneously abiding and diverse actuality, make it possible for God to uniquely uphold this dialectic. What difference does Trinity make? For Dorner Trinity means God is distinct from but not incompatible with created reality.

The reference to divine potentiality can also be used to understand the other side of the question here, the reconciliation of God's inner-trinitarian immutability and God's living relation to the world. As just noted, Dorner's trinitarian ontology opens up a conception of absolute potentiality alongside a notion of divine actuality. This potentiality, which on its own might suggest a kind of lack in God, actually points up the perfection of the relationality of God's being as, in Dorner's words, a 'cycle of life.' Again, it is unlike any potentiality we know, for it exists in God only in perfect unity with the absolute actuality of God's being. But it is nevertheless real in God, as real as the mystery of the trinitarian unity-in-distinctions. The key point is that this ontology supports the connection between the Trinity of God's being and God's living relation to history. Dorner alludes to the connection this way: Out of the self-generating life of God as triune, the perfect realization of God as Father, Son, and Spirit, comes the *new, self-established* good that God wills in the temporal process of creation. This good is new insofar as it pertains to the ongoing relation that God creates with free creatures. It is self-established insofar as it derives from the perennial actuality of the trinitarian relations. Trinity enables a conception of God's involvement with the emergence of the new in created reality. Moreover, the same theme is reiterated in Dorner's notion of the communion of love which God establishes with free creatures.

Having affirmed much in Dorner's use of Trinity for understanding the immutable vitality of God's being and God's living relation to the world, I now offer a critical consideration of Dorner's account. I highlight two problems in what follows. The first problem concerns an inconsistency in Dorner's understanding of immutability. It is relevant to this chapter and the next as I compare Dorner's construal of immutability with the understanding of God's being in Karl Barth's trinitarian theology. The second problem is more important for the larger purpose of this chapter in introducing the central question of this work. Here I consider a limitation in Dorner's application of Trinity to the God-world relation and the need for further reflection on this theme. I begin with the inconsistency in Dorner's idea of immutability.

In part III of the immutability essay Dorner outlines the rationale for God's will to create, specifically to relate to free creatures, through the divine love and the nature of this love in the drive to communicate itself to others. The divine love, we recall, is shorthand for Dorner's ethical concept of immutability. It is in this context that Dorner makes the surprising denial that God's self-imparting love finds its "proper place" in God's being. Rather, its proper setting is only "where purely free original giving takes place, only where there is pure want in the recipient," in the neediness of creatures.[76] Dorner contends that this entails no loss in God, no fundamental change on the part of God's being. Why not? Because "even as [God] posits the world as the end-in-itself of his love, . . . he affirms himself therein as love for the life of love which has its primal reality in him."[77] God is love and God's ways *ad extra* are loving.

But a problem emerges when the statement above on God's self-imparting love and its proper realization in relating to creatures is set against Dorner's previously articulated idea of God's unchanging being in terms of the "intrinsically righteous" nature of God from part II of the immutability essay. God, Dorner states, is the creature's "highest and absolute ethical end."[78] Herein lies the immutable basis which grounds creaturely faith. However, if the realization of God's self-imparting love *among creatures*

76. Dorner, *Divine Immutability*, 178.

77. Dorner, *Divine Immutability*, 181.

78. Dorner, *Divine Immutability*, 119.

becomes the focal point of God's ethical goodness, the unchanging principle of God's being, then a shift of sorts has taken place from what Dorner says in part II of the immutability essay to part III. The locus of God's immutability moves in the event of relating to creation, especially creatures of pure want, from the ethical being of God in eternity to the loving extension of God's ethical nature in time. To be sure, God's character on this view does not change; God acts in accordance with God's loving being. But there is still a notable shift from God's primal, unchanging goodness, to the loving activity of God among us—its 'proper place.'

If God's ethical immutability is the sure grounds of creaturely faith, wherein do those grounds lie? In the eternal, absolute goodness of God's ethical being? Or in the more fitting (for Dorner) extension of this love among us? How reliable is the latter, the manifestation of God's love among us, if the former, the loving reality of God's eternal being, is somehow inadequate in serving as the unshakable grounds of God's ethical immutability? And what secures against the possibility that the locus point of God's immutability, the sure grounds of creaturely faith, will not shift again? Here I only raise these questions. I return to them and offer a proposed solution to the underlying problematic identified in these questions in the following chapter. There I will show that the central problem derives from a fundamental separation between an understanding of divine immutability, on one hand, and the person of Christ and his concrete history, on the other. I argue that Karl Barth's christologically oriented view of election allows for a conception of God's immutable, self-giving love for creatures to *coincide* with God's primal and equally unchanging self-love—and so for a view of immutability different from Dorner's—without undermining the notion of God's (eternal) being as the location of the creaturely grounds for faith.

I turn now to the second problem on Dorner's use of Trinity for understanding the God-world relation. Trinity, as noted above, has two functions in Dorner's essay in relation to the main task of reconciling divine immutability with the vitality of God. I have already shown how the doctrine of the Trinity enables Dorner to conceive of divine immutability and the livingness of God's being together. Likewise, Dorner's allusion to the divine establishment of the new in time in relation to the potentiality of God, a subtle reference to his trinitarian ontology, points up the significance of Trinity for understanding God's living relation to history and creatures in time. But between the two purposes of Dorner's immutability essay, reconciling immutability and the livingness of God's being (*ad intra*) and reconciling immutability with God's revealed vitality (*ad extra*), Dorner more adequately addresses the former problem regarding the being of God *ad intra*. That is, he gives extended attention to divine potentiality as an inner-trinitarian reality that serves to unite God's unchanging nature and eternal (or internal) livingness. Regarding the other problem, reconciling immutability with God's revealed vitality, or the being of God in time, Trinity's application is much more limited. As we have seen, Dorner briefly references divine potentiality in the triune God's way of relating to history. This serves as an allusion to his trinitarian idea of God, and although it allowed me to elaborate above on its implicit meaning, nowhere does Dorner himself fill out the trinitarian dimensions of his subtle reference to divine potentiality. More specifically, Dorner does not make extensive or explicit use of Trinity for reflecting on God's relation to creatures and creaturely reality. Trinity remains a background concept. The point here concerns not only this single reference, however, but all of Dorner's explications of the God-world relation: the application of Trinity to God's living relation to history is underdeveloped in Dorner's immutability essay.

We must be careful with this criticism. The primary task of Dorner's essay is to outline a new conception of divine immutability. His foray into this task is not, at least not initially and explicitly, an endeavor in trinitarian theology. Rather, Trinity is a resource that Dorner avails himself of along the way. And so we might not expect Dorner to put this classical doctrine at the forefront of the solution to the problems he addresses: the reconciliation of immutability and vitality in God *ad intra* as well as immutability and the revealed vitality of God.

This is true. But, in another way, as has been made increasingly clear in the exposition of Dorner's essay and in this concluding section, Trinity remains the point upon which Dorner anchors his doctrine of immutability. Whether stated at the outset or not, Dorner's immutability essay is a work in trinitarian thought. The dialectic of divine actuality and potentiality that undergirds Dorner's concept God's living immutability is rooted in the perennial nature of the trinitarian relations. The contours of God's ethical being— necessary goodness, freedom, and actualization—stand in for Father, Son, and Spirit respectively. Once Dorner avails himself of the classical doctrine of the Trinity, it becomes foundational to both the notion of the inner-vitality of God's being as well as the ethical notion of immutability.

This brings us back to the criticism above. Despite Trinity's foundational place for understanding the immutability of God's being and its connection to the living reality of God, Dorner makes surprisingly minimal use of the resources available to him in his trinitarian theology when it comes to the revelatory activity of God. When Dorner turns from the question of reconciling immutability and vitality in the Godhead to the activity of God *ad extra*, the focal point is not God's trinitarian activity. Rather, it is God's way of relating to ethically independent creatures. Dorner characterizes this relationship in terms of the establishment of a communion of love. The love concept plays the determinative role in God's relation to created reality. Again, special care is called for here. For Dorner's idea of love is not an abstraction but rather summarizes God's ethical (trinitarian) being. The more important point is this: Dorner's near exclusive use of the love concept to articulate God's living relation to creation means that the idea of the trinitarian relations of God, so crucial to his view of God's internal, living immutability, serves primarily as a background notion. For Dorner Trinity more readily *grounds* God's loving relation to creatures; it does not come to expression, or is not put to constructive use, in the same way in terms of the actual history that God lives with others. In Dorner's essay the meaning of this fruitful doctrine for understanding God's living relation to history is a largely untouched possibility for theological reflection.

But as will be expected from the foregoing, the criticism here opens itself up to constructive possibilities. For even as I highlight the subordinate role of particular trinitarian dimensions to the more general idea of love in God's activity *ad extra* in Dorner's account, I have also been able to tease out above one of the possibilities of Trinity for understanding the God-world relation through Dorner's invocation of God's (absolute) potentiality: God generates the good that God seeks to establish in relation to free creatures out of the self-generating fellowship of God's triunity. Dorner's view of the Trinity serves as informative background to the love notion that permeates his idea of God's worldly activity in the immutability essay—to the exclusion, I claim, of utilizing the rich theological resources that the trinitarian idea of God offers for understanding God's worldly activity. But, of course, it need not serve as only informative background. The eternal God is the same one who acts in history. Or in the more contemporary expression, the immanent Trinity *is* the economic Trinity. *How* this God is the same one is a question that I will begin to explore in the following chapter.

What constructive possibilities does Dorner's account open up for theological reflection? Two ideas present themselves here. The first is a simple continuation of Dorner's way of reflecting on the meaning of the trinitarian idea of God for understanding God's being. For Dorner this centered on the reconciliation of immutability and livingness in God. The steadfast vitality of God's being on this view has its primal expression in the unchanging dynamism of the trinitarian relations of God. This way of understanding the internal vitality of God's being through Trinity marks the theological approaches of the four main figures addressed in this study. This leads to the second idea. Again Dorner's two-sided approach to reconciling immutability and vitality is instructive. How does a specifically trinitarian ontology bear not only on understanding the inner-vitality of God but also

God's living relation to history? It is worth noting a relevant epistemological question here that runs in the opposite direction. What determines the
trinitarian ontology? Dorner has largely assumed the creedal confessions
as his source for theological reflection. And in a theological context committed to the church and the reasons for its existence, rightly so. In the following chapters, however, I will engage approaches to the significance of
creedal trinitarian reflection just as much, and often more, attuned to the
scriptural contours that testify to God's self-revelation. For trinitarian reflection on God's relation to the world, this involves a two-fold procedure: first
determining (understanding) the nature of God's triunity through scriptural reflections and a creedal-confessional lens; and second, in the reverse
procedure that takes the truth of God's revelation as truly *self*-revelation,
determining how God relates to history through the trinitarian nature of
God's being. Along these lines trinitarian reflection on the God-world relation is a work in faith seeking understanding.

The second question above—how does a trinitarian ontology bear on
the relation between God and history?—is indebted to Dorner but seeks
to address a theme that is not satisfactorily treated in his account. Dorner
was concerned with the question of reconciling divine immutability with
the revealed vitality of God. In what follows I take up this question in
modified form: How does the doctrine of the Trinity inform the understanding of God's living relation to history? With the treatment of divine
immanence comes the question of God's abiding transcendence. Hence
we will also ask: How does Trinity not only bridge the difference between
the eternality of God's being and God's living history but also maintain
the distinction between God and created reality? In the immutability essay Dorner does not set out a robust enough trinitarian theology to address these questions. However, his account has proved to be a helpful way
forward, both in terms of the possibilities of a trinitarian based view of
God's living history and in refining the key questions and problems to be
addressed in the following chapters.

2

"Ours in Advance"

Trinity and History in the
Theology of Karl Barth

THE REVITALIZATION OF THE doctrine of the Trinity in twentieth century theology is often said to begin with the work of Karl Barth. Barth's decisive move is to situate Trinity at the head of his *magnum opus*, the *Church Dogmatics* (hereafter *CD*), within the doctrine of revelation. For Barth the touch-point between these two theological loci is clear. In the prolegomena to the *CD* Barth asks: Who is revealed in revelation? How does it come about? What happens as a result? His response: God, thrice over: *God* reveals God, both *through* God and *as* God.[1] The relevance of Barth's theology for this work becomes evident at once. The link between this classical doctrine and God's act of self-disclosure indicates the underlying connection of Trinity and God's revelatory history and historical being.

In this chapter I address the relationship between God and history in Barth's trinitarian theology. I survey a select parts of Barth's *CD* with a brief foray into *The Epistle to the Romans*. The basic structure and argument of this chapter is two-fold: (1) I begin with an analysis of Barth's theory of divine correspondence: who God is among us corresponds to the eternal life of God as Father, Son, and Spirit. Barth's theory successfully captures both how God's revelatory activity proceeds from God's eternal being as well as a way that God's unchanging identity holds (immutability) in God's living relation to history. Yet, despite this contribution, there remains a lacuna in Barth's application of Christ's incarnate history to the meaning of God's trinitarian being in the early sections of the *CD*. This lacuna, set alongside Barth's theory of correspondence, leaves his account susceptible to what I describe as a two-fold history, or a kind of ongoing correspondence between God in eternity above and God in time below that ultimately undermines the truth of God's history with us. (2) A corrective to this problem can be found in Barth's doctrine of election in *CD* II/2. I argue that Barth's identification

1. Barth, *CD* I/1:295–96.

of Jesus Christ with the subject of election and his notion of divine obedience entail a divine relation to history that rules out the possibility of a two-track perspective on God's history. Two things are needed to make this claim: first, with Barth, I defend the inclusion of a notion of obedience as proper to the Father-Son relation in the Godhead; and second, I reorient (or, at least, clarify) Barth's construal of election in terms of his notion of an *Urgeschichte*, a primal history of God, in order to avoid a relapse into the previously identified problem of a two-fold divine history.

A few other related topics are taken up for critical consideration in this chapter. At various points I assess similarities and differences between Isaak A. Dorner and Barth on the triune God's relation to history. In the concluding analysis I return to the point from chapter 1 on the way in which Barth's doctrine of election suggests an idea of immutability that holds together God's eternal vitality with the being of God in time. I also attend to Wolfhart Pannenberg's criticism of Barth's notion of divine subjectivity. While the critique is only partly related to the topic of this chapter, my engagement with it opens up a line of criticism on the role of scriptural narrative for understanding the link between Trinity and the God-world relation that plays a decisive role in the following chapters.

Following the basic two-fold structure and argument above, the chapter is divided into two sections. In section 1 I examine the link between Barth's doctrine of the Trinity and the being of God in revelatory history in *CD* I/1. A brief assessment of the second edition of Barth's commentary on the book of Romans prior to this highlights a key problem in the God-world relation that Barth's later trinitarian theology must overcome and provides key background to the major themes that inform Barth's doctrine of the Trinity in *CD* I/1. I then consider the relation between God and revelatory history in *CD* I/1 under Barth's tagline of the triune God as 'ours in advance.' Following this, I look at how Barth applies his trinitarian theology to his doctrine of the divine constancy in *CD* II/1. I conclude section 1 with a critical analysis of Barth's correspondence theory and the role of Trinity in God's relation to history in *CD* I/1 and II/1. In section 2 I attend to Barth's doctrine of election and the meaning of Barth's inclusion of the Son's eternal obedience for conceiving of the relationship between God's pre-temporal eternity and the being of God in time. I conclude section 2 with a constructive reflection on the way that Barth's doctrine of election can be incorporated to both rule out the notion of a two-fold history of God and, more positively, demonstrate the continuity or identity that exists between the eternal Trinity and the being of God with us.

More broadly, this chapter begins to develop the constructive argument of this work through a critical appropriation of Barth's trinitarian theology. The concluding chapter will attempt to bring together the various elements that I argue for in Barth, Pannenberg, and Jenson's theology. Those from Barth's theology pertain primarily to protological aspects of the God-world relation. Above all, I argue that Barth's notions of the antecedent Trinity and his concept of the Son's conformity to the Father's will (based in his doctrine of God's pre-temporal election) can be constructively employed for a theological account of the triune God's living relation to history. Subsequent chapters fill out Barth's protological perspective on election and the divine Son for a more comprehensive understanding of God's involvement in history. Chapters 3 and 4 focus on the inner-historical and eschatological nature of the God-world relation. In chapter 3, I turn to Pannenberg's trinitarian theology and his idea of the monarchy of the Father for a notion of the vitality of God in history. And in chapter 4, I take up Jenson's doctrine of the Spirit and the concept of divine futurity in order to make the case for a trinitarian based idea of divine transcendence.

1: The Eternal Trinity and Revelation History

1.1: *Revelation and God in the* The Epistle to the Romans

Romans II is not a work in trinitarian theology. Barth does not develop his trinitarian thought until his *Göttingen Dogmatics* of 1924–25.[2] However, by the time he develops his trinitarian theology, in both the *Göttingen Dogmatics* and in *CD* I/1, he does so in tandem with some of the central themes from *Romans* II. In the first section of this chapter I briefly consider three such themes: divine revelation, the subjectivity of God, and eternity. I track these themes insofar as they reappear, albeit in modified form, and shape Barth's trinitarian theology in *CD* I/1. The consideration of eternity receives additional attention here. Barth's understanding of eternity from the time of *Romans* II to the appearance of the *CD* undergoes a more critical—and as I argue, welcomed—modification in comparison to the other themes. The stark contrast of eternity with the temporal reality of creatures in *Romans* II makes a conception God's being *in* revelation history nearly impossible. Making this point clear, however, will serve to demonstrate the radical significance of Barth's trinitarian theology in *CD* I/1 for understanding the God-world relation.

As has been explored extensively, the shockwaves created by *Romans* II derive from the evocative way that Barth distances himself from the liberal Protestant tradition that characterized his theological training.

2. Barth, *Göttingen Dogmatics*, 87–130.

In *Romans* II Barth sets his stake on the principle of God's sovereignty. His task is to elucidate the simple but encompassing truth that "God is free."[3] Theology has to do with God, and so, he asserts time and again, it does not ultimately proceed from anthropological or phenomenological insight. Already Barth believed himself to have seen what happens in the anthropocentric approach when several of his teachers, including Adolf von Harnack and Wilhelm Herrmann, willingly signed off on the war plans of Kaiser Wilhelm II.[4] Against this background the main principle of *Romans* II can be understood. *Romans* II is marked by a notion of *diastasis*: the definite contrast between God and the world. Barth writes, the reality of God "touches the world of the flesh, but touches it as a tangent touches a circle, that is, without touching it."[5] Or more fervently, the world is simply not capable of containing what takes place in the event of God's self revelation: "God is pure negation."[6]

Nevertheless, God's revelation happens. And so the question for Barth is how to speak of the absolute subjectivity of God in revelation, or how God remains God in revelation without becoming directly identifiable with revelation's creaturely medium.[7] Barth puts forth this conception of absolute subjectivity by means of a set of dialectical notions. God is known or unveiled within a veil. The revelation of God, he states, "must be the most complete veiling of His incomprehensibility . . . . [God] is made known as the Unknown."[8] In this way revelation reinforces the *diastasis* between God and creature without severing all connection between the two.[9] God remains absolute Lord in the event of God's disclosure, unknown in being revealed. A direct communication of God would do away with the "vast chasm" between God and the world.[10] In his well known reference to Kierkegaard, Barth gives credence to "the infinite qualitative distinction between man and God."[11]

The dialectic of God's being unveiled in a veil secures the sovereignty of God as absolute subject in revelation. A second dialectic in *Romans*

3. Barth, *The Epistle to the Romans*, 92. Hereafter cited as *Romans* II.

4. Barth, "Evangelical Theology," 14.

5. Barth, *Romans* II, 30.

6. Barth, *Romans* II, 141–42.

7. McCormack, *Critically Realistic Dialectical Theology*, 207–8. On Barth's early use of the related phrase, "God is God," see Busch, *Karl Barth*, 87; Jüngel, *Karl Barth*, 31.

8. Barth, *Romans* II, 98, 106.

9. Ruschke, *Entstehung und Ausführung*, 66–68.

10. Barth, *Romans* II, 98.

11. Barth, *Romans* II, 98–99; Barth, *Der Römerbrief*, 73. Translation slightly altered.

II is worth mention here, the dialectic of eternity and time. God and the temporal world exist on two different planes, the unknown plane above and the known world below. In revelation the two planes intersect and leave behind an empty space, a "void."[12] Or, in another of Barth's favored metaphors, the two planes meet and just as soon depart so as to form a "crater made at the percussion point of an exploding shell."[13] The eternal leaves behind no substantial trace of itself in revelation, only lingering impressions. Why? Barth's concern is with creaturely knowledge of God. God is absolute Lord, and so any knowing of God comes in the form of a reoccurring gift; it is not a thing to be possessed.

The concept of eternity in *Romans* II is also significant for understanding the God-world relation. The world of time, Barth states, "is nothing when measured by the standard of eternity."[14] Or, as quoted above, the contact between God and the world in revelation is like the way "a tangent touches a circle, that is, without touching it."[15] Barth follows much of the theological tradition with his timeless notion of eternity. What is distinctive, though, is the radical power of eternity to negate. The implications of this are important. If the eternity of God is radically negating timelessness, then the revelation of God in history, the intersection of two utterly distinct planes, can happen, but *not* in a historical way. Barth's fixation on the momentary nature of revelation (Kierkegaard) means that God's involvement in created reality must always be punctiliar. How does God *live* a history with others if there is nothing temporally abiding to revelation? God is revealed, to be sure, but it becomes nearly impossible to conceive of divine movement within the revealed history of God. "The Lord went in front of (Israel) in a pillar of cloud by day, to lead them along the way, and in a pillar of fire by night" (Exod 13:21). Temporally negating being does not move in history this way.

Shortly after *Romans* II Barth discards the temporally negating dialectic of eternity and time. I return to the significance of this move, as well as what replaces the timeless conception of divine reality in Barth's theology, in the next section. What remains consistent from *Romans* II to the *CD* is the dialectic of the veiling and unveiling of God.[16] In this idea Barth issues forth a conception by which God remains the sovereign subject of revelation.

---

12. Barth, *Romans* II, 29.

13. Barth, *Romans* II, 29.

14. Barth, *Romans* II, 43.

15. Barth, *Romans* II, 30.

16. For other uses of dialectic in this work, see McCormack, *Critically Realistic Dialectical Theology*, 266–80; Beintker, *Die Dialektik*, 55–59.

What changes, however, is the medium of this dialectic. Bruce L. McCormack has traced the shift from the focus on dialectics in Barth's theology to the idea of the analogy of faith in Barth's discovery of the *an/enhypostatic* Christology of the Protestant Scholastics while lecturing at Göttingen in the mid-1920s.[17] Dialectics were not lost, specifically the veiling-unveiling dialectic, but were reconfigured along christological lines in a way that goes beyond anything in *Romans* II. More important for the purposes here, however, is that Barth also finds a suitable place for this form of dialectic, as well as the accompanying and interrelated notions of revelation and divine subjectivity, in his emerging trinitarian theology.

1.2: Revelation and the Doctrine of the Trinity: Church Dogmatics I/1

As stated at the beginning of this chapter, by situating Trinity at the top of his *CD* in the doctrine of revelation, the relevance of this classical doctrine for Barth's understanding of God's relation to history becomes immediately evident.[18] In what follows I outline how Barth's concept of the eternal (antecedent) Trinity from *CD* I/1 (§§8–12) forms the basis for God's revelatory history with an eye toward the development of Barth's theology from *Romans* II to *CD* I/1.

The concept of divine subjectivity from *Romans* II remains central to Barth's doctrine of the Trinity in *CD* I/1. Barth states, "it follows from the trinitarian understanding of the God revealed in Scripture that this one God is understood . . . as person, i.e., as an I existing in and for itself with its own thought and will."[19] The trinitarian dimension of this subjectivity manifests itself in the three-fold nature of revelation. "*God* reveals Himself. He reveals Himself *through Himself*. He reveals *Himself*."[20] In its simplest form the three-fold concept of revelation runs thus: "God reveals

17. McCormack's thesis challenges Hans Urs von Balthasar's proposal that the transition from dialectics to the analogy of faith in Barth's theology occurs with Barth's work on Anslem in 1931 (*Fides Quaerens Intellectum*). McCormack, *Critically Realistic Dialectical Theology*, 1–23. See also Webster, "Interpreting Barth," 12–13.

18. On the significance of Barth's treatment of God as triune before the general doctrine of God (i.e., God's being and attributes), see Jenson, *God after God*, 97–99. On its more general significance within the theological tradition, see LaCugna, *God for Us*, 146–50, 167–69, 213–16.

19. Barth, *CD* I/1:358–59.

20. Barth, *CD* I/1:296. "Revelation means the knowledge of God through God and from God." See also Barth, *Göttingen Dogmatics*, 61.

Himself as the Lord."[21] Revelation as such contains a subject, predicate, and object structure: God, who reveals God, as God. The idea of revelation plays a foundational, even governing role in Barth's trinitarian theology. Barth writes, "we arrive at the doctrine of the Trinity by no other way than that of an analysis of the concept of revelation."[22] The idea of revelation forms "the root of the doctrine of the Trinity."[23] Whether this imposes a non-scriptural or abstract ontology onto the doctrine of the Trinity is a question I return to below.[24]

Because God permeates all of revelation, as its subject, predicate, and object, revelation is nothing other than Godself. "God is identical with His act in revelation and also identical with its effect."[25] Putting a sharper point on this, Barth reemploys the veiling-unveiling dialectic of *Romans* II in view of his trinitarian idea of God. God is sovereign Lord, and so "cannot be unveiled" to creatures.[26] And yet in revelation the self-unveiling of God really happens. How is this possible? The answer lies in God's triunity.

The self-disclosure of God consists of "three moments": the divine "unveiling, veiling and impartation."[27] Each moment corresponds to a "divine mode of being"—Barth's preferred term for divine person or *hypostasis*—in the Godhead.[28] Barth begins by specifying the alterity of the Son from the Father. God as such is free to "differentiate Himself from Himself,

---

21. Barth, *CD* I/1:306.

22. Barth, *CD* I/1:312. Because Barth does not begin his trinitarian theology with the scriptural witness or incorporate the significance of the worship of Jesus the Son in the New Testament, George Hunsinger claims that this leaves Barth's "Trinitarian doctrine with a certain imbalance." Hunsinger, "Karl Barth and Some Protestant Theologians," 296.

23. Barth, *CD* I/1:307.

24. Barth claims that the three-fold notion of revelation aligns with the biblical order of God's self-disclosure. Barth, *CD* I/1:314.

25. Barth, *CD* I/1:296.

26. Barth, *CD* I/1:315.

27. Barth, *CD* I/1:332; Barth, *Die kirchliche Dogmatik* I/1:351. Hereafter *Die kirchliche Dogmatik* is cited as *KD*. English translation slightly altered. In the standard English version's rendering of *Momente* as "elements" something of the logical and sequential ordering of revelation is lost.

28. Barth, *CD* I/1:333, 355–57, 359. Barth's use of the term is meant to stave off the modern notion of person as a distinct center of self-consciousness, and with it, tritheism. Barth's formulation receives criticism from different angles. For a similar reformulation of it, see Rahner, *The Trinity*, 109–11. The criticisms of Jürgen Moltmann and Catherine Mowry LaCugna highlight its modalistic undertones and the loss of God's communal nature and essence; respectively, Moltmann, *The Trinity and the Kingdom*, 139, 143; LaCugna, *God for Us*, 250–55.

to become unlike Himself and yet to remain the same."[29] This internal differentiation in God entails that God is not bound to a self-enclosed eternity, but free to enter into and take on a temporal form in revelation.[30] In this revelation God is disclosed a second time as Father. Barth associates this with the mystery of revelation.[31] God is not another object for creatures to behold. Rather, the Father is the "free ground and free power" of the Son; even in the form of the Son's unveiling, the Father remains within a veil.[32] And lastly, the Spirit. In the veiling and unveiling of God, the divine self-revelation is a concrete event directed toward humanity. The revelation of God in the unveiling-veiling dialectic cannot be grasped, but through the Holy Spirit it addresses creatures and enables the creaturely response to revelation. Barth characterizes this as the "historicity of revelation," the work of the Spirit in time in generating the relation between the creator and creature in Jesus Christ.[33] Each moment of disclosure is the self-revelation of God, for "God is the one God in threefold *repetition* . . . grounded in His Godhead."[34] In this three-fold way God is veiled, unveiled, and imparted to creatures in time.

Based on these preliminary moves in Barth's trinitarian theology, it is clear that the eternal relations of God's being ground God's revelatory activity. The distinction of the Son from the Father, for instance, provides the condition in God for the alterity that characterizes God's involvement with creation. In §§10–12 of *CD* I/1 Barth continues in this mode of reflection and turns to the relation between the eternal Trinity and God's being in salvation history. Barth defines this relationship in terms of a correspondence.[35] The activity of God *ad extra* corresponds to the being of God *ad intra*. The notion is already present, though not developed, in the three moments of revelation: "the question of revealer, revelation and being revealed corresponds to the logical and material order . . . of the

29. Barth, *CD* I/1:320. Cf. Gordon Watson's similar construal of God's hiddenness and disclosure in Barth's theology in terms of God's self-objectivity. Watson, *The Trinity and Creation in Karl Barth*, 50.

30. Barth, *CD* I/1:320–21. See also Barth, *Göttingen Dogmatics*, 59.

31. Barth, *CD* I/1:321, 388–90.

32. Barth, *CD* I/1:324.

33. Barth, *CD* I/1:330. See also 325–26.

34. Barth, *CD* I/1:350, 359. Emphasis mine.

35. Eberhard Jüngel outlines this notion in his commentary on Barth's idea of revelation as the self-interpretive act of God. Jüngel, *God's Being*, 35–37.

doctrine of the Trinity."[36] Who God is among us, Barth puts it, God is "antecedently in Himself."[37]

This time Barth begins with the first divine mode of being. The Father is revealed to us in Christ as creator and thus as the source of all being. God's activity *ad extra*, however, presupposes a "self-grounded and self-reposing possibility" not in God's creative works but in the actuality of the Godhead. Herein lies the corresponding relation. The Father is to the Son and Spirit source and origin; the Son and Spirit are to the Father like "the copy of an original." In the Godhead the Father is—in a way that rules out any temporal or material beginnings in God—"from Himself alone."[38] Already in God the Father is the primal source of the second and third divine modes of being. The Father as such "can set Himself in relation to everything distinct from Him."[39] In other words, as firstly the eternal author of the Son and the Spirit, the Father can be, secondly, the creative force behind all that is not God. "Manifest as the Creator and therefore as our Father," the Father "already is that which corresponds thereto antecedently and in Himself."[40] Who the Father is among us, he is antecedently in Godself.

Barth turns next to the divine Son. The second person of the Trinity is revealed among us as Lord and the object of creaturely faith. Again Barth grounds this point in the eternal relations of God's being. The Son is Lord among us based on his unique relation to the Father. As the Son of the Father, the principle of origin in God, the Son shares in the Father's lordship. "As the Son of this Father," Barth writes, "He *is* the Lord."[41] More specifically, because "the only-begotten Son is according to John 1:18 the one God," the eternal object of the Father from eternity, the Son "can be the object of our faith."[42] The Son is Lord among us because of his Father-enabled lordship in God. The confession that Jesus Christ is Lord,

> is not just an analysis of the meaning of Jesus Christ for us as this is manifested to us in faith. It tells us that grounded in Himself, and apart from what He means for us, Jesus Christ is what He means for us, and that He can mean this for us because quite apart therefrom He is it antecedently in Himself.[43]

36. Barth, *CD* I/1:314.

37. Barth, *CD* I/1:384, 448.

38. Barth, *CD* I/1:394.

39. Barth, *CD* I/1:394.

40. Barth, *CD* I/1:391.

41. Barth, *CD* I/1:406.

42. Barth, *CD* I/1:425.

43. Barth, *CD* I/1:423–24.

Who the Son is for us, he is likewise in God both prior to and in the event of revelation. In this case, the objectivity of the Son in God, his derivative lordship as Son of the Father, provides the grounds for the divine lordship that he manifests among us. It can be added to this that the Son's revelation is for creatures who have turned from God. The Son is revealed as Lord in restoring a disrupted fellowship, and thus the Son's lordship is also his power to reconcile the creature to God.[44]

Finally, Barth understands the appropriated work of the Spirit in setting others free.[45] The redeeming work of the Spirit has its basis in the antecedent communion of God. In begetting the Son the Father also "brings forth the Spirit of love," negating in Godself from eternity "all loneliness, self-containment, or self-isolation."[46] The Spirit is therefore the principle of communion in God. In the traditional Augustinian sense, the Spirit is the bond of love who unites Father and Son from eternity.[47] In revelation the Spirit imparts this love to others.[48] This divine act works in coordination with the Son. The Son reconciles the creature to God; the Spirit brings the fallen creature into the already existing fellowship of the Father and Son based on their antecedent communion. In sum, through the divine modes of the one God's being, who God is from eternity serves as the basis for who God is among us. Likewise, who God is from eternity determines what God does among us. The activity of God *ad extra* always moves in the same direction, from the eternity of God's being to God's revelatory history in creation, reconciliation, and redemption.[49]

To summarize, Barth's doctrine of the Trinity in *CD* I/1 carries over his underlying concern from *Romans* II, the subjectivity of God in revelation, and draws it out along trinitarian lines. This underlying concern is reformulated in the three-fold slogan, 'God reveals Himself as the Lord,' and unpacked through the trinitarian appropriations of Barth's veiling-unveiling dialectic. Barth fills out his concept of the antecedent Trinity with notions of creative lordship, objectivity, and fellowship in God. These latter notions represent Barth's idea of the eternal Trinity as it corresponds to the being of God in revelation. This corresponding relation, and with it, the emphasis on the actuality of God's antecedent, trinitarian being, highlights both the basis of God's revelatory work in God's eternal being as well as the distinction of God from

44. Barth, *CD* I/1:409.
45. Barth, *CD* I/1:448.
46. Barth, *CD* I/1:483.
47. Barth, *CD* I/1:480, 486.
48. Barth, *CD* I/1:470.
49. Barth, *CD* I/1:471.

revelation history, or who God is "apart from what He means for us."[50] Barth himself provides the apt slogan for his trinitarian theology: "as Father, Son and Spirit God is, so to speak, *ours in advance*."[51]

A comparison with *Romans* II elucidates the significance of Barth's formal doctrine of the Trinity in *CD* I/1. The understanding of divine reality in Barth's trinitarian theology stands in stark contrast to the background concept of eternity in *Romans* II. In the *Romans* commentary the eternity of God is understood as a fundamentally negating reality. The divine lordship rests on the polarizing opposition of God to the creaturely sphere. In *CD* I/1 Barth utilizes the trinitarian dialectic of God's being as unveiled within a veil, resting largely on the internal dynamics of the Father-Son relation, to demarcate the divine lordship. The crucial difference: in *CD* I/1 Barth establishes the divine lordship without having to eradicate a sense of God's real relation to the temporal reality of creatures. Why not? Because the dialectic of God's being unveiled within a veil, rooted in the trinitarian nature of God, implies a temporal principle on the part of God's being. Barth does not develop his trinitarian concept of eternity until *CD* II/1, but the sheer fact of God's primal creativity, objectivity, and communal life points up a dynamism and actuality in the being of God that includes movement, change, and flow—characteristics of time—within an abiding structure of identity. To be sure, this time is distinct, for eternal acts like the Son's being begotten are without literal points of beginning, but this does not preclude a unique and genuine sense of temporality that belongs to God alone. Again, Barth has not yet worked out what this fully means for a concept of eternity. But the temporally inclusive idea of eternity suggested in Barth's formal doctrine of the Trinity is a significant advance over against the temporally negating notion of eternity from *Romans* II. For the idea of eternity in *CD* I/1 is more readily able to assist in conceiving of God in relation to history and the process of time.

I take up the more critical engagements with Barth's trinitarian theology in the final part of section 1 of this chapter. In anticipation of the questions to be asked there, it is worth giving some additional attention here to Barth's theory of correspondence. Barth's theory of correspondence rests on a concern for understanding divine freedom. Who God is among us, God already is from eternity through the antecedent Trinity of God's being. Thus revelation is a divinely self-grounded possibility. This notion, I believe, is unobjectionable to any with commitments to the doctrine of

50. Barth, *CD* I/1:423–24.

51. Barth, *CD* I/1:383. Emphasis mine. For a more a detailed account of the theme of antecedence in the *CD*, see Hunsinger, *Reading Barth with Charity*, 8–10, 43–44, 68; Hunsinger, "Karl Barth and Some Protestant Theologians," 294–309.

creation *ex nihilio*. If God is the true source of all being, God is not at the whim of contingent, historical reality. In a fundamental way, God's being does not change or evolve in relation to the ongoing reality of the world, at least not at the level of God's triunity. This need not rule out any sense of becoming on the part of God, specifically in terms of a divine capacity for a living history with creatures—to become incarnate, to answer prayer, and so on—that is *grounded* in Godself.

However, Barth's use of a theory of correspondence for understanding the God-world relation raises some critical questions. The eternal Trinity corresponds to who God is and what God does among us. There is a certain slippage regarding the idea of correspondence. It connects the being of God in revelation with the eternal being of God prior to God's revelatory acts (i.e., the antecedent Trinity). But what are its limits? Does this two-fold portrayal, the antecedent Trinity, on one side, and the revelatory being of God, on the other, itself correspond to a two-fold reality of God? A notion of God above and God below? If so, what would this mean for understanding the truth of God's being and presence in history? If not, what in Barth's trinitarian understanding of God stands in the way of this conception? Does the antecedent Trinity through which God acts in time somehow assume the revelatory history of God into the divine being so that it becomes characteristic of who God is? And what difference would that make for understanding the eternal Trinity's relation to history? I return to these questions below. First, though, I consider how Barth's trinitarian idea of God continues to be developed and employed in new ways in his doctrine of God's being and the divine attributes in *CD* II/1.

1.3: *Trinity and Divine Constancy*: Church Dogmatics II/1

In *CD* II/1 Barth takes up the doctrine of God and the divine attributes. At several points in his treatment of the being and attributes of God Barth draws from and builds on the trinitarian material of *CD* I/1. I focus on Barth's doctrine of the divine constancy in what follows. For while Trinity plays an expansive role in several areas of the doctrine of God's being, Barth's notion of divine constancy provides a helpful link for reflecting on the connection between Barth's theology and Dorner's idea of immutability. Barth notes his indebtedness to Dorner's essay at the beginning of §31.2. He writes, "those who know this essay will recognize . . . how much (inspiration) I owe to Dorner."[52] Moreover, the divine constancy is particularly important for our

---

52. I use Matthias Gockel's translation here which recognizes that Barth makes reference to his own inspiration, and not to that of Dorner's (as in the English translation),

purposes as one of the locales where Barth raises the question of God as the subject of a real relation to the world. Before turning to Barth's account, however, it is important to highlight the maxim which Barth employs for his doctrine of God's being (§28): God is the one who loves in freedom. The significance of this maxim is seen in that Barth structures his treatment of the divine attributes around it.[53] Because of Barth's repeated reference to this leading notion, I pause to briefly summarize it here.

Barth's maxim, God as the one who loves in freedom, breaks down into three parts: First, God who *is*: here Barth takes up the terminology of God as being-in-act (*Gottes Sein in der Tat*), or the traditional idea of God as *actus purus*.[54] Barth claims, God is a deed, a happening, and an event. Moreover, to the notion of God as act, Barth states, "there must be added at least '*et singularis*,'" sheerly unique.[55] As pure act, God is God's "own conscious, willed and executed decision."[56] Barth situates the notion of God's being-in-act in a trinitarian context. Anticipating a point that I return to in section 2 of this chapter, we can note that the being of the triune God as its own decision means that there is no wedge between God's self-determining act from eternity and the triunity of God. Both claims are true: the constitution of God as Father, Son, and Spirit is the divine decision; God's self-determination is based on God's triunity.[57]

Secondly, God *loves* (*Gottes Sein als der Liebende*).[58] God is love, and love fills God's being in the communion of the divine persons. While known through the revelation of the communion God establishes with us, and in keeping with the idea of the antecedent reality of God in *CD* I/1, this fellowship is rooted in the eternal being of God and, in one of Barth's favorite metaphors, "overflows" unto others.[59] In this way the divine love specifies the kind of being-in-act God is. God is being-in-act, being who loves in the fellowship of Father, Son, and Spirit.

---

as a result of reading the immutability essay. Gockel, "On the Way from Schleiermacher to Barth," 491. Barth, *KD* II/1:554; Barth, *CD* II/1:493.

53. The basic structure follows a division between the attributes of the divine love and the divine freedom. This in turn maps onto the traditional distinction in Lutheran and Reformed theology of God's relative and absolute or communicable and incommunicable attributes, respectively. Barth, *CD* II/1, §29. See Štefan, "Gottes Vollkommenheiten," 90–92.

54. Barth, *KD* II/1:288.

55. Barth, *CD* II/1:264.

56. See Barth, *CD* II/1:271.

57. Barth, *CD* II/1:271; Barth, *KD* II/1:304–5. Translation slightly altered.

58. Barth, *KD* II/1:306.

59. Barth, *CD* II/1:273, 281.

Lastly, God is *free* (*Gottes Sein in der Freiheit*).[60] Barth distinguishes between a primary and secondary sense of divine freedom. Primarily, in the sheer plentitude of God's being, the divine aseity, God is free as existing in and from Godself.[61] Secondarily, and included in God's primary sense of freedom, is God's freedom for what is not God, or what Katherine Sonderegger describes as God's freedom to be gracious.[62] The divine freedom includes the capacity to be in relation with the world that "accrues to (God's) glory" and "authenticates His reality" anew.[63] This also has a trinitarian dimension. The divine freedom for others rests on the antecedent alterity of God the Son. The divine Son is the principle of God's secondary absoluteness who serves as the "basis of all divine immanence."[64]

God loves in freedom. This maxim, which Barth incorporates into his construal of the divine attributes, makes for a lively characterization of divine immutability. As Barth writes in a later volume of the *CD*, the divine loving is "immovable (*unbeweglich*)" insofar as "it is an overflowing of love which is in God Himself."[65] Having outlined this maxim, and returning periodically to its place in Barth's doctrine of God in what follows, I now turn to the place of Trinity in Barth's account of the divine constancy.

In his study of Barth on the attributes of God, or what Barth calls the divine perfections, Robert B. Price delineates three sections in Barth's exposition of the divine constancy. The first is Barth's general definition of the divine constancy in relation to Scripture and the classical conception of immutability; the second is the description of constancy through a notion of salvation history; and the third is the concept of divine constancy as affirmed in the history of Jesus Christ and the sub-topic of divine election.[66] I adapt Price's delineations into my reading of the role of Trinity in Barth's account of immutability. First, I analyze how Barth's idea of God as triune underlies his general notion of immutability; second, I draw out the way that Trinity serves as both an implicit as well as explicit concept in Barth's view of salvation history. This concludes the specific analysis of Barth's trinitarian theology in the treatment of divine constancy. In a third and final step, however, I assess the meaning of incarnation for Barth's understanding

---

60. Barth, *KD* II/1:334.

61. Barth, *CD* II/1:301.

62. Sonderegger, *The Doctrine of God*, 124.

63. Barth, *CD* II/1:309.

64. Barth, *CD* II/1:317. For a more detailed account of Barth's maxim, see Gunton, *Becoming and Being*, 186–98.

65. Barth, *CD* IV/2:352; Barth, *KD* IV/2:394. Translation sightly altered.

66. Price, *Letters of the Divine Word*, 129.

of the divine being. This final step is important in tracking the doctrinal development of Barth and setting up the rationale for the turn to Barth's doctrine of election in section 2 of this chapter.

TRINITARIAN IMMUTABILITY

Barth uses the terminology of divine constancy (*Beständigkeit*) in dealing with the doctrine of immutability.[67] By this choice of terminology Barth does not mean that immutability can be reduced to the way God acts. Rather, he also has an ontological claim in view which becomes clear in the introductory statement of §31.2. Barth writes,

> there neither is nor can be, nor is to be expected or even thought possible in [God], the One omnipresent being, any deviation, diminution or addition, nor any degeneration or rejuvenation, any alteration or non-identity or discontinuity. The one, omnipresent God remains the One He is. This is His constancy.[68]

The constancy of God is interchangeable with the essential immutability of God's being. Moreover, the role of the divine freedom and love in Barth's idea of constancy is also immediately evident. Divine constancy in fact reinforces them. Freedom and love belong to God because "they are the freedom and the love of the One who is constant in Himself."[69] Constant in the divine being, God is free to demonstrate Godself among us anew. As the one who is free in the divine loving, God is the "living God."[70] Barth states, "immutability includes rather than excludes life. In a word it is life."[71] In a way that echoes Dorner's notion of God's "living immutability," Barth describes God as "unchangeably alive (*unveränderlichen Lebendigkeit*)."[72] Thus when Barth references the idea of God's immutable essence, it should not be read as a "lapse" from his dynamic concept of constancy into a static notion of immutability.[73] The constancy of God is the immutable perfection of the divine freedom and love.

67. Barth, *KD* II/1:552.

68. Barth, *CD* II/1:491.

69. Barth, *CD* II/1:491.

70. Barth, *CD* II/1:491.

71. Barth, *CD* II/1:495.

72. Barth, *CD* II/1:511; Barth, *KD* II/1:574. Dorner, *Divine Immutability*, 175. See Sang Eun Lee and Robert Shermann on the different ways that Barth makes use of Dorner's immutability essay: Lee, *Karl Barth und Isaak August Dorner*, 153–98; Sherman, "Isaak August Dorner on Divine Immutability."

73. Russell, "Impassibility and Pathos," 226n8.

More important for the purposes here, Barth conceives of the living nature of God's immutability along trinitarian lines. One of the foundational rules in Barth's doctrine of God is that the "relation between subject and predicate is . . . irreversible."[74] The subject, God, defines the predicate, immutability. Barth's incorporation of Trinity language into the concept of constancy exemplifies this. His trinitarian reference to God's immutability, however, is only implicit. The unchanging life of God as constant in the divine being takes place, he writes, "in eternal self-repetition."[75] Here, Barth, like Dorner before him, intentionally interweaves a previously articulated theme into his account of immutability that derives from his trinitarian understanding of God. The language of self-repetition in God harkens back to CD I/1.[76] There Barth writes, "the name of Father, Son and Spirit means that God is the one God in threefold repetition . . . grounded in His Godhead."[77] As Father, Son and Spirit, God is repeated, thrice over, as the one God. Repetition language, while inclusive of some level of distinction, and therefore appropriate for trinitarian reflection, emphasizes sameness in God. Given Barth's concerns to affirm the traditional character of God's immutable being from the introductory comments of §31.2, his recourse to the idea of repetition in God comes as no surprise. It illuminates the divine unity and underscores the unchanging identity of God in three divine modes of being. As Barth writes, the self-repetition of God rules out the idea of "alteration in [the] Godhead."[78]

Barth follows this allusion to his trinitarian theology of CD I/1 with a claim concerning the capacity of God to remain the same in relation to others. The inner, self-repeated life of God "will go out from the peace, return to the peace, and be accompanied, upheld and filled by the peace, which He has in Himself as the only really living One."[79] The implicit references to Barth's trinitarian theology in the introductory section stop at this. What is clear, though, is that the trinitarian underpinnings of the divine constancy afford Barth a way of defining immutability in terms of the vibrant actuality of the divine life and in tandem with the revealed vitality of God. Barth's rejection of the notion of God as the pure *immobile* in the Protestant orthodox theologian, Amandus Polanus, reflects this point. Even more telling, Barth

---

74. Barth, CD II/1:448.

75. Barth, CD II/1:492.

76. For more on Barth's way of relating concepts and doctrines at different stages of the CD, see Hunsinger, *How to Read Karl Barth*, 28.

77. Barth, CD I/1:350.

78. Barth, CD I/1:350.

79. Barth, CD II/1:492.

posits the idea of a "holy mutability."[80] This mutability is not the haphazard capacity for change in God. Barth references the scriptural accounts of divine repentance (e.g., Gen 6:6–7; 1 Sam 15:11). But this repentance is not an imperfection. Determined by the loving perfection of the divine life, God's holy mutability works this way: God changes in relation to the changing attitudes of humanity. Admittedly, the latter ideas are not laid out in trinitarian terms. But, at the same time, it is not too much to say that Barth's initial references to the trinitarian nature of the divine constancy play a supportive role in these formulations and in Barth's efforts to outline the vitality of God's immutable nature.

SALVATION HISTORY

In the second division of §31.2 Barth turns to the connection between God's immutability and salvation history. Barth's trinitarian theology surfaces in both explicit and implicit ways. He begins with God's act of creation. Created reality is marked by a sense of novelty, for it derives exclusively from the act of God. Barth traces this novelty back into God's being. Creation, writes Barth, is "an expression and confirmation of [God's] constant vitality."[81] Through God "all new things in this reality exist." The basis of this created novelty lies in the fact that God is "the One who is eternally new."[82] Barth's language here invokes the earlier terminology of God's self-repeated being. This understanding of God's unique vitality shapes other aspects of God's relation to the world. Barth asks, "what new thing can the world offer, lend or be to Him, when the ground of the novelty of its existence, and all of the novelties in its essence, is in Himself[?]"[83] In other words, because God is the ultimate origin of the new—creation comes from nothing but God—God can relate to the genuinely new of creation without either being overcome or taken by surprise by it. God, who is at once living in an immutable way, remains the same in creating a complex world full of development and change.

There is no explicit reference to Trinity here. But the connection between these claims and Barth's trinitarian theology is clear. The novelty through which God creates is rooted in the eternal newness of God's being. In the parallel language of divine repetition that Barth employs, this novelty lies in the thrice-repeated being of God. The self-repeated being of God the Father is not twice-more Father but the divine modes of being in God as

80. Barth, *CD* II/1:496–98.
81. Barth, *CD* II/1:499.
82. Barth, *CD* II/1:500.
83. Barth, *CD* II/1:499–500.

Son and Spirit, different from the Father but nevertheless living repetitions of the one God's being. As we saw in *CD* I/1, the Father is the eternal author of the Son and Spirit, and so a unique form of origination—without material beginning—applies to the Godhead.[84] The eternal newness of God's being is concretely trinitarian. Barth spells this out in his later doctrine of creation from *CD* III/1: God's creative work "denotes the divine action which has a real analogy, a genuine point of comparison, only in the eternal begetting of the Son by the Father, and therefore only in the inner-life of God Himself."[85] God's creative activity corresponds to the eternal Trinity.

After detailing the link between God's creative work and the divine constancy Barth moves to the topics reconciliation and revelation. Reconciliation, Barth notes, sheds a light backward on the purpose of creation, communion with the fallen creature, and a light forward to its end in redemption, the consummation of this fellowship. Between the act of creation and its eschatological end, God lives a history with others, the history of reconciliation. God, Barth writes, is the "real subject of this real history."[86] In this history God "leads the world to a future redemption."[87] Barth keeps two poles in view here: on one end is the susceptibility of humanity toward self-destruction; on the other is the internal harmony of God's being. It is the latter, the inner-unity of God's being, that both enables God's relation to the world and makes God's reconciling history with others effective.

Specifically, the trinitarian nature of God's being grounds God's reconciling history. Here Barth is explicit: the constancy of God consists of the "perfect, original and ultimate peace between the Father and the Son by the Holy Spirit."[88] This inner-trinitarian peace is a life generating principle of God's being. In contrast to the self-sustaining nature of God's being, the creature who defects from the purposes of the creator encounters the possibility of "self-annulment."[89] The creature is not self-supportive but relies on the life generating nature of God, the source of the creature's being. In other words, God cannot not be; the creature can not be. God in the perfect fellowship of Father, Son, and Spirit is at peace; the creature is contingent being, and so, given the corruption of sin, faces the possibility of ultimate destitution.

---

84. Barth, *CD* I/1:392–93, 433.
85. Barth, *CD* III/1:13–14.
86. Barth, *CD* II/1:502.
87. Barth, *CD* II/1:502.
88. Barth, *CD* II/1:503.
89. Barth, *CD* II/1:503.

Barth conceives of reconciliation here in terms of encounter between God and the creature. God relates to the creature through the peace that characterizes God as Father, Son, and Spirit. Inasmuch as the creature "rejects the preserving grace of God," Barth writes, God "opposes the opposition of the creature to Himself." God confronts the creature and befriends it, for "the fact of resistance to God in the sphere of creation does not involve any conflict in God Himself."[90] God relates to the conflicted creature, and as constant, the divine peace holds. The living nature of God's peace is unchanging; it is the eternal iteration, and reiteration, of the everlasting harmony of God as Father, Son, and Spirit. In relation to it "sin cannot oppose anything new."[91] Thus as creator God leads the creature toward its rightful end in redemption. The result is the history of reconciliation that God lives with others. Because of God's triunity, God can be the "real subject of this real history" without undergoing a fundamental change in God's being.[92] The constancy of God's being is synonymous with God's triunity.

Before turning to the final section on election I highlight some of the connections and note a difference between Dorner and Barth on the use of Trinity in their respective accounts of immutability. I offer a more general analysis of the relation between Dorner and Barth at the end of section 1. Like Dorner, Barth makes recourse to the Trinity in order to specify the immutable reality of God. There is, as Barth affirms, no 'diminution or addition' in God; God is unchangeable. The difference that Trinity makes in this conception lies firstly in the inherent vitality of the divine constancy. As already noted, like Dorner's idea of God's living immutability, the being of God for Barth is "unchangeably alive."[93] The unchanging but complex reality of God as triune serves as a basis for God's living relation to history. Again, Barth's approach mirrors Dorner's by establishing the grounds for God's activity *ad extra* in the eternal being of God. Specifically, the novelty and peace of God's inner-being for Barth parallel Dorner's understanding of the actualized potentiality in God by which God brings about the good in time.[94]

The differences between their accounts are somewhat of a trade-off. Dorner is more explicit about the trinitarian basis for God's activity *ad extra*. Barth utilizes Trinity in a similar way, but at times only implicitly and the point must be drawn out, as I have done above. Conversely, Barth more

---

90. Barth, *CD* II/1:503, 515.

91. Barth, *CD* II/1:505.

92. Barth, *CD* II/1:502.

93. Barth, *CD* II/1:511.

94. Elsewhere Barth also makes use of a qualified idea of potency in God's eternity as simultaneous with divine actuality. See Barth, *CD* II/1:612.

readily conceives of the actuality of God in history, specifically the history of reconciliation between God and fallen creatures, in trinitarian terms than Dorner does in the immutability essay. This is an important advance on Dorner's account, although it does not pervade all aspects of Barth's account of the God-world relation. For now I leave these general observations here. I return to the difference that Barth's account makes over against Dorner's for understanding God as the subject of a living history with others below.

Jesus and Election

In the third and final division Barth turns to the particular history of Jesus Christ. The significance of this history, in Barth's words, is that in it one lives "in obedience to God" in the uniqueness of the "full possession of all the divine perfections."[95] Although hidden in its revelation, the life of Christ is identical to the life of God. As such, the incarnation is the distinct act of God that forms the presupposition for all of the work of God *ad extra*. However, for all of the focus on the incarnate history of Jesus and its tie to the perfections of God's being, Barth does not develop his notion of the divine constancy in a new way in the final division of §31.2. Rather, Christ's incarnate history serves to confirm what has already been said. Barth writes,

> Without abrogation of the divine unity, there is revealed in [the incarnation] the distinction of the Father and the Son, and also their fellowship in the Holy Spirit. [God becomes and is one with the creature] as the Creator because the incarnation is as such the confirmation of the distinctive reality of creation; for in the fact that God becomes one with creation there is revealed that God and creation as such are two distinct realities, and that the creature has its own reality over against God. He does it finally as Reconciler and Redeemer, because the incarnation as such confirms and explains the fact that God has befriended and continually befriends fallen creation, and will lead it on to a full redemption.[96]

God's act of incarnation is based on the same reality as God's other works *ad extra*: as the particular act of God it "is the decisive and final demonstration of what His being is—His free love."[97] The revelation of the incarnation is "the manifestation of the immutable vitality of God."[98] Barth repeats these

95. Barth, *CD* II/1:514.
96. Barth, *CD* II/1:515.
97. Barth, *CD* II/1:512, 514.
98. Barth, *CD* II/1:513.

ideas in his exegesis of the *kenosis* theme from Philippians 2. The self-emptying act of God speaks more to revelation and the capacity to become incarnate based in the divine love and freedom than it does in adding new insight into the constancy God's being.[99]

Regarding the development of Barth's theology, his final comments on election are more telling. While composing *CD* II/1 Barth was in the process of reconceiving his understanding of divine election. He provides a personal account of this period later in the *CD*.[100] The key statement from his final comments on the divine constancy is this: "Jesus Christ Himself (is) . . . the one reality of the divine decision."[101] Election is the self-determining decision of God; it gives shape to who God is. It means, conceptually speaking, that Barth lifts the historical identity of the man Jesus into the eternal reality of the Godhead. It also shapes the understanding of how God, based on God's eternal identity, acts among us. As Barth writes, it is possible to conceive of this decision as the "basis for the doctrine of the *opera Dei.*"[102] Overwhelmingly, Scripture locates the telos of the divine decree in history. "I am God . . . declaring the end from the beginning . . . I will put salvation in *Zion*, for Israel my glory" (Isa 46:9–13). The mystery of God's will is "set forth in Christ, as a plan for the fullness of time" (Eph 1:9–10).[103] Barth does not fill out these ideas in the treatment of the divine constancy. Nevertheless, the beginnings are evident here of a concept of election that will come to bear significantly on Barth's doctrine of God and the understanding of the God-world relation in view of the particularities of Jesus Christ's concrete history.

In what precedes I have drawn out the trinitarian contours of Barth's doctrine of divine constancy. Barth continues in the style of *CD* I/1. Who God is among us God is already—'in advance'—in the antecedent Trinity of God's being, namely, the unchangeably living one. Specifically, the novelty and harmony that characterize God's worldly activity align with who God is from eternity. In short, the notion of a correspondence between the eternal Trinity and the being of God in time, one of the central motifs from Barth's trinitarian theology in *CD* I/1, applies also to his account of

---

99. For a similar analysis of Barth's exegesis, see McCormack, "The Actuality of God," 233.

100. Barth, *CD* II/2:188–94. Similarly, see Barth's preface to Pierre Maury's *La Prédestination*. For other analyses of this period, see Gockel, *Barth and Schleiermacher*, 158–64; McCormack, *Critically Realistic Dialectical Theology*, 455–58.

101. Barth, *CD* II/1:521.

102. Barth, *CD* II/1:522.

103. Emphasis mine. Barth also includes Ps 2:7–8; Eph 1:12; and Acts 2:23; 4:27–28; Barth, *CD* II/1:521.

immutability. Having laid out Barth's formal doctrine of the Trinity and an application of it in Barth's treatment of the divine perfections, I now turn to the first of two assessments in this chapter of Barth on the relation between the triune God and history.

1.4: Initial Analysis

My initial analysis of Barth on the relation between Trinity and history is divided into four sections: A summary of Barth on the Trinity and revelation history; a constructive engagement with Wolfhart Pannenberg's criticism of Barth on the doctrine of the Trinity and divine subjectivity; an analysis of Barth's theory of correspondence; and some observations on the significance Barth's doctrinal development. The final observations on doctrinal development in Barth's theology lead us into section 2 of this chapter on Barth's notion of divine election and its implications for understanding the God-world relation.

SUMMARY AND POSITIVE CLAIMS

Trinitarian theology emerged within Christian thought to solve a practical problem: which side of the creator-creature divide does the Son, Jesus, land on? Fundamental questions regarding worship, prayer, and salvation hinge on the question of whether or not he is of one being with the Father. A similar practical orientation, perhaps one that can be seen to build on the Nicene affirmation of Jesus as *homoousios* with the Father, characterizes Barth's approach to trinitarian theology. By situating Trinity within his doctrine of revelation, Barth allows this classical doctrine to serve the purpose of identifying God. The name of God as Father, Son, Spirit, in short, offers a summary expression of God's being, of who God is; it tells us, *from* who God is among us, who God has always been. If Father, Son, and Spirit are the truth of who God is in the depths of God's being, given to us as the basic metaphysical fact, then Trinity, as Robert W. Jenson says of Barth's theology, takes on a "wider role as the frame within which ancient and new theological puzzles can be resolved."[104]

For Barth, the Trinity of God's being orders God's activity *ad extra*. We saw this in Dorner's theology as well, and it reaches back into the theological tradition, such as in Thomas Aquinas' claim that the historical missions of the divine persons are included within the eternal processions, but with the

---

104. Jenson, "A Theological Autobiography," 50.

addition of a temporal term.[105] Barth applies this idea to several sides of the God-world relation. The hidden-revealed dialectic of God's self-disclosure is grounded in the eternal relation of the Father and Son; the difference of the Son from the Father provides the basis for God to create a world as other than God; the divine peace enables a way out of the creature's self-inflicted discord in encounter with the triune God. In these ways Barth demonstrates the practical nature of trinitarian reflection. Nor does Trinity merely ask for the assent of the faithful as they move on toward more lush theological pastures. Rather, trinitarian theology carries out the purpose of making the relations between God and us revealed in Christ intelligible. It does not prove the truth God's real presence and relation to history—revelation does. But it reinforces the point by demonstrating how the activity of God among us is grounded in God's own being. Trinity gives expression to the way that God creates, reveals, and saves; it clarifies the reality of God who is, in Barth's words, as "ours in advance."[106]

Divine Subjectivity and History

Barth's trinitarian theology teaches that God is ready for history. However, his account of the Trinity's relation to revelatory history is not without its conceptual difficulties. I begin here with a criticism of Wolfhart Pannenberg on Barth's notion of divine subjectivity. Barth utilizes this notion to maintain a concept of the sovereignty of God in revelation, first in *Romans* II and then transcribed into his subsequent trinitarian theology. According to Pannenberg, Barth's notion of subjectivity mirrors the tradition, running back to Augustine, of construing the doctrine of the Trinity in psychological analogies. In *CD* I/1 Barth distances himself from this conventional approach, taking the derivation of the Trinity from a general notion of thought to be a form of natural theology. Similarly, Barth criticizes Hegel for identifying God with "the self-movement of the thinking of the human subject." The risk here, Barth writes with some wit, is that humanity risks becoming God's idol.[107] Nevertheless, Pannenberg claims that Barth's way of relating the subjectivity of God with divine revelation has much in common with the tradition Barth so vehemently rejects.

The root of the problem, on Pannenberg's view, is that Barth attributes logical priority to the divine subjectivity in his doctrine of the Trinity. Pannenberg cites a telling passage from *CD* I/1 noted above: "it

105. Aquinas, *Summa Theologica*, 1.43.2.3.

106. Barth, *CD* I/1:383.

107. Barth, *Protestant Theology*, 404–5.

follows from the trinitarian understanding of the God revealed in Scripture that this one God is understood . . . as person, i.e., as an I existing in and for itself with its own thought and will."[108] The derivation of God's single subjectivity from the three-fold nature of revelation, or God as the subject, predicate, and object of revelation, means that the divine I stands behind Barth's way of conceiving of God's trinitarian disclosure.[109] For, as Pannenberg argues, the subjectivity of God is not only derived from the three-fold or trinitarian nature of revelation, but the subjectivity of God in fact defines the revelation event itself. In Pannenberg's words, "if the doctrine of the Trinity should depict, according to Barth, the indissoluble subjectivity of God in his revelation, then the I of God, as the I of the Lord, must form its 'root,'" that is, the root of the doctrine of the Trinity.[110] Whether knowingly or not, in giving primacy to the divine subjectivity, Pannenberg says, Barth follows the path of speculative idealism.

In Hegel, for instance, revelation is the self-objectification of the subject in its self-consciousness. At least in intention, Barth distances himself from this starting point. Trinity is not deduced from a general concept but from revelation itself. Pannenberg notes his explicit agreement with Barth on this point. However, Pannenberg asks, is not the thrice-repeated subjectivity of God in revelation, and specifically in its subject, predicate, and object structure, or even as revealer, revelation, and being revealed, analogous to a model of self-objectification?[111] Catherine Mowry LaCugna echoes much in Pannenberg's analysis when she states, "Barth's view is a hybrid of the Latin theology of the Trinity in which the one divine substance exists in three persons, and the idea of God as Absolute Subject who exists under the aspects of self-differentiation and self-recollection. . . . For Barth, the essence of God is uni-personal."[112]

Pannenberg identifies several implications of Barth's view. For the purposes here the most important is Pannenberg's claim that absolute subjectivity leads to the idea of a heteronomous relation between God and the world.[113] For if God is absolute single subject and, as is safe to presume for Barth, not one and the same with the world (pantheism), then the divine being is conceived

108. Barth, *CD* I/1:358–59. Emphasis mine.

109. Barth, *CD* I/1:304, 306–7.

110. Pannenberg, "Die Subjektivität Gottes," 100. Translation mine.

111. Pannenberg, "Die Subjektivität Gottes," 101–2. See also Pannenberg, *Problemgeschichte*, 256–57.

112. LaCugna, *God for Us*, 252.

113. Pannenberg, "Die Subjektivität Gottes," 104–5. Similarly, Pannenberg, "Das Heilige in der modernen Kultur," 22.

as the transcendent correlate of the world.[114] The self-objectification model so reifies the single subjectivity of God as to make the divine relationality secondary, the very means by which God relates to the world. This results in a conception of God pitted against the created world.

Is this right? Is Barth's model analogous to a concept of absolute single subjectivity that downplays the import of divine relationality and leads to a heteronomous notion of the God-world relation? Pannenberg is right, I think, to note the way that Barth gives priority to the divine unity over the distinctions of the divine persons. Barth's language for the divine *hypostases* as 'modes' of the one God's being indicates this much. And to be sure, Barth's concept of divine personhood, which does not follow the Greek tradition of associating divine personality with the first person of the Trinity, or at least associating the origin of divine personhood with the Father, raises questions around a notion of God's personhood lurking behind the revealed modes of God's being. But the problem of relating single subjectivity and diversity in Barth's doctrine of the Trinity is not a clear-cut thing. After he outlines the root of trinitarian doctrine in revelation, Barth goes on in *CD* I/1 to lay out the constitutive place of the eternal relations in the Godhead (§§10–12). More telling, however, and more closely related to Pannenberg's objection, is Barth's handling of the idea of the divine lordship. Here I draw on Eberhard Jüngel's adaptive rendering of Barth's trinitarian theology.

According to Jüngel, Barth has the essential relationality of God's being in view from the beginning of his treatment of the lordship of God in revelation. Jüngel points to Barth's formula for the three-fold nature of revelation (the 'root' of the doctrine of the Trinity): "God reveals Himself as the Lord."[115] Jüngel argues that the formula corresponds to the classical notion of the eternal relations of origin in God. 'God reveals Godself as Lord' can be broken down into "(a) a whence of revelation, (b) a becoming revealed of God which is grounded in this whence, and (c) a being revealed of God which is grounded in this whence *and* in the becoming revealed."[116] (a) The Father is the whence of revelation; (b) the Father becomes revealed through the begotten Son; and (c) the Spirit is the being revealed grounded (or one in deity) with the Father and Son. As in God's own being, the analogous activity of God in revelation contains an origin and two distinct ways of being issued in relation to that origin. In other

---

114. Pannenberg, "Die Subjektivität Gottes," 110. See also Pannenberg, "Das christliche Gottesverständnis," 275. Fred Sanders provides a similar reading of Pannenberg's critique in *The Image of the Immanent Trinity*, 98–99.

115. Barth, *CD* I/1:306.

116. Jüngel, *God's Being*, 37–42, esp. 39.

words, who God is and what God does in revelation corresponds to the eternal relations of the Father, Son, and Spirit.

The point stands to note that relationality is not an add-on or subsequent to the subjectivity of God in revelation in Barth's formal doctrine of the Trinity. This does not remove all conceptual difficulties. There remain strong statements about the singular personality of God that present a challenge for understanding how three divine modes of being relate to the one divine nature. More to the point here, though, is that the inclusion of God's essential relationality in Barth's concept of the divine lordship takes the edge off Pannenberg's charge that Barth's account leads to a conception of God as the transcendent correlate of the world. Contrary to Pannenberg's criticism, the eternal relations of God underlie Barth's account of the divine singularity in such a way that absolute subjectivity as a one-to-one contrast of God over against the world does not apply, or at least not nearly to the extent that Pannenberg claims. That said, I believe Pannenberg's critique of Barth on the divine subjectivity remains important, but for a much more straightforward reason.

The majority of the problems that Pannenberg identifies in Barth's doctrine of the Trinity derive from what Pannenberg perceives as an unscrutinized concept of divine subjectivity. On top of this, however, Pannenberg states that Barth moves too quickly from the foundational concept of revelation to his doctrine of the Trinity.[117] This leads Barth to overlook certain elements of God's revelatory history and their significance in his configuration of the eternal Trinity. One plausible reason for this lies in Barth's concern with the immediate nature of revelation. Barth fixates on maintaining a notion of divine sovereignty in the event of God's self-disclosure. At any rate, Pannenberg claims that the haste with which Barth treats the particulars of God's saving history means that Barth's account passes over how God's self-disclosure in the Bible culminates in a final, eschatological revelation of God.[118] For a theological account of God's relation to history, why does this matter?

By overlooking the historical progression of revelation in favor of a notion that attends to its immediacy—such as God's being unveiled in a veil which Barth maps onto the dialectic of the Father-Son relation—Barth's doctrine of the Trinity does not adequately identify the divine basis for God's historical activity. This is not to discount the value of the concepts Barth employs. With Barth, revelation in Scripture occurs here and now, and so aligns with his emphasis on the immediacy of revelation. Rather, it

117. Pannenberg, *Problemgeschichte*, 257.
118. Pannenberg, *Problemgeschichte*, 257–58.

is to ask for more, for revelation in Scripture also pushes toward a culmination of the final disclosure of God as "all in all" (1 Cor 15:28). To be sure, Barth's trinitarian theology advances on the concept of God from *Romans* II. I argued that in *Romans* II the God-world relation must, as a result of Barth's concept of eternity, be conceived in a punctiliar way, and not in terms of movements internal to or that coincide with history itself. The trinitarian idea of God in *CD* I/1 no longer contains the negating idea of eternal timelessness from *Romans* II. Barth's notion of divine being at the outset of the *CD* rightly shows how God relates to us through the divine alterity, lordship, and communion of the antecedent Trinity. These notions go a long ways in helping to conceive of the compatibility between God and history, particularly the latter notion of divine communion that God establishes with creatures. However, what is missing here, and what is likely the result of Barth's neglect of scriptural narrative, is the way in which the Trinity enables God's forward-moving history in time. Barth's notion of God's eternal communion could be adapted to address this point, for eternal fellowship implies a sense of movement internal to God's being, but it would not quite capture how the precise *ordering* of the eternal relations, gleaned from God's revelatory work, lends itself to a notion of God ready to live an eschatologically oriented history with others. For this conception of the eternal relations of God's being we will need to look elsewhere. I return to this problem in chapter 3. There we will see that even a general notion like divine lordship, run through the scriptural narrative for the sake of understanding God's eternal being, has the potential to serve as a concept for conceiving of God's eschatologically mediated history.

DIVINE CORRESPONDENCE

I concluded the overview of Barth's doctrine of the Trinity in *CD* I/1 above with some critical questions on his theory of correspondence. For Barth, divine correspondence ensures a sense of ontological identity between the eternal or antecedent Trinity and the being of God in time. Insofar as God's revealed being in time corresponds to the antecedent Trinity, it is *this* God, the eternally triune God, who is made known to us in revelation. However, the correspondence notion that Barth employs lacks a certain level of precision in specifying how God relates to the world. The concern here lies in the way that a correspondence notion leaves open a sense of ontological distance between the antecedent Trinity and the being of God in time, which in turn raises questions around the reality or truth of God's being with us. This distancing between the eternal Trinity and God's being in time can be understood in different ways. In one way, which is not problematic, the antecedent Trinity relates to the being of God in time as simply that, the prior reality of God through which God acts among us. Granted that the relation between eternity and time is not a straightforward thing, this is merely to acknowledge the priority of God's eternity over time. In the terminology that is used in later chapters of this work, this can also be understood as affirming the role of the immanent Trinity in theological reflection on the God-world relation.

The question of a potential distance between the eternity of God and the history God lives with others becomes problematic in the understanding of this corresponding relation as ongoing in revelation itself. This too needs to be specified. It is one thing to say, as Barth does, that who God is and what God does among us correspond to the antecedent Trinity. This can be taken to mean that God, as said before, simply acts through the antecedent Trinity of God's being; it is God who acts here, present among us, as the selfsame one God has always been. But it is another thing to say that the correspondence between the eternal Trinity and the being of God in time continues or holds specifically in the *present* of God's revelatory acts. At stake here is the reality of divine presence. For to say that who God is and what God does in revelatory history correspond to the inner-being of God *in* that history itself, as it takes place, can suggest not only that God acts *from* the antecedent Trinity of God's being, but that the divine being remains in a higher, corresponding reality, untouched by this history. It suggests not a lived history of God, but histories, or a corresponding reality of God, running alongside the being of God in history. Revelation history risks becoming simply a duplicate of eternal history. While this raises a general concern for using a notion of correspondence, the more immediate question is this: is this true of Barth's doctrine of the Trinity?

On the whole the answer is no. Barth remains consistent on the point that Jesus Christ has a reality apart from us, but this pertains to who he is "antecedently in himself."[119] Correspondence in Barth's trinitarian theology is primarily between the antecedent Trinity of God's being and the subsequent reality of God in revelation history. "Manifest as the Creator and therefore as our Father," the Father "already is that which corresponds thereto antecedently and in Himself."[120] The link lies primarily between who God is prior to revelation history and this history itself. We must be careful therefore not to overdo the criticism here. The more precise claim to be made is that Barth does not preclude the idea of an ongoing

119. Barth, *CD* I/1:414, 423–24.
120. Barth, *CD* I/1:391.

correspondence between the eternal Trinity and the being of God in time. His trinitarian theology does not rule out the idea of an ongoing correspondence that holds in the present of God's revelation, the reality of the inner-life of God at a remove from revelation history. It may even be asked if Barth's account suggests it, given his strong affirmation of a notion of Jesus Christ apart from us in *CD* I/1. And it can be asked for mainly one reason: Barth does not go far enough in showing the determinative place of Jesus Christ's life and history for God, such as the meaning of the Son's incarnation for understanding God's eternal being.

In short, the moorings are simply not in place in Barth's doctrine of the Trinity to stave off the conception of an ulterior (corresponding) history of God, one that hovers above God with us below. Correspondence is a fluid notion, and it requires greater specification than Barth allows for in understanding the God-world relation. One can detect in Barth's account, as James Cone puts it, a persistence toward the "early theme of God's absolute transcendence."[121] If this concern is to be alleviated, it must be made clear that the revelatory history of God in Christ matters in such a way that God assumes it into the divine life so as to be *this* God, God with us, without any possible 'God behind God' scenario. This is not a wholesale indictment on the use of a correspondence notion. Kathryn Tanner, for example, employs the language of a repetition and correspondence between the eternal relations of God's being and the divine activity in time. However, she makes this important qualification.

> Even if the very same [triune] relations are simply being extended into the mission they undertake for us, when they incorporate the human in a situation of sin and death through the Word's incarnation, the relations that the members of the trinity have with one another come to reflect that fact.[122]

What happens in revelation history is assumed into the character of the relations of the divine persons.[123] This helpfully rules out the specific kind of ontological distance between the eternal Trinity and the activity of God in history that undermines a notion of God's authentic presence. It does, because this history becomes part of the divine life.

Again, the criticism should be fit to scale. It is too much to say, as Jürgen Moltmann does, that Barth retains a notion of God as a "closed circle" in relation to the world, which would more directly imply an ulterior

---

121. Cone, *God of the Oppressed*, 107.

122. Tanner, *Christ the Key*, 180.

123. Similarly, see Bonhoeffer, *Christ the Center*, 105.

history of God running alongside revelation history than I take to be the case in Barth's trinitarian theology.[124] The worry is more accurately put by saying that Barth does not adequately ward off this idea. And thus Barth's use of a notion of correspondence in his trinitarian theology is susceptible to the idea of an ulterior history that undermines claims on the reality of divine presence. What is required is a better account of the way that revelation history bears on God's being, even as God transcends that history. And this requires not simply fixing the loose ends of a correspondence theory, but to take seriously the second person of the Trinity who becomes flesh, who we know in the Godhead as one and the same Son, the man Jesus. This is essential in order to speak of revelation as *God's* history, or in Barth's terms, of God as 'ours in advance'; truly there for us in advance—no problem there for Barth—but also truly *ours*.

Doctrinal Development

The last thing to consider here, which is also a point for transitioning to section 2 of this chapter, concerns the development of Barth's theology. By far, and as elaborated upon enough above, the emphasis in Barth's trinitarian theology falls on God's being as the *grounds* of God's revelatory history. The point is accented in terms of Barth's focus on the antecedent nature of the triune God. And it is reinforced by the regularly occurring expressions around the manifestation of God anew in the world. "What is revealed under the name of Jesus Christ is the confirmation and manifestation of the immutable vitality of God."[125] Barth's trinitarian understanding of the God-world relation is close to Dorner's view in the immutability essay here. For Dorner, God relates to created reality through the realized potentiality of God's ethical (trinitarian) being. God's self-imparting acts to creatures confirm the being of God as such. Notably, Barth goes beyond Dorner by applying the triune idea of God to God's own involvement in history, particularly in his treatment of the divine constancy; whereas for Dorner this relation is mediated through ethically independent creatures, not primarily in terms of Dorner's trinitarian doctrine of God. This is a step forward. But the idea of the being of God as manifest and demonstrated anew in history, of God's being as the grounds for God's activity *ad extra*, remains the primary way that Trinity is employed for understanding God's relation to history in both Barth and Dorner. Barth's more direct application of Trinity to God's involvement in history is an advance on

---

124. Moltmann, *The Crucified God*, 255; see also 240.

125. Barth, CD II/1:513. See also Barth, CD I/1:391, 423–34, 499, 515.

Dorner's immutability essay, but not a big one. How the trinitarian being of God, for instance, enables God to live a history with others, to be present by moving therein, remains an open question.

More specific to the purposes here, however, is the meaning of Jesus Christ's actual history for understanding the inner-relations of God's being. Even a sympathetic interpreter of Barth like Price notes, Barth "remains disappointingly vague about what particularity Christ's dying reveals about the unchangingly lively divine nature."[126] The implications of this lacuna were laid out above. What is important to highlight here is that by the end of Barth's treatment of the divine constancy in *CD* II/1, there are positive suggestions that Barth has this very point in view. There Barth asserts that Jesus Christ is the content of the divine decree. Barth does not develop this claim, but there are hints that he will. The claim that Jesus Christ is the content of the divine decree, Barth writes, can be taken as the "basis for the doctrine of the *opera Dei*."[127] This suggests a doctrine of God with a more robust christological configuration, that is, a configuration more attuned to the specifics of Jesus Christ's concrete history. And in turn this conception, taken up into the understanding of God's trinitarian being, provides the basis for a theological account of the triune God's self-grounded history with us. The same conclusion follows from another approach. If God *is* the divine decision, as Barth states in his being-in-act ontology, and Jesus Christ *is* the decree, then the doctrine of God's being that follows needs only to be unpacked accordingly: the assumption of Jesus Christ and the meaning of his salvific history into God's being. Barth's doctrine of election, as I show below, does precisely this.

2: Trinity, Election, and History

In section 2 of this chapter I turn to Barth's doctrine of divine election. Barth states that election is "the sum of the gospel."[128] For it involves a divine decision that, at its most specific point, illuminates the general purposes of God's activity *ad extra*.[129] At the same time, as Barth said in *CD* II/1, election provides a basis for the works of God in revelation. Its significance for the doctrine of God is clear: this decision extends to God's "innermost being,

---

126. Price, *Letters of the Divine Word*, 139.

127. Barth, *CD* II/1:522.

128. Barth, *CD* II/2:10. See also Barth's exegesis of Ephesians 1 and related New Testament passages: Barth, *CD* II/2:60.

129. Barth, *CD* II/2:8.

willing and nature."[130] It is God's decision to elect "the man of Nazareth, that he should be essentially one with Himself in His Son."[131]

In what follows I consider how Barth's trinitarian theology is shaped by the christological focus of his doctrine of election and what this means for understanding God's relation to history. Barth conceives of the eternal obedience of the Son as it applies to the eternally electing will of God and the actualization of election in Jesus' history. The constructive claims of this chapter hinge on the concept of the Son's obedience or conformity to the will of God. For I argue that a necessary corrective to the problems identified at the end of section 1 of this chapter, specifically around Barth's theory of correspondence and the potential conception of a two-tiered history of God, can be found here. I also show how the notion of the Son's conformity to the Father's will factors into an understanding of the vitality of God in the relation between pre-temporal eternity and revelation history.

2.1: *The Election of Jesus Christ*: Church Dogmatics II/2

ELECTION AND TRINITY

In §33 Barth puts forward his constructive understanding of divine election. The central theme is the relationship between election and the person and history of Jesus Christ. Particularly significant is the way that Barth unpacks the meaning of this doctrine in view of the divine Word's identification with Jesus of Nazareth. In other words, election not only bears on the incarnate existence of God but also gives shape to God's eternal being. I pay close attention to this two-way relation, the eternal decision to become incarnate and the way this history determines God's identity, in the reading of Barth's doctrine of election below.

In his initial exegesis Barth turns to the Johannine prologue. Crucial for the identification between the Word of God and the subject of the gospel are the parallels in John 1 between the eternal *Logos* and the man Jesus.[132] John suggests no clear or implied break in identity between the three-fold claim on the *Logos* in John 1:1, the Word with God in the beginning who was God, and the incarnate being of the Word in 1:14. The Word does not merely assume the flesh of the man Jesus, but *becomes* flesh. Perhaps more significant though is the claim of Colossians 1:17 in which the Son, in the explicit context of his incarnate existence, is characterized as existing

130. Barth, *CD* II/2:5–6.

131. Barth, *CD* II/2:11.

132. Barth, *CD* II/2:95–99.

"before all things." Or, likewise, in Hebrews 1:2–3 where Christ, the "heir of all things," is described as the one through whom God creates and "sustains all things by his powerful word."[133] Jesus is both "the first and the last, the beginning and the end" (Rev 22:13, 16).

The divine Word is one and the same with the man Jesus. For Barth the selfsame identity of the Word with Jesus means more than that from eternity the Son wills to become incarnate in time. Election is also consequential for God's being. As Barth puts it, the presence of the divine Word, identified with the man Jesus, indicates a "subjective self-determination" of God.[134] The divine decision, to be sure, takes place within the confines of the divine love and freedom. Nevertheless, it is a decision so profound, so basic to God that it uniquely defines what it means for God to be God. Election determines God's being—all the way down.

Barth's characterization of the relation between eternity and God's electing decision requires specific attention. Barth takes liberties throughout §33 in using temporal expressions to describe election, even while acknowledging that divine election occurs in the sphere of God's eternity, or in the beginning of God's ways *ad extra*.[135] According to Barth, the being of God is being-in-act. God's act and being are not two divisible things. Rather, they constitute the one reality God is. Therefore election, as the primal act of God, bears in the most intimate of ways on the nature of God's being. Importantly, Barth elevates the theological significance of election to the plane of God's eternal triunity. Among Barth's interpreters, how best to understand the relationship between election and the triunity of God has incited some significantly different renderings.[136]

George Hunsinger distinguishes between two prominent ways of interpreting Barth on the ordering of election and God's triunity. As Hunsinger recognizes, the categories are generalizations with a fair amount of differentiation and nuance on each side. On one side are those who hold that for Barth the pre-temporal event of the election of Jesus Christ presupposes both the being of God as Father, Son, and Spirit as well as a notion of the divine *Logos* in-and-of-itself, distinct from its relation to the man Jesus—the "traditionalists." The being of God as Father, Son, and Spirit, on this view, is clearly prior to the self-defining decision of God in election. On the other are those who take God's triunity to presuppose the pre-temporal election

---

133. Barth, *CD* II/2:99.

134. Barth, *CD* II/2:100.

135. Barth, *CD* II/2:117.

136. Several important contributions to the debate on the relation between Trinity and election in Barth can be found in Dempsey, *Trinity and Election in Contemporary Theology*.

of Jesus Christ, making election, in one way or another, a self-constituting event—the "revisionists."[137] The latter side ranges from understanding election as giving rise to the triunity of God's being to the view of election and the constitution of God's triunity as simultaneous in God.

Several reasons animate the differences in such readings. The *CD* is an unfinished, monumental theological endeavor. The sheer length of it begs the question of the degree and the significance of Barth's theological development. It is clear that Barth's experiences leading up to the composition of *CD* II/2, which he himself reflects on, as well as the importance of election throughout the various loci of subsequent volumes of the *CD*, makes his treatment of this classical doctrine something of a watershed moment in his thinking.[138] Moreover, Barth's own claims complicate the matter, offering a set of at least ostensibly diverging statements that make the synthesizing work of interpreting this material a particularly difficult challenge. Barth writes, the "primal decision (*Urentsheidung*)"[139] of God means "we cannot and should not say the word 'God' without at once thinking of it."[140] Likewise, "God Himself does not will to be God, and is not God, except as the One who elects. There is no height or depth in which God can be God in any other way."[141] Claims such as these back up the revisionist reading. And yet Barth also states, "that Jesus Christ is the Son of God does not rest on the election."[142] Similarly, "the subject of this decision is the triune God—the Son of God no less than the Father and the Holy Spirit."[143] Such claims lend support to the traditionalist reading.

On the whole I find most convincing a version of the revisionist reading of Barth's theology that posits election and divine triunity as equally basic to God's being, with logical priority given to God's triunity.[144] Most significant for the purposes here, however, is the way that Barth conceives

---

137. Hunsinger, "Election and Trinity," 179; Hunsinger, *Reading Barth with Charity*, xi–xvi. Hunsinger's position is laid out further in "Election and Trinity." Other traditionalist positions include Driel, "Karl Barth on the Eternal Existence of Jesus Christ"; Molnar, "Can the Electing God Be God without Us?" The foundational work in this debate, and within Hunsinger's categorizations, the key revisionist perspective, is Bruce L. McCormack's essay, "Grace and Being."

138. Barth, *CD* II/2:188–94.

139. Barth, *CD* II/2:103; Barth, *KD* II/2:110.

140. Barth, *CD* II/2:8.

141. Barth, *CD* II/2:77.

142. Barth, *CD* II/2:107.

143. Barth, *CD* II/2:110.

144. On this view see Hector, "God's Triunity and Self-Determination"; Hector, "Immutability"; Jones, "Obedience," esp. 145–55.

of the divine decision to fundamentally shape the eternal identity of God as triune. For instance, in *CD* IV/1 Barth writes that it is not only "pointless" but even "impermissible" to reflect on the inner-being of God, or an abstract idea of the *Logos asarkos*, apart from the divine decision.[145] Accordingly, I believe that Paul Daffyd Jones is right when he ascribes "equivalent *dogmatic* importance" for Barth to both the being of God as Father, Son, and Spirit and the decision to become incarnate in Jesus.[146] Upon the electing decision, the trinitarian being of God can only be conceived in light of Jesus and his concrete history. The closer alignment of the eternal Trinity with Jesus as a figure in space and time is crucial for the argument of this chapter. For as I show below it has broad implications for reconceiving of Barth's notion of the antecedent Trinity, and with it, his theory of divine correspondence, in relation to the criticisms that I leveled against these notions in section 1 of this chapter.

Election and the Obedience of the Divine Son

I return now to some of the central ideas in Barth's doctrine of election. The key point from Barth's exegesis in §33 is the identification of Jesus with the divine Word at the beginning of God's ways and works *ad extra*. Barth proceeds to sift out the meaning of this identification through addressing Jesus as both the subject and object of God's electing decision. In what follows I focus on Barth's claims on Jesus Christ as the subject of election and their implications for understanding God's relation to history.

Jesus Christ is the electing God. He is this, according to Barth, because he was present with God at the beginning. Barth also comes at this point another way. Election is a *divine* decision. As a self-determining decision, one that belongs to the being-in-act that God is, its ramifications reach into the fullness of God's being. The "being (of God) is decision," writes Barth, and insofar as the decision is identical to Jesus and his history of faithfulness to the Father's will, Jesus is not just election's object but also the subject of the divine decree.[147] Barth writes,

> The election of Jesus Christ is the eternal choice and decision of God. And our first assertion tells us that Jesus Christ is the electing God. We must not ask concerning any other but Him. In no depth of the Godhead shall we encounter any other but Him. There is no such thing as Godhead in itself. Godhead is

145. Barth, *CD* IV/1:52.
146. Jones, *The Humanity of Christ*, 81.
147. Barth, *CD* II/2:175.

always the Godhead of the Father, the Son and the Holy Spirit. But the Father is the Father of Jesus Christ and the Holy Spirit is the Spirit of the Father and the Spirit of Jesus Christ. There is no such thing as a *decretum absolutum*. There is no such thing as a will of God apart from the will of Jesus Christ.[148]

The force of this claim lies not so much in the assertion that Godhead is always triune, significant as this point is, but rather in that all the trinitarian coordinates of God's being are linked to the individual, Jesus Christ. What Barth says can be fashioned along the lines of Athanasius' famous dictum: The Father is Father only in relation to *Jesus*, and likewise with the Spirit. Election is a self-constituting decision, basic to the divine being.

As a divine decision rooted in God's eternity, Barth moves freely between descriptions of election as undertaken by Jesus and the eternal Son. Furthermore, because election is identical to Christ's concrete history, Barth characterizes the divine decision as an act of faithful obedience on the part of the Son. Accordingly, the Father-Son relation lends itself to two perspectives regarding one divine act. On one hand, election is understood as the way that "the Son of God (is) given by the Father" for the purpose of being united with human flesh.[149] Divine agency centers on the Father's initiating will on this view, such as in the scriptural characterization of the Father's sending of the Son into the world. On the other, and equally important, the divine Son freely renders his obedience to the Father's will. From the command he receives from the Father, he lays down his life of his own accord (John 10:18). To the giving of the Son by the Father in God there corresponds the self-giving of the Son to the will of God. In the "harmony of the triune God," Barth writes, Jesus Christ "elected to be man, and as man, to do the will of God" in an act of "free obedience to His Father." The act is fully trinitarian insofar as the Spirit of God is the "Spirit of obedience itself."[150] Election determines God's "whole being," the being of God in anticipation of fellowship with humanity.[151]

Barth's treatment of election also covers the God-world relation, specifically the relation between eternity and history. The just noted theme of election as a self-determining decision of God is relevant here. The election of Jesus Christ, Barth writes,

tells us that before all created reality, before all being and becoming in time, before time itself, in the pre-temporal eternity

148. Barth, *CD* II/2:115.
149. Barth, *CD* II/2:105.
150. Barth, *CD* II/2:105–6.
151. Barth, *CD* II/2:162.

of God, the eternal divine decision as such has as its object and
content, the existence of this one created being, the man Jesus
of Nazareth, and the work of this man in His life and death, His
humiliation and exaltation, His obedience and merit.[152]

The historical existence of Jesus of Nazareth is the 'object and content' of
the eternal decision. Barth assumes Christ's history into the eternal being of
God. His history colors what God wills from eternity, and what God wills, as
we have seen, is the decision constituting God's being. In other words, what
God wills from eternity shapes who God is, such that the election of Jesus
becomes so basic to God's identity that this individual is *there* from eternity;
he is the maker of this decision as the second person of the Trinity. It follows
that the eternal decision of God and the actual history of election among us
are joined together in the most intimate of ways.

This last point is perhaps most evident in Barth's description of the
pre-temporal election through the cryptic term of a "primal history (*Urgeschichte*)" in God's being.[153] Barth raises the notion of a primal history in
the context of explaining the order of God's relations to the world and the
person of Christ. The God-world relation is real, Barth says, but it has "no
independent signification." Rather, the God-world relation

takes place in the interests of the primal history which is played
out between God and this one man and His people. It is the
sphere in which this primal history is played out. It attains its
goal as this primal history attains its goal.[154]

The primal history of God is the electing decision, a decision that, according to Barth, not only gives creation its ultimate purpose but that also unfolds and comes to fulfillment within created reality. There is, however, a
tension here. On one hand, election is played out through the God-world
relation, signifying the historical character of the divine decision and its
execution. On the other, the characterization of election as a primal history
risks denoting the eternal decision as a history unto itself, above and apart
from the this worldly character of the enactment of election in time. The
nature of election as a primal history, in other words, comes with a certain
level of ambiguity. Barth's comments in the immediate context of his statement on the primal history of God in *CD* II/2 fail to clear up the confusion.
Without further details that fill out this notion of a primal history of God,
we are left with the question of where the real heart of election lies: in the

152. Barth, *CD* II/2:116.
153. Barth, *CD* II/2:8; Barth, *KD* II/2:6.
154. Barth, *CD* II/2:8.

pre-temporal eternity of God or in the actualization of election among us? I touch on this question below and return to a fuller analysis of it in the final sub-section and show how it connects to my critical assessment of Barth's theory of correspondence from section 1.

Barth returns to the relation between election and history at the end of §33. Here Barth characterizes election as "divine activity in the form of history, encounter and decision between God and man."[155] As we have seen, election shares both eternal and temporal features. It is rooted in the eternal being of God, and as such it is identical to the activity of God in the inner-relationships of Father, Son, and Spirit. This activity, however, is transitional: it moves "from God's being in and for Himself to His being as Lord of creation."[156] What happens with God among us "is merely an over-flowing of His inward activity and being." Barth asks, "what else can that be but activity and event?"[157] This sheds some light on the nature of election as history. Election coincides with the self-determination of the triune God to be God for us. This activity, as trinitarian activity, is also a history in God, the history of the divine persons in their inner-relationality. But this activity or divine history also coincides with the trinitarian activity of God among us. How Father, Son, and Spirit are unto one another in God, based on the once-for-all decision of election, reflects how God is among us in the encounter with the creatures God loves and saves. Barth writes, "the eternal will of God which is the predestination of all things is God's life in the form of the history, encounter and decision between Himself and man . . . which are already willed and known from all eternity, and to that extent, prior to all external events, are already actual before Him and for Him."[158]

Election therefore has a lodging point in the eternity of God's being. However, Barth remarks, "as the content of eternity before time was, it can-not remain beyond time."[159] Barth explains this in different ways. At a basic level, election becomes historical because "Jesus Christ was in the begin-ning with God."[160] The primal will of God is the union of the eternal Son with Jesus of Nazareth. More elaborately, Barth maps election onto his sche-matic of divine eternity from *CD* II/1 as the simultaneously pre-temporal, supra-temporal, and post-temporal life of God.[161] Reflecting the nature of

---

155. Barth, *CD* II/2:175.
156. Barth, *CD* II/2:175.
157. Barth, *CD* II/2:175.
158. Barth, *CD* II/2:175.
159. Barth, *CD* II/2:188.
160. Barth, *CD* II/2:175–76.
161. See Barth, *CD* II/1:608–40.

eternity, the electing decision of God is "not left behind by time" when it comes to be in creation. Rather, it is "above time" even as it "accompanies" and "outlasts" time.[162] It is before, in, and the goal of time, and reaches beyond time as well. Election reflects the divine actuality that impacts us in all of its states. Barth writes, election "occurs in the very midst of time no less than in that far distant pre-temporal eternity."[163] Lastly, election has a directionality. The divine decision "can never belong only to the past."[164] It is oriented toward the "foundation and existence and guidance of Israel and the Church," to the salvific proceedings of God in history that culminate in the death and resurrection of Jesus and the proclamation of salvation in his name. Election, in a word, "takes place in time."[165]

In sum, in the doctrine of election Barth conceives of God's being in light of the identification of Jesus Christ with the divine Word before time. This leads Barth to set forth a christologically centered account God's trinitarian being. The point is epitomized in the way that Barth posits an act of divine obedience on the part of the eternal Son to the will of the Father. Barth also considers the meaning of the divine Word's identification with Jesus for conceiving of the God-world relation in several different ways. In the final analysis of this chapter I turn to the significance of Barth's doctrine of election for addressing some of the open-ended questions from the critical assessment of section 1 above, mostly around Barth's theory of divine correspondence, and evaluate Barth's theology of election for understanding God's relation to history.

2.2: Concluding Analysis

I concluded section 1 of this chapter with the observation that Barth's formal doctrine of the Trinity and the surveyed sections of Barth's doctrine of God give inadequate attention to the meaning of Christ's incarnate history for understanding God's triune being. Barth's doctrine of election makes an important contribution in addressing this problem in his doctrine of God. From eternity the divine Son conforms to the Father's will for the purpose of saving the creaturely beings God loves. This notion of conformity or divine obedience is a result of Barth's conscription of the incarnate life of Jesus, present at the beginning of all things, into the identity of the eternal Trinity.

162. Barth, *CD* II/2:183.
163. Barth, *CD* II/2:185.
164. Barth, *CD* II/2:184.
165. Barth, *CD* II/2:186.

In the analysis that follows I argue that Barth's way of positing an obedience in the Godhead helps to overcome some of the previously identified problems in his conception of the God-world relation, particularly the notion of a two-track history of God. I also address one of the remaining points of ambiguity for understanding God's relation to created reality that arises with Barth's idea of a primal history in God. I show how the relation between the concepts of election and God's primal history in Barth's theology must be amended, or at least clarified, in order to critically appropriate his account of election for an understanding of God's relation to history. The analysis is divided into five sub-sections: A final comparison of Barth and Dorner on divine immutability; a defense of Barth's application of divine obedience to the inner-relations of God; an assessment of divine correspondence in light of Barth's notion of divine obedience; a critical reflection on Barth's concept of primal history; and some general considerations on the relationship between Trinity, the pre-temporal eternity of God, and history.

DIVINE IMMUTABILITY

Before I consider the significance of Barth's trinitarian doctrine of election for understanding God's relation to history, I return to the ancillary thread on divine immutability from chapter 1. This sub-section picks up on one of the criticisms of Dorner's theology and brings it into dialogue with Barth's doctrine of election. In the previous chapter I noted a significant inconsistency that appears in Dorner's account of divine immutability. Dorner initially locates the immutability of God in the internal love of God's being, God's self-love, which in turn provides the secure and unchanging grounds for creaturely faith. In contrast to this, in part III of the immutability essay Dorner claims that divine love finds its "proper place" not in the divine being itself but in the manifestation of God's self-imparting love toward creatures in need. Through this self-imparting love, Dorner writes, a "purely free original giving takes place" that corresponds to the "pure want in the recipient."[166] But if the divine love, once rooted in the self-love of God's being, now finds its 'proper place' outside of God and in relation to creatures, then this implies a kind of shift in the unchanging nature of God's being. It entails a change to the supposedly unchanging foundation of faith. What then serves as faith's security amidst the unpredictabilities of creaturely life? Is the immutability of God's love really unchanging if this shift, this kind of mutability, takes place?

166. Dorner, *Divine Immutability*, 178.

Barth's account of election provides an alternative solution to the problem. This involves an understanding of God's self-imparting love as an overflowing of the divine love. What creatures experience of God is a surplus of the divine love that originates in the eternal fellowship of the divine persons. But there is a way that Barth takes this point a step further, or at least enables a further step to be taken, by more closely linking the internal fount of divine love *with* the love of God for creatures in need. This results in an account of immutability that overcomes the fissure in Dorner's essay between the immutability of the divine love in Godself and the way that this love applies to fallen creatures. In other words, it does not entail a shift from God's essential immutability, God's self-love, to a higher form of immutability encapsulated in God's relation to free creatures. It is a single vision of immutability, and therefore more readily provides the stable grounds for faith. Admittedly, what follows depends largely on the way one renders the relation between Trinity and election in Barth's theology, a disputed point among Barth's readers. Below I follow through on an implication of the account I proposed above, shared with others, which attributes dogmatic equivalency to God's triunity and the self-constituting nature of election, or both Trinity and election as basic to God's being.

For Barth, election is a self-determining decision. It is *at once* a decision of the triune God, and a decision that determines God's triunity. As the triune decision is basic to who God is, there is no going behind it. Christian theology possesses this fact as a starting point for its reflection on the nature and purposes of the living God. What does this mean for the doctrine of divine immutability? First, it means something we have already seen in Dorner: the immutability of God's being is identical to the unchanging nature of God as expressed in the divine self-love, the inner-trinitarian fellowship of God as Father, Son, and Spirit. Election, as a decision of the triune God, is a self-confirming act of the divine love. We can affirm this point: there is nothing higher or more concrete and unchanging than God's triunity and the love shared by the divine persons. And second, and here Barth's account carries us beyond Dorner's, we take note that the second person of the Trinity in the electing decision does not have a questionable identity. Election, as a self-determining decision of the triune God, means that the second person of the Trinity is Jesus of Nazareth. Therefore we can equally affirm this point: as *this* one from eternity, the man Jesus, all creaturely beings in need of reconciliation are in God's sight from eternity. Because the second person of the Trinity is the man Jesus, the gracious inclusion of the creatures God loves and wills to save belongs to God's very being. Properly speaking, their inclusion awaits the actualization of election in time, but the decision to give them a share in the divine life shapes the trinitarian identity of God from eternity.

How this overcomes the shifting nature of immutability from Dorner's essay should now be clear. Barth's doctrine of election allows us to speak of divine immutability in terms of the eternally grounded and abiding love of the Trinity, on one hand, and, on the other, in terms of the purposes of God to save in reconciling fallen creatures. They are distinct but not separable. To make the point more clear, the two dimensions of God's immutability are *not* successive states, so to speak, in which God's primal immutability, the self-love of the divine persons, comes to find its 'proper place' in the self-imparting love of God for creatures. They are not sequentially ordered in this way because the self-determining decision of election includes both.[167] There is then no shift from a primal mode of divine immutability in eternity to another mode in relation to creatures in time. This view would ultimately undermine the role that divine immutability plays as a resting point for faith, for it highlights the possibility that what appears unchanging about God may in fact change again. The view of immutability that I argue for here envisions the unchanging nature of God as a singular reality. It posits that Trinity has logical priority over election, yes; but, all importantly, it holds that insofar as election is a decision basic to God's being, we cannot truly conceive of Trinity apart from God's creaturely love—apart from Jesus Christ. Divine immutability is the self-love of God, expressed in the internal fellowship of Father, Son, and Spirit. And because the identity of the second person of the Godhead is Jesus, this self-love includes God's self-giving love for others. The eternal love of God's being is unchangingly directed toward us.

Divine Obedience

Barth's characterization of the eternal Son's relation to the Father in terms of divine obedience allays concerns around a two-fold conception of God's history, one above and one below. But before addressing this point we should ask whether it is appropriate on dogmatic grounds to speak of an obedience in God at all. Obedience implies a certain responsiveness on the part of the second person of the Trinity, and therefore raises the question of whether the divine Son wills something apart from the Father to the extent that we must speak of not one but two wills in God. The latter notion clashes with the traditional conception of the one divine will proper to God's single nature.

167. For a similar view, see McCormack, "The Actuality of God," 222–23.

Guy Mansini, among others, takes this position against Barth's way of ascribing both obedience and humility to the Son. According to Mansini, these relational qualities belong not to the eternal Son but to the humanity that he assumes, specifically, to the created, human will of the man Jesus.[168] Mansini draws on Gregory of Nyssa's idea from *Ad Ablabium*, mediated through Thomas Aquinas, on the unity of operation that characterizes the works of God. For Gregory, the singularity of God follows from the unity of operation of the three divine persons. Each divine act is numerically one. If the Son obeys and the Father commands, Mansini argues, then there are operations in God proper to each that do not belong to the other. The result of which would be differences in operation and power in God that amount to two different wills, two divine natures, and thus "two Gods." On the contrary, Mansini claims, "each Person does the one operation wholly and completely."[169]

In response to this charge, however, it should be noted that in *Ad Ablabium* Gregory construes the operation of God within the ordering of the trinitarian relations: every divine operation begins with the Father, proceeds through the Son, and comes to completion by the Holy Spirit.[170] Gregory upholds two points. First, as noted above, each divine act is numerically one. Second, each divine act follows the internal structure of God's trinitarian being. In light of this, the obedience of the Son can be understood as the way in which the divine will begins with the Father's command and concludes in the perfecting activity of the Spirit. More specifically, the Son's obedience is a Spirit-perfected response to the initiating will of the Father. Or from another angle, the obedience of the Son is his perfect conformity to the Father's being, the self-donating gift of deity that the Son receives from the Father and that, as divine nature itself, includes the Father's will. In this way the Son both receives and perfectly exhibits the Father's being and will through the Spirit's power. "Whoever has seen me has seen the Father" (John 14:9). "I seek not to do my own will but the will of him who sent me" (John 5:30). The Son's obedience is active receptivity. If the point here seems at all a stretch, we might consider the possibility of mutual love in God. Love in God runs not only from the Father to the begotten Son, but from the Son to the Father as well. The Son is loved by,

---

168. Mansini, "Can Humility and Obedience Be Trinitarian Realities?," 97. See also White, "On Christian Philosophy and Divine Obedience," 286–88; White, "Intra-Trinitarian Obedience and Nicene-Chalcedonian Christology," 377–402.

169. Mansini, "Can Humility and Obedience Be Trinitarian Realities?," 90–91.

170. Gregory of Nyssa, *Ad Ablabium*, 155.

and actively loves, the Father (John 14:31). The Father begets the Son "so that he will have someone . . . to love and be loved by."[171]

Barth does not approach the question of divine obedience in the Godhead this way. Rather, Barth mostly assumes the reality of the Son's eternal conformity to the Father based on the meaning of the revealed relations of the divine persons for understanding God's being.[172] One other reason for suggesting a divine obedience on the part of the eternal Son is worth noting. The revealed relation of the Son's obedience to the Father in the Spirit is compatible with classical trinitarian doctrine. Trinitarian theology hinges on the fact that the being of God is unity-in-distinctions, that real diversity, albeit unique to God alone, applies to the divine unity. It is the character of this diversity that allows for a form of obedience, of command and response, or of loving and being loved, to exist in (and as) God's being. In the diversity of the divine relations the Father issues the divine will to the Son. The Son in turn proceeds from the Father and receives what he is therein, his very life and deity. In this way it is natural for the Son to conform perfectly to the Father's loving will. Clearly, this obedience is without analogy, for it is bracketed by the simultaneous unity of God. It is a command of will that flows from the Father to the Son who is the natural manifestation of the Father's being. The Son's obedience is true obedience, but it is also, to borrow a phrase from Tanner, the Father's will as "the teaching of (Jesus') own heart."[173] Darren O. Sumner makes the same point that I argue for here. Drawing on Barth's trinitarian theology, he asserts that the thrice repeated being of God entails that God acts in three modes of being in diversity "despite the fact that their subjectivity, and therefore their will, is one." As unique being that exists in unity-in-distinctions, "God has it within himself to 'command' and to 'obey' within the structure of that relation."[174] In short, a notion of the Son's obedience need not imply three distinct powers or wills in God, and certainly not three gods. Who and how God is for us, God is in Godself.

DIVINE CORRESPONDENCE

In the assessment from section 1 of this chapter I identified a point of ambiguity in Barth's use of a theory of correspondence for understanding the God-world relation. For Barth, the being of God in revelation history

171. Tanner, *Christ the Key*, 195.

172. See esp. Barth, *CD* IV/1:192–210.

173. Tanner, *Christ the Key*, 185.

174. Sumner, "Obedience and Subordination in Trinitarian Theology," 140–41.

corresponds to the antecedent Trinity. The issue here does not pertain to the fact that God acts in history from the antecedent (corresponding) nature of God as triune. The Trinity of God's being grounds, and therefore precedes, what God does among us. Rather, the problem lies in the idea of a correspondence that holds *in* the revelatory activity of God itself. In this way the corresponding relation leads to a notion of the eternal Trinity and the being of God with us in history as running alongside one another, a two-tiered history of God.

In *CD* I/1, of course, Barth does not conceive of such a clear break between the eternal Trinity and God with us. He consistently conceives of the divine correspondence between the antecedent or prior reality of the Trinity and the being of God in time. However, in his formal doctrine of the Trinity Barth does not adequately stave off the idea of an ongoing correspondence liable to the two-tiered understanding of God's history. In one way, this is simply to point out something that Barth does not do, though perhaps he should have, and need not be overstated. In another way, however, the problem is more significant. It can be linked to the deficit in Barth's application of the particulars of Christ's incarnate history to the understanding of God's being, as I pointed out in Barth's doctrine of the divine constancy in *CD* II/1. The problem of an ongoing correspondence in the sense of a two-track understanding of the God-world relation arises only when it becomes unclear whether the eternal God makes the creaturely history God's own. Positively, a two-tiered notion of the God-world relation can be avoided when it becomes clear that God, in some way, assumes the creaturely history into the eternal life of God. Apart from this basic claim, the possibility remains that statements about the real presence of God are not truly indicative of God *with us*, but rather reference something only analogous to authentic divine presence.

This latter point on the assumption of Christ's incarnate history into the divine being is therefore, among other reasons, what makes Barth's doctrine of election so significant. In *CD* II/2 Barth begins to track more closely with God's revealed history and what it allows us to say about the second person of the Trinity. The eternal Son does not have a vague identity. On scriptural grounds, we cannot conceive of the Son apart from the life, death, and resurrection of Jesus. For the author of Colossians, Christ is "before all things"; he is "the firstborn of all creation" (1:15, 17). The fourth gospel makes no qualifications about the identity of the antecedent reality of the Word become flesh: "*Jesus* said to them, 'very truly, I tell you, before Abraham was, I am'" (John 8:58).[175] In John's apocalypse the risen Jesus bears the

---

175. Emphasis mine.

exact characteristics of the divine being as "the first and the last" (Rev 1:8, 17). When Barth speaks of a divine obedience on the part of the Son in the pre-temporal decision of election, then, it is simply a consequence of the fact that the individual Jesus is the subject of the election. One cannot parse the identity of Jesus and the divine *Logos* so as to conceive of the latter apart from the former, or the eternal Word apart from the Son in the revelation of Jesus' concrete history.[176] The eternal Word is Jesus.

Barth's inclusion of a divine obedience in the eternal Trinity, following from the claim of Jesus as election's subject, has further implications for understanding God's relation to history that I turn to below. Here it stands to note that this rendering of obedience indicates for Barth how God assumes a defining feature of what is revealed in Jesus' incarnate relation to the Father into the divine life. The obedience of the divine Son is a relation proper to the Godhead that manifests his readiness to save the fallen creature. It is the obedience by which the Son in fact saves the fallen creature in time. Moreover, the inclusion of this obedience in the eternal Trinity staves off the idea of an ongoing correspondence, two histories of God, one above and one below, in revelation itself. It staves off this idea insofar as it purges a concept of correspondence of any suggestion that God does not make revelation history God's own. To adapt the line from Tanner used in the critical assessment from section 1, the eternal relations of the divine persons incorporate Jesus' humanity into the Godhead through the Word's incarnation such that their inner-relations come to reflect that fact.[177] Correspondence does not entail a two-fold history insofar as God assumes features of the revelatory history of God into the divine life; revelatory history is God's own. From eternity, the self-constitution of God is such that God is *this* God, God present with us in Jesus by the Spirit. Effectively, this removes the impulse or temptation to conceive of an ulterior history of God in the divine life mirroring the history God lives with us. For it is clear from the pre-temporal identity of the Trinity that God wills to be our God—to be, so to speak, 'ours in advance.'

ELECTION AND HISTORY

Barth's concept of the Son's obedience goes a long ways in overcoming the problem I have identified with the notion of correspondence. This opens up the possibility for constructively appropriating Barth's trinitarian doctrine of

176. It is notable that following election Barth eschews reflection on the *Logos asarkos* concept. See Barth, *CD* IV/1:52.

177. Tanner, *Christ the Key*, 180.

God for understanding God's relation to history. There remains, however, a final point to consider. In some ways it is the problem that Barth creates not by the lack of attention given to the meaning of Christ's incarnate history for understanding God's being in his formal doctrine of the Trinity (*CD* I/1), but what happens when he does in the doctrine of election (*CD* II/2). This has to do with Barth's peculiar idea of a primal history (*Urgeschichte*) of God. All the efforts above were aimed at overcoming the troubling notion of a two-track understanding of God's relation to history, or a history of God above running parallel to the revelatory history of God below. The identification of the second person of the Trinity in terms of a divine obedience allays this concern. The characterization of the pre-temporal election of God in terms of a primal history potentially rekindles it.

Likewise, descriptions of election in terms of a decision that "occurs in the very midst of time no less than in the far distant pre-temporal eternity" of God do little to clarify the matter.[178] Perhaps what Barth has in view here is the fact that the temporal realization and vitality of election in time cannot override its point of origin in the actuality of God's being. Or more likely, such descriptions follow from the kind of concrete characterization that Barth makes of Jesus Christ as not only the object but the living subject of election; Jesus Christ elects. The laudable point in Barth's doctrine of election is the absence of an unidentified *Logos asarkos*. At any rate, such characterizations of election as occurring in time 'no less than' in the pre-temporal eternity risk confusing what is proper to eternity and what is proper to time, or at least how God's eternal will is enacted in time. Specifically, such characterizations risk making the history of God with us into a thing of secondary importance, a copy of the original that occurs not primarily among us but in the 'far distant pre-temporal eternity.'

The point has not been lost on Barth's critics. Both Pannenberg and Jenson take note of it. Pannenberg takes Barth's account to succumb to the bifurcated view outlined above. The primal history of God, he writes, belongs "to a dimension which is 'oblique' to ordinary history . . . if, indeed, it has not remained in an archetypal realm above the plane of history."[179] Jenson gives more attention to Barth's doctrine of election than Pannenberg but arrives at a similar conclusion. As Jenson sees it, since Christ is the revelation of the eternal history of God, described here as God's primal history, Barth's depiction threatens to make the reconciling history of God a reality above the plane of history itself.[180] I give further attention to

178. Barth, *CD* II/2:185–86.

179. Pannenberg, "Redemptive Event and History," 41–42.

180. Jenson, *Alpha and Omega*, 162–63.

Jenson's criticism, alongside his assessment of Barth's doctrine of eternity, in chapter 4. Alan E. Lewis captures the sentiment of these criticisms well: "Has indeed *everything* significant already happened in eternity within the Trinity, needing now only to be recapitulated and revealed so that we might know what has primordially occurred?"[181]

To be sure, when Barth describes election in terms of two simultaneously occurring phenomena without proper distinction, he runs the risk of positing two realities of God: a pre-temporal reality of God, and a reflection of this more basic pre-temporal reality in revelation history. Still, there is another side to this. Election "takes place in time"; there is a primal history, but even it is "enacted in time."[182] It seems to me that Pannenberg, Jenson, and Lewis catch hold of a real tension in Barth's account of election. The whole thing, it appears, can be construed as something that ultimately resides above and beyond (before) us in pre-temporal eternity. Barth really seems to mean this. However, the electing decision is thoroughly characterized by the incarnate life of Jesus. Election is enacted in the process of creaturely time. Barth really seems to mean this. We are left with conflicting conceptions. There is a stark sense of ambiguity in Barth's doctrine of election when it comes to the relationship between eternity and time. Much is at stake in how election and the eternity-time relationship is conceived. Revelatory history retains its integrity as the real history of God with us when this relationship more closely approximates the view of an eternal decision enacted in time. In sharp contrast, revelatory history as the real history of God with us is diminished when this relationship more closely approximates the view of an outplaying of the more pristine, eternal (primal) history of God in time.

If Barth's doctrine of election is to be incorporated into a conception of God's living relation to history, as I attempt in the next sub-section, then the distinction between what God wills in pre-temporal eternity and its actualization in history must be maintained with greater consistency than Barth himself does. What God wills from eternity is a self-constituting decision. It is basic to God's being; it defines the contours of God's triunity, even as the Trinity is the subject of this decision. The decision stems from the actuality of God, or what Barth calls God's being-in-act. But the actuality of this decision in no way downplays its realization in time. The decision defines who God is and is rooted in the actuality of the Trinity. However, in the pre-temporal eternity in which the decision is made, it remains in its own way not yet. It is *not yet* insofar as what God wills is a

---

181. Lewis, *Between Cross and Resurrection*, 212–13.
182. Barth, *CD* II/2:106, 186.

history with us. God wills to be the subject of a reconciling history that has a beginning, middle, and eschatological point of consummation. It is a simple point, but it must be upheld with all seriousness if the understanding of the God-world relation is to do justice to the scriptural account of revelatory history as the real history of God with us.

TRINITY AND HISTORY

In this final sub-section I begin with a summary of the critical analysis of Barth's trinitarian theology offered so far. I conclude with a final statement on the significance of Barth's inclusion of a concept of divine obedience in the Godhead for understanding the relationship between the triune God and history.

In section 1 of this chapter I outlined how Barth conceives of God's relation to the world through the Trinity of God's being. As Father, Son, and Spirit the triune God is 'ours in advance.' Trinity serves the purpose of making intelligible various aspects of the God-world relation manifest in revelation. For instance, as Barth suggests in his doctrine of the divine constancy in *CD* II/1, the restoration of the proper order between God and fallen creatures stems from the internal harmony of the three divine modes of being. In the parlance of Barth's doctrine of the Trinity from *CD* I/1, God's relation to us is understood through a correspondence between the antecedent or eternal Trinity and the being of God in revelation. However, I argued that in utilizing a notion of correspondence it is important to specify how God's worldly involvement impacts or is received into God's eternal being. Left unspecified, the idea of a two-fold history of God, one above and one below, looms in a way that risks undermining the truth of a theological account of the God-world relation. More practically, this bears on the truthfulness of the foundationally important pastoral claim: 'God is here, with you.' Barth remains susceptible to this criticism because, at least in part, he does not adequately apply the meaning of Christ's incarnate history to the being of God in his trinitarian doctrine of God in *CD* I/1 and *CD* II/1. This critique overlaps with Pannenberg's assessment that Barth passes by the scriptural history of God with us too quickly, specifically the eschatological movement of revelation, in formulating the basis of his doctrine of the Trinity. The result is that Barth does not sufficiently address the grounds in God by which God is able to abide and move in an eschatologically oriented history with others. Nor does Barth make a significant advance on Dorner's use of Trinity for understanding the God-world relation.

Much of this changes with Barth's doctrine of election in *CD* II/2. There Barth takes the New Testament witness to the identity of Jesus Christ at the beginning of all things into his understanding of the divine being. Consequently, Barth posits a divine obedience on the part of the Son in the eternal Godhead, an obedience that reflects the posture of the man Jesus in relation to the Father evident in his temporal mission. This obedience, which by extension belongs to the command of the Father and the Son's conformity to the divine will, is real in God, albeit unique to God alone. As I argued, it is compatible with the unity-in-distinctions that characterize God's triune being. More central to my argument, it also overcomes the ambiguity that underlies Barth's use of a notion of correspondence in *CD* I/1. For it is clear that the eternal obedience of the Son, or his conformity to the Father's will to be God *this* way, as the one who saves fallen creatures, rules out the idea of an ulterior or corresponding history of God running alongside God's revelatory history with us. However, Barth's characterization of election as the primal history (*Urgeschichte*) of God raises another set of questions. While I am sympathetic to the criticisms of Barth's doctrine of election suggesting that the real vitality of God's life lies in pre-temporal eternity, I think the matter more muddled as to whether Barth's account actually entails this or if the real directionality of election is that of an identity defining decision in eternity *to be enacted* in time. At any rate, a constructive appropriation of Barth's account ought to move forward without the concept of a primal history.

I conclude the analytical assessment of Barth's trinitarian theology with a statement on the significance of Barth's inclusion of the concept of Jesus Christ's obedience to the Father in the eternal Godhead.

From Barth's doctrine of election we can glean a way of understanding the continuity that exists between the triune God in pre-temporal eternity and the being of God in history—God before all things and God with us. We can, insofar as the obedience that pertains to the Godhead from (pre-temporal) eternity, the result of the eternal identity of the divine Son as the man Jesus, extends into Christ's incarnate history. We might say that the obedience of Jesus to the Father in time corresponds to the eternal conformity of the Son to the Father; or we might leave out the correspondence notion here altogether. For what the second person of the Trinity does among us is nothing other than the natural outcome and the execution of the divine decision. In this way Christ among us manifests and confirms the antecedent or eternal reality of God's being. What is more, as the extension of the eternal obedience of the Son among us, the activity of God *ad extra* confirms the being of God *ad intra* without the thought that God remains closed off from us or untouched by the revelatory history God lives with us.

What the Father wills and the Son obeys in the Spirit from eternity—a living history with us—the triune God faithfully enacts in time. With this we can return once more to the tagline of this chapter, thus giving due weight to both aspects of the claim that as Father, Son, and Spirit, God is, so to speak, ours *in advance*, and indeed, truly *ours*.

Conclusion

In this chapter I have sought to demonstrate how Karl Barth conceives of the revelatory history of God to proceed from the eternal Trinity. Who God is among us corresponds to the antecedent Trinity of God's being. I considered how Barth's lack of attention to scriptural narrative in his trinitarian idea of God from *CD* I/1 restricts the way he is able to use this doctrine for understanding the eschatological movements of God in history. I also highlighted a missing component in Barth's application of Christ's incarnate history to the being of God and how this leaves open the problematic idea of a two-tiered understanding of God's relation to the world. However, by tracing this line of doctrinal development into Barth's doctrine of election in *CD* II/2, I argued that this problematic notion is overcome through the way that Barth shapes his conception of the eternal Trinity in terms of the incarnate Son's conformity to the Father's will. In the final part of the chapter I showed how Barth's treatment of election, particularly his view of the Son's obedience, provides a way to understand the revelatory history God lives with us as Father, Son, and Spirit as the natural expression of the eternal liveliness of God's being.

3

"The Trinitarian Mediated History of God"

Trinity and History in the Theology of Wolfhart Pannenberg

In this chapter and the next I turn to a pair of theologians following in the wake of Karl Barth's theology and their respective accounts of the triune God's relationship to history. I begin with the theology of Wolfhart Pannenberg, for whom the doctrine of the Trinity becomes a crucial focal point starting in the 1970s. The relevance of this classical doctrine to the central theme of this study in Pannenberg's theology is clear. Pannenberg asserts that the doctrine of the Trinity "formulates the relationship of God to history in general."[1] With Pannenberg's theology we shift gears from a focus on the pre-temporal life of God to eschatology and the notion of the vitality of God in history itself.

The purpose of this chapter is three-fold: (1) I revisit Pannenberg's critique of revelation and divine subjectivity in Barth's doctrine of the Trinity (*CD* I/1) in order to pick up on two lines of thought developed in the previous chapter: the role of the scriptural narrative in formulating the doctrine of the Trinity and the theological use of Trinity for understanding God's relation to the world, specially the historical contours and directionality of the God-world relation. These engagements serve as the backdrop for understanding Pannenberg's eschatological view of the Trinity and the way that God relates to history. (2) I then turn to Pannenberg's notion of the mutual relations of the divine persons. The essential constructive claim of this chapter is that Pannenberg's idea of the dependent monarchy of the Father can be used to articulate a conception of God's forward moving or eschatologically shaped history; that is, a notion of the livingness of God *in* history. (3) And, finally, I offer a critical assessment of Pannenberg's doctrine of eternity. I show how a set of ambiguities surround the concept of eternity in Pannenberg's theology, with resonances of eternal timelessness. This in turn will set up the transition to the following chapter on the theology of Robert W. Jenson and a trinitarian view of divine transcendence.

1. Pannenberg, "Der Gott der Geschichte," 122. Translation mine.

This chapter contains four sections. Since the paragraph above out-lines the main argumentative movements of this chapter, I list mainly the contents of the four sections here: In section 1 I return to Pannenberg's critique of Barth on the divine subjectivity. Section 2 looks at the notions of history and eschatology in Pannenberg's early work. This section com-pares Pannenberg's understanding of revelation and history with Barth's and also introduces two important themes in Pannenberg's theology, di-vine futurity and the principle of the unity of deity and lordship in God. In section 3 I consider the main components of Pannenberg's trinitarian theology and the key concepts that he employs for understanding God's relation to history. Drawing from the above, I set forth my constructive application of Pannenberg's trinitarian thought in section 4. I identify how Pannenberg's trinitarian theology helpfully upholds two poles of the God-world relation regarding divine immutability and God's historical presence. I then move beyond Pannenberg, while utilizing his trinitarian formulations, to argue for a concept of the triune God in the movement of history and the process of time. Section 4 concludes with the critical assessment of Pannenberg on the doctrine of eternity.

This chapter continues to develop the argument of this work. To recap, in chapter 1 I highlighted how the central problem of this work, the use of the doctrine of the Trinity to conceive of God's living relation to history, emerges from Isaak A. Dorner's way of reconciling divine immutability with the revealed vitality of God. Chapter 2 served both to further situate the question on Trinity and history in the work of Karl Barth by examining aspects of his trinitarian doctrine of God and divine election. I argued that Barth's doctrine of election, centered on his christological understanding of God's being, provides the means to conceive of the continuity and vitality that underlie the relationship between the pre-temporal being of the Trinity and the being of God in history. This chapter turns to the eschatological nature of God's relation to history, with a focus on the way that the future orientation of the God-world relation opens up an understanding of the vitality of God in history itself. While holding these appropriations loosely, if the emphasis in Barth's protological account of God and history can be said to fall on the conformity of the Son to the divine will, here, as I show, it rests on the dependent rule of the Father.

1: Subjectivity, Eschatology, and History

Before considering Pannenberg on the triune God's relation to history, I first return to his criticism of revelation and divine subjectivity in Karl

Barth's doctrine of the Trinity. The critique appears in an essay from 1977 entitled, "The Subjectivity of God and the Doctrine of the Trinity: An Essay on the Relation between Karl Barth and the Philosophy of Hegel." Around this time Pannenberg was beginning to work out a developed doctrine of the Trinity. In another significant essay from the same year, "The God of History," Pannenberg sets forth the notion of God as triune as the answer to the question of how to conceive of the unity between the being of God and God's historical activity.

To recap the critique (laid out in the previous chapter), Pannenberg claims that Barth's view of divine subjectivity constrains his trinitarian formulations. Pannenberg writes, "if the doctrine of the Trinity should depict, according to Barth, the indissoluble subjectivity of God in his revelation, then the I of God, as the I of the Lord, must form its 'root,'" that is, the root of the doctrine of the Trinity.[2] Despite Barth's efforts to the contrary, as Pannenberg sees it, Barth continues in the tradition of describing the Trinity according to psychological analogies that are undergirded by a form of natural theology. The prized place of the divine subjectivity overshadows the reality of the divine relations of God's being, which in turn leads to the idea of God as the transcendent correlate of the world.[3] God does not relate to the world through the complex unity of God's being, but rather, because of God's sheer singularity, stands over against it in a heteronomous relation.

I claimed in response that Pannenberg overstates the case here. With the help of Eberhard Jüngel's paraphrasing of Barth's doctrine of God I showed how in CD I/1 Barth has the creedal understanding of the divine relations in view in his initial formulations on the trinitarian nature of revelation. The trinitarian diversity of God, in other words, is not made subordinate to an imported concept of subjectivity, or at least the divine relations are elevated to a place in Barth's trinitarian theology that complicates Pannenberg's assertions around the heteronomous God-world relation in Barth's theology. However, there is a more direct and helpful criticism that underlies Pannenberg's suspicions. Pannenberg claims that Barth passes over the scriptural narrative too quickly in formulating his doctrine of the Trinity. Barth's concern for the immediacy of God's self-disclosure overlooks the progressive or eschatological nature of revelation.[4] I believe Pannenberg is right. The scriptural foundation for Barth's doctrine of the Trinity is thin. His articulation of God's abiding lordship in revelation, the centerpiece of

---

2. Pannenberg, "Die Subjektivität Gottes," 100. Translation mine.

3. Pannenberg, "Die Subjektivität Gottes," 110. See also Pannenberg, "Das christliche Gottesverständnis," 275.

4. See Pannenberg, Problemgeschichte, 257.

his doctrine of the Trinity in *CD* I/1, lacks a temporal dimension. Barth does not adequately identify the grounds in God by which God can be among us in history, particularly the history of revelation as oriented to a future in which God will be "all in all" (1 Cor 15:28).

Jürgen Moltmann brings this criticism into sharper focus. According to Moltmann, Barth takes over the personalism of Wilhelm Herrmann and applies it theologically to the non-objectifiable nature of God. In distinction from Pannenberg, though, Moltmann claims that Barth does not simply transfer notions of selfhood and personal reflection to the idea of God. The trinitarian being of God as revealed in another eschews such notions.[5] However, according to Moltmann, Barth's concept of God's self-disclosure and his concern to articulate a notion of divine lordship take priority over developing an idea of revelation along trinitarian lines. The lordship of God, as Barth describes it, is a kind of "self-contained *novum*," with a foundation and basis in God's own being, or what God is "antecedently in Himself."[6] In this way Barth makes the source and the aim of revelation one and the same: namely, God. Or as Moltmann puts it, "to understand the revelation in Christ as self-revelation of God, is to take the question as to the future and the goal indicated by revelation, and answer it with a reflection on the origin of revelation, on God himself."[7] Barth leaves the eschatological dimension of revelation untouched, as well as the question of how the revelation of God in the resurrection of Christ denotes a future that is, at least in some sense, still open.[8] If the revelation of God occurs in history, and thereby takes historical shape, what is the relationship between the being of God and the still outstanding future?

Unlike Moltmann, Pannenberg's criticism of Barth on the divine subjectivity does not center on the structuring of the divine relations. But Pannenberg would certainly agree with Moltmann's claim on the circularity of revelation in Barth's account, or the way in which the reflexive nature of revelation prioritizes divine origins to the extent of overlooking the telos and eschatological end of God in revelation. The criticisms of Moltmann and Pannenberg end up in the same place. Barth's lack of attention to scriptural narrative in his formal doctrine of the Trinity in *CD* I/1, as I have argued, constrains the ability to conceive of the eternal Trinity as the means by which God has a history and ushers in the eschatological end. Pannenberg's trinitarian theology, which is at least partly driven by his criticism of Barth's

---

5. Moltmann, *Theology of Hope*, 55–56.

6. Barth, *CD* I/1:306, 384.

7. Moltmann, *Theology of Hope*, 58.

8. Moltmann, *Theology of Hope*, 58.

theology, works to conceive of God's being in a way that is more congenial to God's historical activity.[9] This leads Pannenberg to consider the significance of God's eschatological activity for understanding God's being and God's relation to time. Furthermore, it leads Pannenberg to advance a notion of reciprocity in the divine life, or a concept of the internal becoming of Father, Son, and Spirit, consistent with the relational activity of the divine persons in salvation history. In a programmatic claim, Pannenberg writes,

> [The] reciprocity in the relationship of the trinitarian persons provides the foundation for the compatibility of the salvation-economical view of the Trinity with the immanent Trinity which precedes all time and world history.[10]

In section 3, I consider the notion of mutuality in Pannenberg's trinitarian theology. But first I turn to some of the foundations in Pannenberg's early work that support this turn to eschatology. This will also shed light on Pannenberg's eschatological concepts of God and revelation and allow me to draw out the basic themes that I will incorporate into the critical appropriation of Pannenberg's trinitarian theology in the concluding section of this chapter.

2: Early Notions of Revelation, History, and Futurity

In what follows I consider a pair of themes in Pannenberg's early work that play an important role in his mature account of the triune God's relation to the world: history and eschatology.[11] The first sub-section briefly outlines Pannenberg's idea of revelation as history. The second sub-section attends to the connection between deity and lordship as well as Pannenberg's early concept of eternity. Each part serves to illuminate Pannenberg's eschatological understanding of God. I also track some relevant points of doctrinal development in Pannenberg's work that factor into this chapter's critical assessment of his theology.

9. Pannenberg, "Der offenbarungstheologische," 16.

10. Pannenberg, "Problems of a Trinitarian Doctrine of God," 252. See also Pannenberg, *Systematic Theology*, 1:333. Hereafter cited as *ST*. Wenz, *Introduction to Wolfhart Pannenberg's Systematic Theology*, 66–67n1.

11. On Pannenberg's different engagements with the concept of history, such as his understanding of the historical veracity of the resurrection event or his adaptation of the historical-critical method, see Pannenberg, "On Historical and Theological Hermeneutic," 156–59; Pannenberg, "Redemptive Event and History," 38–80; Pannenberg, *Jesus—God and Man*, 88–105. Carlos Blanco provides an overview of the range of historical perspectives that Pannenberg treats. Blanco, "God," 305–7.

2.1: *History and Revelation*

During the 1950s Pannenberg and a cohort of scholars from the fields of biblical studies and theology formed a working group that came to be known as the 'Pannenberg Circle.' The collection of essays entitled *Revelation as History* is the product of their collaborative work. In this text Pannenberg, the systematic theologian of the group, claims that biblical revelation should be understood as both indirect and historical. Pannenberg has Barth in view. In conceiving of revelation as indirect, Pannenberg distances himself from the sense of immediacy and instantaneous completion in Barth's view of revelation.[12] I will return to this contrast at the end of this sub-section. It is also important to note Pannenberg's criticism of Barth on election, laid out in the previous chapter. Under the notion of a 'primal history' in God, Pannenberg takes Barth to conceive of the reality of the incarnation in "a dimension which is 'oblique' to ordinary history . . . if, indeed, it has not remained in an archetypal realm above the plane of history."[13] In contrast, Pannenberg seeks to characterize the nature of revelation as thoroughly historical. The revelation of God happens in history through a series of interconnected, temporal events.

Likewise, the indirect nature of revelation points to its more encompassing and historical framework, putting Pannenberg at odds with some of the demythologizing strands in the exegetical-theological program of Rudolf Bultmann.[14] For example, the biblical notion of the word of God, Pannenberg claims, is not an unmediated revelation of God, but takes shape as the apostolic kerygma (Luke-Acts) and the prophetic witness of Jesus (Rev 19:10, 13).[15] Moreover, individual events of revelation in Scripture are not complete in-and-of themselves, and the intention of God in revelation is not always transparent. God "will carry out many things which cannot be foreseen, and they will point back to the origin, though in different ways." At an even more basic level, Pannenberg writes, "God's activity illuminates the being of God only in a *partial* way."[16] This means that a definitive self-revelation of God occurs only with the totality of God's actions, that is, at the endpoint of history.

12. Pannenberg, "Introduction," 4–8.

13. Pannenberg, "Redemptive Event and History," 41–42. Pannenberg has Barth's commentary on Romans in view here, but his comment in 41n73 of this essay specifies that his claim applies to the *CD* as well.

14. Pannenberg, "Dogmatic Theses," 130–31.

15. Pannenberg, "Introduction," 7, 10–11.

16. Pannenberg, "Introduction," 14–16.

Pannenberg supports his thesis by evidencing the widening scope of God's self-vindicating actions in the history of Israel up through the early Christian movement. Of particular importance here is the promise-fulfillment schematic of the deuteronomisitic history and the later exilic vision of the future revelation of God, authenticating the prior acts of God in history (Deut 4:37–40; Isa 2:2–4; 25:26–28; Zech 2:11).[17] In the non-canonical literature of apocalyptic Judaism, Pannenberg sees the continuation of this eschatological movement in a final revelation of the divine glory and the resurrection of the dead (2 Bar 21:25).[18] The connection between God's eschatological glory and the resurrection is repeated, albeit in a unique way, in the New Testament (Rom 8:23; 2 Cor 3:8–11, 4:6; 1 Pet 4:14).[19]

All of this gives revelation its historical, future-oriented shape. Revelation is not a one-time unveiling of God, but "the defined goal of the present events of history."[20] Pannenberg writes,

> Since knowledge of God's divinity was no longer expected from single events but from one final occurrence which would gather together all earlier, single events into one single history, this ultimate knowledge had to be placed at the end of all history. Only when all occurrence is ended can the divinity of God be known on the basis of the connection of history. So one may say that only the last, the eschatological, event which binds history into a whole brings about final knowledge of God.[21]

In other words, the mediation of God's self-revelation, not through isolated occurrences, but in a series of interrelated events, means that the disclosure of God comes to completion only at the end of history. Furthermore, the revelatory actions of God come to a point of fulfillment. Thus Pannenberg is ultimately concerned with history as a meaningful whole, or history that comes to a unity under the auspice of God's activity. Pannenberg finds extra-theological support for the priority of the whole in the idea of establishing the meaning of the parts in both Martin Heidegger's existential philosophy

---

17. Pannenberg, "Dogmatic Theses," 125–27; Pannenberg, "Redemptive Event and History," 18.

18. Pannenberg, "Redemptive Event and History," 20; Pannenberg, "Dogmatic Theses," 132–33; Pannenberg, "The Revelation of God in Jesus," 121–22. See also Wilkens, "The Understanding of Revelation," 62–64. Christiaan Mostert gives extensive attention to the theme of apocalyptic in Pannenberg's theology. Mostert, *God and the Future*, 27–54.

19. Pannenberg, "Dogmatic Theses," 129.

20. Pannenberg, "Dogmatic Theses," 131.

21. Pannenberg, "The Revelation of God in Jesus," 122.

and, particularly, in Wilhelm Dilthey's hermeneutics.[22] Pannenberg's interest in history as a totality, though, is ultimately theological and grounded in the forward-looking nature of divine revelation.

This notion of history finds support in the resurrection event of Jesus. According to Pannenberg, the key to understanding the resurrection, as well as much of the New Testament's prophetic message, lies in apocalyptic Judaism's view of history as a whole. The resurrection of Jesus is significant insofar as in it the eschatological end of history occurs in advance. What God does by raising Jesus from the dead, God will do for all in the future resurrection of the dead. Jesus' resurrection is therefore proleptic in nature, and indicates that "the perfection of history has already been inaugurated."[23] In this way the resurrection event serves to substantiate Pannenberg's concept of history as a totality. Insofar as it stands at the center of God's revelatory actions in time, it also points to the final boundary of revelation, and with it, history itself, in the general resurrection of the dead. At the same time the resurrection of Jesus means that all of God's dealings in history are forward moving. By definition, history is eschatological; or conversely, history *is* because God acts eschatologically.[24]

As will become clear, these notions of revelation and history shape Pannenberg's doctrine of God. A brief comparison with Barth is helpful here. Barth's doctrine of the Trinity, both in *CD* I/1 and in the *Göttingen Dogmatics*, follows from his concept of revelation that reaches back to his commentary on Romans. Barth's idea of revelation is concerned with the lordship of God and the immediacy of God's disclosure. It is not surprising therefore that Barth makes these notions central to his trinitarian idea of God. Pannenberg explicitly contrasts his understanding of revelation with Barth's. Revelation, according to Pannenberg, is not immediate but indirect. Where immediacy dominates in Barth, and a notion of God's absolute lordship follows, for Pannenberg aspects of process and movement, a sense of the future as open, and the notion of historical fulfillment play vital roles in the formulation of his theological concept of God. As I show

22. Dilthey writes, "one would have to wait for the end of history to have the material necessary to determine its meaning." Dilthey, *Selected Writings*, 236. Pannenberg engages with Dilthey and Heidegger regularly in his work. See, e.g., Pannenberg, "On Historical and Theological Hermeneutic," 161–74.

23. Pannenberg, "Dogmatic Theses," 141–42. See also Pannenberg, *Jesus—God and Man*, 108, 321n96, 391. Ronald D. Pasquariello lays out the emergence of the idea of prolepsis in Pannenberg's early work. Pasquariello, "Pannenberg's Philosophical Foundations," 341–46.

24. See also Pannenberg's assessment on the proclamation of the kingdom of God in Jesus' ministry as following the same proleptic pattern of the resurrection. Pannenberg, *Theology and the Kingdom of God*, 53–54, 64–65.

in the next sub-section, and more fully in section 3 of this chapter, Pannenberg's idea of revelation leads him to a concept of God compatible with the eschatological nature of history.

2.2: Futurity and God

In *Revelation as History* Pannenberg sets out to detail the link between the eschatologically oriented history of God and the specific mode of God's self-revelation. Already in this early work there are strong hints that Pannenberg will attempt to work out a theological vision that includes the doctrine of God's being from the locus point of the future. The end of history, and not the course of history itself, he writes, is "at one with the essence of God."[25] What does this mean? I address this question by considering two themes in Pannenberg's early eschatological notion of God: the unity of deity and lordship and Pannenberg's concept of divine eternity.

DEITY AND LORDSHIP

We now turn to what Roger Olson has coined "Pannenberg's Principle."[26] The deity of God is inseparable from the divine lordship. Pannenberg takes this idea as axiomatic to the understanding of God: "God's being and existence cannot be conceived apart from his rule."[27] The idea of God is intricately linked to a notion of power; God devoid of power is no god at all. The principle, while basic, is of decisive significance, and follows in part from Pannenberg's notion of revelation. The biblical God, according to Pannenberg, is revealed through an eschatologically oriented history. The future, over and above the present, is the locus point of God's historical revelation. Yet if the manifestation of the divine lordship is still future, then the deity or the being of God lies in the future. But how so?

Pannenberg's principle has two different applications. The principle of the unity of God's deity and lordship has a more straightforward epistemic meaning: because the revelation of God's lordship is eschatological, the being of God is ultimately disclosed at the end of history. To say that the being of God lies in the future in this way means only that the divine lordship, in the midst of the vicissitudes of history and the struggle to overcome sin, has not yet been fully made known. But it will be, and in that sense the being of God, or the creature's true knowledge of God, lies in the future. But Pannenberg

25. Pannenberg, "Dogmatic Theses," 133.
26. Olson, "Wolfhart Pannenberg's Doctrine of the Trinity," 199.
27. Pannenberg, *Theology and the Kingdom of God*, 55.

also intends a stronger, ontological claim. In one of Pannenberg's most pro-
vocative statements he writes, it is true to say "in a restricted sense . . . God
does not yet exist." The being of God "is still in the process of coming to be."[28]
The claim needs to be unpacked. Concerning God's existence, it is possible
to avoid a great deal of misunderstanding here by pointing to a claim from
another essay of Pannenberg during this time. He writes, "everything that
already exists, all being, can be fundamentally called into question."[29] This,
however, does not apply to the being and existence of God if understood eschatologically. A being that really *is*, but that is not "present at hand (*Vorhan-
denheit*)," is unsurpassable.[30] To say that God does 'not yet' exist is different
from saying that God does not exist. Rather, for Pannenberg it means that
God exists distinctly in the future, such that the present existence of God can
be affirmed only through specific qualifications.

Furthermore, Pannenberg is articulating a novel idea of divine transcendence. A being that is not 'present at hand' lies beyond what is. But God
is not beyond what is by the sheer removal of temporal, creaturely properties,
such as in the idea of eternity as God's timeless reality. Rather, through the
futurity of God's being God lies *ahead* of what is. The idea is not fully developed in Pannenberg's early theology. In one of the more detailed descriptions
of the eschatological being of God, Pannenberg writes, "God, through the
realization of the historical future at a given time, pushed this away from
himself as the power of the ultimate future and in this way mediated himself to it in his own eschatological futurity."[31] The terminology of God as the
power of the future is common in Pannenberg's theology. Regarding God's
transcendence, the being of God who "exists only in the way in which the
future is powerful over the present" thus covers both the present and the
future.[32] By the divine futurity God transcends present reality; and yet, at the
same time, as the power of the future God mediates the here and now. God is
therefore intimately involved in every momentary present.

Philip Clayton summarizes Pannenberg's notion of futurity and divine
being.

28. Pannenberg, *Theology and the Kingdom of God*, 56; Pannenberg, "The God of
Hope," 242.

29. Pannenberg, "The God of Hope," 241.

30. Pannenberg, "The God of Hope," 241.

31. Pannenberg, "The God of Hope," 244. Cf. Pannenberg, *Theology and the Kingdom of God*, 54.

32. Pannenberg, "The God of Hope," 242. See also Pannenberg, *Theology and the
Kingdom of God*, 56.

God must be in some sense fully actual; he cannot be deficient in being; he cannot be solely located in the future, for he must be vitally involved with every Now of history; yet he is so dependent on the future that it can be spoken of as the locus of his being. Hence he is God now in anticipation of the God he will show himself to be (have been?) at the end of history.[33]

Clayton captures the tension in Pannenberg's early eschatological idea of God here. God is so fully enraptured by the future that it can be described as the locus of God's being. There is a kind of go-between in the literal and figurative understandings of God's futurity as Pannenberg works out a view of divine transcendence. Futurity corresponds to something in the reality of God. However, as some commentators maintain, divine futurity does not mean that God is simply identical to the future.[34] Rather, Pannenberg intends something more complex than this reduction allows. The being of God incorporates the future as well as the present. God is the *power* of the future, and thereby, albeit not in an entirely clear way, straddles present and future time by means of God's eschatological being.

This notion of futurity comes to expression in a similar way in Pannenberg's idea of Jesus' retroactively confirmed unity with God.[35] What happens in the resurrection event sheds a light backwards on the life, ministry, and death of Christ. While Jesus' unity with the Father does not begin in the resurrection event, his pre-Easter authority is, in its historicity, contingent upon his life coming to a point fulfillment in which his being one with the Father (as the Son of God) is revealed.[36] Pannenberg's notion of retroactive permanence, the confirmation of Jesus' unique relation to the Father in the resurrection, attempts to make sense of a real becoming of God in history alongside a notion of God's unchanging being, or at least a sense of ontological stability in the history of Jesus as mediated by God's future.[37] At times it appears that Pannenberg's claims around the futurity of God in his early theology are rather context specific. In an engagement with the process philosophy of Whitehead and Hartshorne, for instance, Pannenberg specifically rules out a notion of development in God: "what turns out to be true in the future will then be evident as having been true all along."[38] Part of the ultimate

---

33. Clayton, "Being and One Theologian," 665–66.

34. See, e.g., Bloesch, *Essentials of Evangelical Theology*, 31; Hill, *The Three-Personed God*, 157, 160–61.

35. Pannenberg, *Jesus—God and Man*, 322; see also 320–21.

36. Pannenberg, *Jesus—God and Man*, 135–37.

37. Cf. Pannenberg, *Jesus—God and Man*, 157, 320–21.

38. Pannenberg, *Theology and the Kingdom of God*, 62–63. On the distinction

revelation of God in the future includes the fact that God does not change in God's history with us. Nevertheless, through the futurity of God's being, God is actively involved in history and the process of time.

Divine Eternity

Pannenberg also outlines a notion of eternity that follows from his eschatological concept of God. God as the power of the future means that the divine being is the future of every present moment, both here and now and for every present moment now past. This notion of futurity brings into view an idea of the whole that approximates Boethius' concept of eternity as the simultaneous totality of life. For insofar as God both is and has been present to every temporal moment as its divine future, no moment of time, present or past, is lost on God. Rather, it is included within God's future, its divine source.[39] God precedes every historical present as the power of its future, and thus the dynamics of temporality, from past to future, are present to God as a whole. Again, the eternity of God is not timeless. Insofar as divine eternity includes the dimensions of time in itself, it is at least compatible with temporal reality.[40] The futuristic concept of eternity, however, also lends itself to another view or modality of the relationship between eternity and time. On this view eternity is itself imminently temporal for Pannenberg. The futurity of God, as described above, straddles present and future. Therefore, from the focal point of God's eternity, the divine futurity, God generates the process of time from within (or alongside) time itself.

Both of these early views of Pannenberg on futurity and divine eternity undergo modifications that I track in the remainder of this chapter. At this point I simply note that Pannenberg's early divine ontology contains a more temporal or historically resonant concept of God than Barth's trinitarian theology from *CD* I/1. According to Pannenberg, God intimately relates to history and the process of time and transcends temporal reality from within time itself. In Pannenberg's account this follows from the future orientation of God's dealings in history as well as the principle of the unity of deity and lordship. But the concept of futurity in Pannenberg's theology is not without its problems. Futurity has a structural basis in revelation, but it is also highly abstract; it is functional but lacks substantial content. Theological ontology

---

between becoming and development in Pannenberg's idea of God, see Ford, "The Nature of the Power of the Future," 78; Mostert, *God and the Future*, 157–61.

39. Pannenberg, "The God of Hope," 243–44; Pannenberg, *Theology and the Kingdom of God*, 62.

40. Pannenberg, *Theology and the Kingdom of God*, 62–63.

is meant to provide some help in answering a fundamental question of faith: *Who* is God? Or, here, who is this futurity? As Christoph Schwöbel notes, "one can only believe in a deity, honor and serve it, pray to it, with a known identity." Worship is impossible, or at least loses its core sense of meaning, without an adequate response to the question of who God is.[41]

In short, Pannenberg's idea of futurity is promising insofar as it offers a concept of eternity and transcendence along temporal lines. In this way it avoids the problem outlined in the previous chapter of a two-tiered history of God. But it can be of theological use only if we can say more about who the God of the future is. This points up the significance of Pannenberg's developed trinitarian concept of God to which I now turn.

3: Trinity, History, and Eschatology

In section 1 of this chapter I looked at Pannenberg's critique of Barth on the divine subjectivity. I judged that Pannenberg overstates the case in his criticism that Barth's account leads to a heteronomous relation between God and the world. Pannenberg, however, rightly detects that Barth's concern with the subjectivity of God leads to an oversight regarding the essential place of eschatology in the formulation of his doctrine of the Trinity, stemming also from a lack of attention to scriptural narrative. In this section I consider Pannenberg's constructive response and the way in which he, beginning with Jesus' relation to the Father, conceives of the mutuality that characterizes the trinitarian relations as "the foundation for the compatibility of the salvation-economical view of the Trinity with the immanent Trinity."[42] The first sub-section gives an overview of the exegetical basis of Pannenberg's trinitarian theology and his concept of the mutuality or reciprocal self-distinctions of the divine persons. The second sub-section considers some of the essential concepts in Pannenberg's understanding of the relationship between the immanent and the economic Trinity.

3.1: The Trinity of Persons and the Eternal Relations of God

In line with the question from Christoph Schwöbel above, Pannenberg takes the doctrine of the Trinity to indicate "who the God is who has revealed himself in Jesus Christ."[43] This, moreover, designates the starting point of trinitarian reflection in the Spirit-filled relation of Jesus to the Father. Prior

41. Schwöbel, "Trinitätslehre," 407. Translation mine.
42. Pannenberg, "Problems of a Trinitarian Doctrine of God," 252.
43. Pannenberg, *ST*, 1:300.

to addressing that relation, Pannenberg raises a question that lies at the heart of any trinitarian theology: What is the exegetical basis for establishing the idea of the consubstantial relation between Jesus the Son and the Father, as well as the deity of the Spirit? A full account of Pannenberg on the equality and sameness of deity between the divine persons lies beyond my task here. My focus in what follows is limited to the way in which Pannenberg's solution to this problem gives way to his construal of the eternal relations of God in terms of the mutuality of the divine persons.

I begin with Pannenberg on the inner-trinitarian relations. The classical doctrine of the Trinity conceives of the divine relations in two fundamental ways: first—logically, not temporally—in terms of the eternal begetting or generation of the Son from the Father and, secondly, the Spirit's procession from or being breathed by the Father (and, in the west, the Son; John 3:16; 15:26; 20:22). These eternal relations are sharply distinguished from the sendings or the missions of the Son and the Spirit in the economy of salvation. But, as Pannenberg notes, the exegetical basis for such a distinction is thin. The Spirit is breathed on the disciples in the presence of the risen Jesus. And the begetting statements primarily serve to designate the unique quality of Jesus' sonship in the events of his baptism and resurrection (Matt 3:17; Luke 3:22; John 3:16; Acts 13:33).[44] Each has a historic, not an eternal, reference point. For Pannenberg, these relations remain important for understanding the eternal triunity of God insofar as God's eternal being is inferred from the revelatory history of God. However, according to Pannenberg, a more definitive basis within the revelatory history of God itself is needed if the Son, and likewise, the Spirit, are to be conceived on equal terms with the deity of the Father.[45]

It is against this background that Pannenberg puts forward his thesis that the equality of the divine persons belongs to their personal self-distinctions. This leads not only to the concept of the mutuality of the divine persons as basic to God's being, but also to a qualified idea of divine monarchy within the traditional construct of the eternal relations of origin (e.g., the Father's begetting of the Son).

Pannenberg's account of divine relations starts from the revelation of God in Christ. Particularly important for Pannenberg is the witness of Jesus' life and Jesus' proclamation of the exclusive sovereignty of God and

44. Pannenberg, *ST*, 1:305–6.

45. Pannenberg, *ST*, 1:264–65, 307; *Systematic Theology*, 2:371. Pannenberg notes that the sending claims give greater specification to the eternality of the second and third persons of the Trinity insofar as they imply pre-existence. However, the ontological relation between sender and those being sent remains unclear apart from further consideration of the divine economy. Pannenberg, *ST*, 1:305, 307.

God's coming reign. "No one is good but God alone," Jesus confesses (Mark 10:18). While one with the Father, Jesus nevertheless declares the Father to be greater than himself (John 10:30; 14:28). He is resolved to obey the Father's will and to trust himself into the Father's care (Mark 14:36). On Jesus' relation to the Father, Pannenberg writes,

> Precisely by distinguishing himself (*sich unterscheidet*) from the Father, by subjecting himself to his will as his creature, by thus giving place to the Father's claim to deity as he asked others to do in his proclamation of the divine lordship, he showed himself to be the Son of God and one with the Father who sent him.[46]

The self-distinction of the Son in relation to the Father is not, however, unilateral. In what is perhaps Pannenberg's most novel exegetical move, he turns to the way in which the Father grants "all authority" and "all things" to the Son (Matt 28:18; Luke 10:22). The Father gives the rights to the divine kingdom to the Son. And the Son, the recipient of the Father's gift, carries out his mission until, in the consummation of all things, he returns the kingdom to the Father in order that "God may be all in all" (1 Cor 15:15, 28).[47]

The distinction of the Son from the Father follows from his proclamation of the divine lordship and his obedience to the divine will. Conversely, in the manifestation of the Son's deity in relation to the Father, a similar self-distinction applies to the Father in relation to the Son. The divine rule, the Father's kingdom, hinges on whether "the Son glorifies him and actualizes his lordship by fulfilling his mission."[48] In other words, the deity of the Father depends on the obedience of the Son. This point is also in keeping with the previously elaborated principle on the unity of deity and lordship in God. If the deity of God is identical to the divine sovereignty, then the deity of God somehow rests on the realization of God's kingdom in the work that the Father entrusts to the Son. The self-distinction of the Father is manifest in his dependency on the Son's establishment of the kingdom of God.

Pannenberg posits a similar self-distinction of the Spirit. The farewell discourse of John (14–17) exhibits the basic pattern of the Spirit's unique activity. Just as the Son distinguishes himself from the Father in honoring him, so the Spirit glorifies the Son and, through him, the Father by shedding light on the Father-Son relation (John 16:14). In bearing witness to the Son,

---

46. Pannenberg, *ST*, 1:310; Pannenberg, *Systematische Theologie*, 1:337.

47. Pannenberg, *ST*, 1:312.

48. Pannenberg, *ST*, 1:313; Pannenberg, *Systematische Theologie*, 1:340. English translation slightly altered. See also *ST*, 2:29–30. Ángel Cordovilla Pérez offers a similar rendering of Pannenberg's trinitarian idea of God. Pérez, "The Trinitarian Concept of Person," 137.

the Spirit testifies to the one through whom the Father is known (John 14:6; 15:26). Likewise, the Spirit has the same goal as the Son in glorying the Father and bringing about his rule, such that every aspect of Jesus' work is driven by the Spirit.[49] In this way the Son-mediated rule of the Father applies to the Spirit as well. The Spirit plays a similar role in mediating the Father-Son relation in raising Jesus from the dead (Rom 1:4; 1 Tim 3:16).[50] As the medium of their fellowship, the Spirit cannot be reduced simply to the "we" of the Father and Son's communion. The Spirit has its hypostatic identity over against them as the principle of their unity, or as their common Spirit.[51]

Beginning with Jesus' relation to the Father, Pannenberg draws out the mutuality that characterizes the inner-relations of the triune persons in the divine missions. Herein lies for Pannenberg the answer to the question of the sameness and equality of deity between the divine persons: none possess it on their own. This is not to say that the Father is not God, and likewise with the Son and Spirit. Rather, it is to make a point that follows from the self-deferential way that the divine persons relate to one another. The Father, for instance, is God, but never as a member of the Trinity in abstraction from the Son or the Spirit. The deity of the Father hinges on the honor that he receives from the Son in the Spirit, or concretely, on the establishment of the divine rule among us. Ted Peters aptly captures Pannenberg's intention when he describes the deity of the divine persons as "*dependent* divinity."[52]

Pannenberg incorporates his trinitarian conception of God into the traditional schematic of the eternal relations of origins. He writes,

> the Father does not merely beget the Son. He also hands over his kingdom to him and receives it back from him. The Son is not merely begotten of the Father. He is also obedient to him and he thereby glorifies him as the one God. The Spirit is not just breathed. He also fills the Son and glorifies him in his obedience to the Father, thereby glorifying the Father himself.[53]

---

49. Pannenberg, *ST*, 1:317.

50. Pannenberg, *ST*, 1:314–15, 330; Pannenberg, *The Apostle's Creed*, 138–39.

51. Pannenberg, *ST*, 1:315–17, 358. See also Pannenberg, *ST*, 2:32. In reducing the Spirit to the common principle of the Father and Son, their "we," Pannenberg has Heribert Mühlen's *Der Heilige Geist als Person* in view. Pannenberg cites Moltmann's criticism of Mühlen in which the Spirit, conceived as the first person plural, leads to only a constitutive duality in God. Pannenberg, *The Trinity and the Kingdom*, 245n73.

52. Peters, "Trinity Talk," 136. The notion of dependent deity also illuminates Pannenberg's affinity for Athanasius' axiom that the Father is not Father without the Son. On this theme, see Pannenberg, *ST*, 1:273, 275, 311–12, 322; *ST*, 2:367.

53. Pannenberg, *ST*, 1:320; Pannenberg, "Die Subjektivität Gottes," 110.

Pannenberg thus complements the traditional notions of the Son's begetting and the Spirit's procession with a simultaneous response of the Son to the Father mediated by the Spirit.[54] The relations between Father, Son, and Spirit, Pannenberg states, "cannot be reduced to relations of origin."[55] Rather, the obedience of the Son and the indwelling of the Spirit who glorifies the Son in his obedience to the Father gives more concrete expression to the perichoretic relations of the divine persons. Furthermore, Pannenberg holds that the persons are not "identical simply with any one relation. Each is a catalyst of many relations."[56] Pannenberg follows through on this invitation to understanding the relational complexity of God's being through a revised (expanded) conception of divine monarchy in God. The difference from the traditional schematic is that the Son and Spirit not only derive from the unoriginate origin in God, the Father as the divine monarch, but that this monarchy is constituted by the reciprocal nature of the divine relations. Going back at least to Athanasius, it becomes a norm in the tradition to say that the Father is Father only in relation to the Son. In this way the essential being of the Father depends on the Son. Pannenberg takes this a step further in articulating the dependency of the Father's monarchy on the way in which the Son and the Holy Spirit respectively glorify the Father from whom they proceed. The Father is Father as such always and only as affirmed by the Son in the Son's Spirit-filled conformity to the Father's will.[57]

In sum, beginning with Jesus' relation to the Father, Pannenberg maintains that a notion of mutuality or reciprocal self-distinction applies to God's trinitarian being. But Pannenberg's aim is not only to delineate the basic distinctions in God for a doctrine of the Trinity. As we will see, he intends to show how the "reciprocity in the relationship of the trinitarian persons provides the foundation for the compatibility of the salvation-economical view of the Trinity with the immanent Trinity."[58] In one way,

54. Linn Tonstad denies that the kind of dependence Pannenberg articulates "enacts genuine reciprocity and mutuality." Tonstad compares Pannenberg's conception to a "boss (that) depends on his subordinates for his status as boss," and doubles down: "Indeed, that is the case." Tonstad, "'The Ultimate Consequence,'" 392. However, an important point is left out of Tonstad's metaphor. For Pannenberg, lordship and deity are one and the same. A more genuine notion of reciprocity obtains if, in keeping with Tonstad's metaphor, the boss not only relies on the worker, but even goes so far as to put the whole fate of the company in the hands of the latter.

55. Pannenberg, *ST*, 1:320.

56. Pannenberg, *ST*, 1:320.

57. Pannenberg, *ST*, 1:325, 421.

58. Pannenberg, "Problems of a Trinitarian Doctrine of God," 252. See also Pannenberg, *ST*, 1:333; Wenz, *Introduction to Wolfhart Pannenberg's Systematic Theology*, 66–67n1.

however, Pannenberg has already begun this work in articulating the notion of mutual dependency in God. For the establishment of the divine rule by the Son, the specific act which manifests the Father's dependency on the success of the Son and his mission, fills out part of Pannenberg's early notion of revelation as history in trinitarian terms. According to Pannenberg's doctrine of revelation, the climatic disclosure of God in the eschatological end is the driving force of history. Within a trinitarian constellation: the revelation of God in the eschaton, or the arrival of the Father's rule as mediated by the Son through the Spirit, is history's rationale. Accordingly, Pannenberg entitles the paragraph which follows his treatment of the mutuality of the divine persons in *Systematic Theology* 1, "The World as the History of God and the Unity of the Divine Essence." In the following section I turn to Pannenberg's way of applying his trinitarian idea of God to the relation between the immanent and the economic Trinity.

3.2: The Immanent Trinity and the Economic Trinity

By the second half of the twentieth century, following the appearance of Karl Rahner's 1967 work, *The Trinity*, it became commonplace to describe the link between the eternal Trinity and the being or activity of God in revelation as the relation between the immanent and the economic Trinity. The basic slogan of Rahner's trinitarian theology is the claim that the immanent Trinity is the economic Trinity, and vice versa. The claim, which Rahner describes as his *Grundaxiom*, lends itself to various interpretations and uses in the theological history that follows. Pannenberg explains the appeal of Rahner's *Grundaxiom* in the following way:

> This thesis [the immanent Trinity is the economic Trinity, and vice versa] means that the doctrine of the Trinity does not merely begin with the revelation of God in Jesus Christ and then work back to a trinity in the eternal essence of God, but that it must constantly link the trinity in the eternal essence of God to his historical revelation, since revelation cannot be viewed as extraneous to his deity.[59]

In other words, not only does the axiom grasp the fact that God is known in God's self-revelation; it also asserts that God is involved in salvation history. God assumes this history into the divine life, and the eternal Trinity of God's being must be understood accordingly. For this reason Rahner asserts that the specific activity of becoming incarnate in the man Jesus belongs uniquely

---

59. Pannenberg, *ST*, 1:328.

to the divine Son and should not be merely appropriated to his person in distinction from the Father and Spirit.[60] Pannenberg, however, is critical of certain elements in Rahner's application of the *Grundaxiom*. Most important for our purposes is Pannenberg's claim that, according to Rahner, God the Father possesses no direct involvement in the history of revelation. To "give life" to Rahner's thesis, Pannenberg claims, requires an understanding in which the Father is himself implicated in the economy of salvation.[61]

Pannenberg's concern to conceive of the Father's genuine involvement in salvation history follows from his analysis of the reciprocal self-distinctions of the divine persons. The decisive point here lies in the dependency of the Father's monarchy. The begetting of the Son hinges on his obedience to the Father's primal act. In the economy, the Father's rule rests on the success of the Spirit-filled mission of the Son. The Father's rule is thus at stake in the activity of the divine persons. With both Jüngel and Moltmann, Pannenberg notes how this pattern comes to expression in both Jesus' death and resurrection as well as the eschatological arrival of the kingdom. The Son succeeds in his mission; his life does not end in death, because of the life giving power of the Father who raises him from the dead through the Spirit. The Father also relates to the world in his dependency on the Spirit's ongoing witness in order that the divine reign, the Father's rule, be realized among us, both now and in the consummation of all things.[62] In both cases, Christ's death and resurrection and the eschatological arrival of the kingdom, the reciprocal self-distinctions of the divine persons underlie the involvement of the Father in revelation history.

However, Pannenberg does not put forward his own distinct formulation on the relationship between the immanent and the economic Trinity. Rather, Pannenberg identifies specific concerns that govern his construal of the immanent-economic Trinity relation. The two most prominent concerns are these: First, Pannenberg states his intention to maintain a notion of identity-in-distinction between the immanent and economic Trinity. The need to distinguish the immanent from the economic Trinity lies in the fact that equating the two would entail "the absorption of the immanent in the economic Trinity," which in turn "steals from the Trinity of salvation history all sense and significance."[63] God is not only God in revelation, but is God from eternity. It is from God's creative power, rooted in God's eternity, that

60. Pannenberg, *ST*, 1:328.

61. Pannenberg, *ST*, 1:330.

62. Pannenberg, "Problems of a Trinitarian Doctrine of God," 252; Pannenberg, "Der Gott der Geschichte," 122–28.

63. Pannenberg, *ST*, 1:331–32.

the world comes into being and is given its purpose and meaning. Neverthe-less, the being of God in revelation *is* God. "God is the same in his eternal essence as he reveals himself to be historically."[64] The two sides of identity-in-distinction coalesce in Pannenberg's claim that the immanent Trinity is "to be found" in the economic Trinity.[65]

The second concern has to do with Pannenberg's eschatological the-ology. Given Pannenberg's account of God, revelation, and history from the previous section, it does not surprise that he agrees with Moltmann's analysis (and also, though less clearly, with Robert W. Jenson's) on the trinitarian life of God as consummated in the eschatological end of history. "When all things are in God and God is 'all and all,' then the economic Trinity is subsumed into the immanent Trinity."[66] This does not entail, Pan-nenberg writes, a "divine becoming in history, as though the trinitarian God were the result of history and achieved reality only with its eschatological consummation."[67] There is a sense in which with the creation of the world, God is dependent, even "radically dependent on this creation and on its history."[68] But this latter point pertains mainly to the proof of God's exis-tence and the principle of the unity of deity and lordship, and does not mean that God becomes triune in time. Pannenberg writes, "the eschatological consummation is only the locus of the decision that the trinitarian God is always the triune God from eternity to eternity."[69] The economic Trinity is finally revealed as one with the immanent Trinity, but revealed in such a way as to disclose their unity at every moment—their unity across time—in the triune God's relation to the world.

An important question remains unanswered here. Eschatology clearly retains priority of place in Pannenberg's mature theology. Only in eschato-logical consummation is the truth of God's existence settled once for all. But it is not entirely clear where God stands, so to speak, in relationship to the world. In light of the notions we explored from Pannenberg's early theology, what is the connection between God's being and divine futurity? The early Pannenberg envisions God to be somehow future; God transcends what is, and yet intimately relates to the world, to every momentary present, as the productive source of its future. To get a better grasp on this issue, as well

64. Pannenberg, *ST*, 1:331.

65. Pannenberg, *ST*, 1:331; Pannenberg, "Divine Economy and Eternal Trinity," 84–85.

66. Pannenberg, *ST*, 1:330.

67. Pannenberg, *ST*, 1:331.

68. Pannenberg, "Problems of a Trinitarian Doctrine of God," 255.

69. Pannenberg, *ST*, 1:331.

as the broader conception of the immanent-economic Trinity relation, we will need to consider other dimensions of Pannenberg's trinitarian idea of God and the way it shapes his understanding of the God-world relation. In what follows I turn to four basic themes on the relationship between the immanent and the economic Trinity in Pannenberg's theology: Pannenberg's idea of the true Infinite; the self-actualization of God in the world; the link between deity and lordship; and divine eternity.

THE TRUE INFINITE

The notion of the infinite plays a governing role in Pannenberg's treatment of the divine attributes. He divides this treatment into, first, the attributes that designate the general form of the divine nature (omnipresence, eternity, etc.) and, second, those that culminate in the divine loving and the revealed character of God (righteousness, patience, etc.) as the concrete form of the divine essence.[70] The infinity of God belongs to the former set of attributes, the general form of the divine nature. The infinity of God's being for Pannenberg underlies the concept of divine transcendence. Insofar as God is infinite being, God lies beyond what is, finitude and all of created reality. But transcendence does not mean simple difference from the world. It implies a point from which God transcends, and therefore also a relationship with something other than God. Here Pannenberg makes use of the paradoxical structure of Hegel's idea of the infinite. On this view that which is authentically infinite, in distinction from the mathematical infinite, not only stands in opposition to finite reality, but "must be conceived both as *transcendent* in relation to the finite and as *immanent* to it."[71] As Hegel puts it, "if God has the finite only over against himself, then he himself is finite and limited." Finitude is "posited in God himself, not as something insurmountable," but as that which God sublates.[72] True infinite being, as by definition the exclusion of all contrastive limitations, includes the finite within itself, even as it transcends all that is.[73]

70. See Pannenberg, *ST*, 1:384–96.

71. Pannenberg, *Metaphysics and the Idea of God*, 36; Pannenberg, *ST*, 1:357, 400.

72. Hegel, *Lectures on the Philosophy of Religion*, 406. Pannenberg remains wary of a conflation between the infinite or God and the world in Hegel's system of thought. Hegel, according to Pannenberg, slips into an identification of God and the Idea that realizes itself in the self-unfolding of the logical concept in nature, a mistake that eliminates the difference of God and the world. See Pannenberg, *Metaphysics and the Idea of God*, 147–52, esp. 152.

73. A similar point follows from the traditional concept of God as beyond genus. See Tanner, *God and Creation in Christian Theology*, 36–80, esp. 37–48.

According to Pannenberg, the trinitarian idea of God coheres with the idea of the true Infinite. For the distinction between the infinite and the finite, and the incorporation of the latter as a moment that exists within the former, aligns with both the trinitarian distinctions in God and the way in which the divine persons relate to one another in revelation history. "The transcendent Father works in the world through the Son and the Spirit."[74] Pannenberg conceives of the Father's relation to the Son and Spirit as that of a tension between two poles through which God occupies the world—in the Son and Spirit—that God simultaneously lies above and beyond—in the Father.[75] In this way, as the "true Infinite," God "transcends the antithesis to what is distinct from it," the created reality that God indwells.[76] The relationship between these two poles, however, is fluid. In their perichoretic union, the transcendent Father is present to the world and, conversely, the divine Son and Spirit are not confined to the finite structure of created reality.[77] Finally, it is likely that Pannenberg has Barth's account of the divine subjectivity in view here. In the abstract concept of unity or divine singularity, God stands in contrast to the plurality of the world. A trinitarian concept of the Infinite, as that which includes (indwells), and simultaneously transcends, what is other than itself, is more readily relatable to the idea of the world in its finitude and complex diversity.[78]

Divine Self-Actualization

Pannenberg's engagement with the divine attributes culminates in the divine love, the basic form of the divine essence. This means that while the idea of the true Infinite governs Pannenberg's initial treatment of the divine attributes (omnipresence, eternity, etc.), it remains at somewhat of a general level without delving into the specifics of the immanent-economic Trinity relation. Pannenberg describes the relation between the immanent Trinity and the divine economy more concretely through the idea of divine self-actualization (*Selbstverwirklichung*).[79] In keeping with his pervious assertions on the unity of the immanent Trinity and the eschatological activity of God, Pannenberg maintains that God's self-actualization in history does not

---

74. Sanders, *The Image of the Immanent Trinity*, 99.

75. Pannenberg, *ST*, 1:415.

76. Pannenberg, *ST*, 1:445. For a similar construction, though with greater emphasis on divine omnipresence, see Baker-Fletcher, *Dancing with God*, 66.

77. Pannenberg, *ST*, 1:415, 431.

78. Pannenberg, *ST*, 1:445.

79. Pannenberg, *Systematische Theologie*, 1:418.

mean that God works out God's being in time. He compares God's worldly activity to the developing sense of selfhood among creaturely beings. For creatures, the I is always *on its way* to identification with the self, which for creatures applies only to the point at which life comes to an end and one's identity is established once for all. For God, however, there exists a perfect harmony between the divine being and the self-determinations of God.[80] Hence, unlike creatures, the divine self *to be* actualized, to become the result of its own actualization, is "already actual" from the starting point of the action.[81] Divine self-actualization does not mean self-discovery, at least in a constitutive way. While the notion of act, as we will see, remains important in Pannenberg's conception of the God-world relation, the idea here is closer to a notion of divine self-expression or self-manifestation.

Divine action connects the immanent and the economic Trinity. Pannenberg writes, in action "the one who acts is with another on or toward which he or she acts." Pannenberg applies the basic notion of act here to the relation between God's being in itself (the immanent Trinity) and who God is for us (the economic Trinity): the concept of divine action links "the intratrinitarian life of God with the economic Trinity, the active presence of Father, Son, and Spirit with their creatures in the economy of salvation."[82] This intratrinitarian life is the divine fellowship of Father, Son, and Spirit, through which the self-actualization of God in the world takes concrete form.[83] Pannenberg expresses this point in light of the divine monarchy.

> Already in the eternal fellowship of the Son with the Father the Son subjects himself to the Father as the King of eternity. The divine lordship is not first set up in God's relation to the world. It has its basis in his trinitarian life. By his subjection to the monarchy of the Father the Son is what he is from eternity, the Son of the Father, bound to him in the communion of the Godhead.[84]

Kent Eilers is thus right to point out that Pannenberg conceives of the relation between the immanent and economic Trinity as asymmetrical.[85] God acts among us through God's trinitarian being; the divine lordship 'has its basis in his trinitarian life.' While there is a way that Pannenberg's concern is strictly God's being in relation to the world, a point that comes to the fore in his exegetical basis for understanding the inner-life of the Trinity, this does

---

80. Pannenberg, *ST*, 1:390.

81. Pannenberg, *ST*, 2:393; Pannenberg, "Christologie und Theologie," 142.

82. Pannenberg, *ST*, 1:388.

83. Pannenberg, *ST*, 2:393–94.

84. Pannenberg, *ST*, 1:421; see also 313; Pannenberg, *ST*, 2:392–93.

85. Eilers, *Faithful to Save*, 41; see also 45, 53, 67–70.

not preclude a concept of the antecedent Trinity. Regarding Pannenberg's early concept of God, William J. Hill writes, "of the *Deus in se*," the being of God in itself, "nothing whatsoever can be said."[86] This has, at best, only a restricted application in Pannenberg's mature theology. Pannenberg has a definite concept of the immanent Trinity, and can even claim that the Son's mediation of the Father's rule among us is "a repetition or reiteration of [God's] eternal deity in his relation to the world."[87]

God does not become triune in the world. God acts among us through the immanent Trinity of God's being. But to these largely protective measures in conceiving of the Trinity of God's being in the worldly activity of God, Pannenberg also takes note of the historical nature of the divine acts. The Father's monarchy, he claims, is "God's absolute lordship."[88] In honoring the Father the Son serves the Father's lordship, as does the Spirit by glorifying the Father and the Son. In this temporal activity, "the monarchy of the Father is mediated by the Son, who prepares the way for it by *winning form* for it in the life of the creatures, also by the Spirit, who enables creatures to honor God as their Creator."[89] In terms of priority, the eternal monarchy of God comes first. However, this does not prevent Pannenberg from laying out the temporal quality of the kingdom's establishment in the world. The quote that follows encapsulates both of these notions:

> God actualizes himself in the world by his coming into it. For this his eternal existence in the fellowship of Father, Son, and Holy Spirit is presupposed and his eternal essence needs no completion by his coming into the world, although with the creation of a world God's deity and even his existence become dependent on the fulfillment of their determination in his present lordship.[90]

Moreover, Pannenberg retains his eschatological distinctive in this account. The self-actualization of God is linked to the eschatological future. The "action of God" is evident in the "signs of his in-breaking lordship" through coming into the world. In this divine action, according to Pannenberg, "God does not look ahead from the beginning of the world to its consummation as to a distant future." Rather, "the future of the world is the mode of time that stands closest to God's eternity."[91] The action of God

86. Hill, *Three-Personed God*, 157.

87. Pannenberg, *ST*, 1:389.

88. Pannenberg, *ST*, 1:389.

89. Pannenberg, *ST*, 1:389. Emphasis mine.

90. Pannenberg, *ST*, 1:390.

91. Pannenberg, *ST*, 1:390.

that occurs in the Son's mediation of the Father's rule approximates the eschatological future. Therefore, the antecedent Trinity is not only the prior reality of God in acting toward the world. Insofar as "the goal of the world and its history is nearer to God than its commencement," there remains a sense in which God precedes the world eschatologically.[92] In a way that smacks of Pannenberg's early concept of deity, it appears on this rendering that God is somehow ahead of us, located in the future.

Deity and Lordship

The principle of the unity of deity and lordship plays a pivotal role in Pannenberg's early concept of God. As noted before, the principle has two sides. First is the epistemic side. Insofar as the sovereignty of God over all creation, over the dominion of sin and resistance to God, is not yet complete, so the truth of God's deity (or goodness) remains a point of dispute for creatures until the eschatological consummation. This point fuels much of the debate between theism and atheism. The other side is ontological. Insofar as the lordship of God is not yet fully established, God's deity is somehow at stake until the eschatological consummation, when the divine lordship over the power of evil is complete and God is "all in all" (1 Cor 15:58). The full realization of the divine lordship, at one with God's deity, hinges on the divine triumph over sin and death in God's creation. What role do the two sides of Pannenberg's principle play in his mature theology?

The epistemic side of the principle of the unity of deity and lordship remains largely the same in Pannenberg's later work. Pannenberg continues to reflect on the question of the debatability of God's existence.[93] The eschatological future remains decisive regarding the ultimate revelation of the truth of God's existence. Pannenberg writes,

> The eschatological future of the consummation of history in the kingdom of God . . . has a distinctive function in establishing belief in the trinitarian God if on the basis of this event a decision is made concerning the existence of God from eternity to eternity, i.e., before the foundation of the world.[94]

The final demonstration of God's being, therefore, has retrospective value. In the eschatological end it becomes clear to the creature that God not only

---

92. Pannenberg, *ST*, 1:390.

93. See Pannenberg, *ST*, 1:58–59, 95, 176.

94. Pannenberg, *ST*, 1:331–32.

is but has always been the living God. This settles the debate on the truth of God's lordship and whether God exists.

There is slightly more development in Pannenberg's theology in relation to the ontological side of the principle. In his early theology this principle rests on the truth of God's lordship in light of created (and historical) reality and its resistance to God; if God creates a world, God is God only as Lord over it. As a whole this notion remains intact in Pannenberg's later work. He claims, "the rule or kingdom of the Father is not so external to his deity that he might be God without his kingdom."[95] What changes is that his trinitarian account of God specifies how the ontological side of the principle of the unity of deity and lordship works. Having outlined his exegetical basis for the doctrine of the Trinity, this is already familiar territory for us. The deity and lordship of the Father depend on the success of the Son in establishing the divine rule among us, first in Jesus' life, death, and resurrection, and definitively in the eschatological consummation. The lordship of God the Father depends "on whether the Son glorifies him and fulfills his lordship by fulfilling his mission."[96] The Son's mission is driven by the Spirit, whose ongoing activity in the interim period between Pentecost and eschatological consummation functions analogously to the establishment of the Father's rule in the mission of the Son. In short, in Pannenberg's later theology God's deity remains tied to the divine lordship, specifically to the Son's and the Spirit's execution of the Father's lordship in time.

Thus Pannenberg maintains the ontological side of his principle but within a more refined trinitarian scheme. The other point to note here is that in his mature theology Pannenberg often pairs the unity of deity and lordship with his concern, noted previously, to highlight the immutable nature of God's being in time. For instance, Pannenberg asserts that the link between deity and lordship has a basis in the triune relations. The unity of deity and lordship "has its place *already* in the intratrinitarian life of God, in the reciprocity of the relation between the Son, who freely subjects himself to the lordship of the Father, and the Father, who hands over his lordship to the Son."[97] The point is notable insofar as in his early work Pannenberg's principle often indicates the radical way in which God's being depends on the divine activity in the world for the actualization of the divine lordship. Pannenberg's later trinitarian idea of God supplements this notion with a grounding point in the eternality of God's being. Nevertheless, the principle on the unity of deity and lordship in Pannenberg's later thought shows that

95. Pannenberg, *ST*, 1:313.
96. Pannenberg, *ST*, 1:313.
97. Pannenberg, *ST*, 1:313. Emphasis mine.

God's temporal activity draws God's being into the divine plan in the world. While the divine monarchy has a basis in the antecedent or eternal Trinity, it remains true, as noted in the section on divine actualization, that the Son establishes this lordship in a *new* way in time "by winning form for it in the life of the creatures." The same point applies to the Spirit in its interim activity, "who enables creatures to honor God as their Creator."[98] I unpack this point further in the concluding section of this chapter. For now we can note that Trinity, within the broader context of Pannenberg's principle on the unity of deity and lordship, allows him to conceive of God's abiding identity in time and why history matters for God's being.

DIVINE ETERNITY

In section 2 I outlined Pannenberg's early notion of eternity. Pannenberg's early conception of eternity revolves around God's presence to the distinct moments of time in light of God as the power of the future. I claimed that Pannenberg's notion of eternity attempts to conceive of God's transcendence in view of the futurity of God's being. In *ST* 1, Pannenberg addresses the themes of eternity and futurity, with a focus on the presence of time to God as a whole. Like the idea of the true Infinite, under which the notion of eternity belongs, Pannenberg conceives of eternity within the framework of the relationship between the immanent and the economic Trinity.

In his mature theology Pannenberg continues to contrast the eternity of God with a notion of eternal timelessness. Pannenberg conceives of time past and time future to be included within the scope of God's eternity.[99] Here Pannenberg takes Scripture's often repeated title for God as the "first" and "last" (Isa 44:6; 48:12; Rev 2:8; 21:6; 22:13) as lending support to the idea of God's eternity as that which "embraces (*umgreift*)" the dimensions of time.[100] Likewise, the passages that speak of a future salvation of the faithful that is experienced in the present underscore eternity's "entanglement (*Verschränkung*)" with time (Rom 6:5; Col 3:3).[101] Particularly important for Pannenberg is Psalm 90:4: "for a thousand years in your sight are like yesterday when it is past." 'Yesterday' entails both a sense of completion and proximity to the beholder. In the eternity of God, writes Pannenberg, "all time is before the eyes of God as a whole (*als Ganzes*)."[102]

---

98. Pannenberg, *ST*, 1:389.

99. Pannenberg, *ST*, 1:403.

100. Pannenberg, *ST*, 1:403; Pannenberg, *Systematische Theologie*, 1:435.

101. Pannenberg, "Zeit und Ewigkeit," 201. Translation mine. See also, Pannenberg, *ST*, 3:604–5.

102. Pannenberg, *ST*, 1:401; Pannenberg, *Systematische Theologie*, 1:434.

For Pannenberg, the inclusion of time in God's eternity finds suitable expression in Plotinus' notion of the "presence of the totality of life."[103] This idea enters the Christian tradition with Boethius and goes on to play an important role in the work of figures who adapt Boethius' definition of eternity, like Thomas Aquinas and Karl Barth. In Pannenberg's accommodation of Plotinus' notion, the concept of eternity presupposes the distinct dimensions of time and their presence to God's eternity, although this is unique insofar as God is near to past, present, and future time at once.[104] Importantly, this idea of eternity indicates God's *relation* to time from beginning to end, and not eternity itself as any kind of temporal-finite whole. In *Metaphysics and the idea of God* Pannenberg clarifies this point: "God is not the whole of what exists finitely," but rather the "unifying unity of the totality of the finite."[105] God for Pannenberg is a whole, a unity; but this unity is to be set in stark contrast to the unity of the temporal world. Nevertheless, the whole or unity of God's being gives temporal reality its wholeness. As the ground of created life, there is an intimate, incorporating relation between God and temporality. "God's eternity includes the time of creatures in its full range, from the beginning of creation to its eschatological consummation."[106] Eternity "is itself simultaneous (*gleichzeitig*) with all events, and, indeed, in the strict sense of this word."[107] God is present to the dimensions of time, past, present, and future, according to their temporal positions.[108]

The emphasis here clearly falls on the idea of the whole or the simultaneous presence of all things to God. But one also finds assertions in Pannenberg's mature theology that resonate with the notion of futurity from his early work. God is "absolute future," Pannenberg claims, and "does not have ahead of him any future that could be distinguished from his present."[109] Divine eternity entails that God "has no future outside himself.

---

103. Pannenberg, *ST*, 1:403–4. Pannenberg's use of Plotinus' concept of eternity follows his understanding of the relation between theology and philosophical theology. His adaptation of Plotinus' concept of eternity to the doctrine of the Trinity is exemplary. See Pannenberg, "The Appropriation of the Philosophical Concept of God," 139–40; Pannenberg, *Metaphysics and the Idea of God*, 41–42; Mostert, *God and the Future*, 65–69.

104. Pannenberg, *ST*, 1:405–6; Pannenberg, *Metaphysics and the Idea of God*, 76–78.

105. Pannenberg, *Metaphysics and the Idea of God*, 142–43.

106. Pannenberg, *ST*, 1:405–6.

107. Pannenberg, *ST*, 2:91; Pannenberg, *Systematische Theologie*, 2:113. English translation slightly altered.

108. Pannenberg, *ST*, 1:405.

109. Pannenberg, *ST*, 1:410; Pannenberg, *Systematische Theologie*, 1:443. English translation slightly altered.

His future is that of himself and of all that is distinct from him."[110] God stands in possession of God's own future, and is thus unlike creaturely beings "subject to the march of time."[111] These claims align with what we saw in Pannenberg's account of divine self-actualization. Particularly, "God does not look ahead from the beginning of the world to its consummation as to a distant future." On the contrary, "the future of the world is the mode of time that stands closest to God's eternity."[112] One of the major challenges in Pannenberg's theology, as I explore later, is bringing together this notion of futurity with the previously addressed concept of eternity as God's simultaneously structured relation to time.

The Christian theological idea of eternity that borrows from Plotinus' concept is only fully realized, Pannenberg claims, with the doctrine of the Trinity.[113] The doctrine of the Trinity provides the structural grounds for the differentiated nature of the concept of eternity as a totality. As stated above, "God's eternity includes the time of creatures in its full range, from the beginning of creation to its eschatological consummation."[114] The distinct moments of time are present to God at once. This simultaneous presence of God to time in its differentiated moments finds suitable expression in the "intrinsically differentiated unity" of God's being, that is, in the unity-in-distinctions of the divine persons of the immanent Trinity.[115] This also allows Pannenberg to articulate his notion of divine eternity in keeping with the idea of God's infinity. Eternity is a "paradigmatic illustration . . . of the structure of the true Infinite," he writes, insofar as on trinitarian grounds the similarity between eternity and time holds without obfuscating the distinction between them.[116] Pannenberg follows Barth here by including the trinitarian idea of God in his notion of eternity. He even lauds Barth's way of speaking of an "order" and a "before and after" in God's eternity, although Pannenberg, unlike Barth, does not utilize Trinity for understanding the successive nature of time in his temporally inclusive concept of eternity.[117]

Despite the absence of an articulated understanding of time's successive nature as grounded in the eternity of the triune God, Pannenberg conceives of a positive relation between divine eternity and the temporally

110. Pannenberg, *ST*, 1:410.

111. Pannenberg, *ST*, 1:410; Pannenberg, *Systematische Theologie*, 1:443.

112. Pannenberg, *ST*, 1:390.

113. Pannenberg, "Eternity, Time, and the Trinitarian God," 70.

114. Pannenberg, *ST*, 1:405–6.

115. Pannenberg, *ST*, 1:405.

116. Pannenberg, *ST*, 1:408.

117. Pannenberg, *ST*, 1:405. See also Pannenberg, "Eternity, Time, and Space," 102.

structured creation. The coherence of God's eternity and God's simultaneous presence to all time, he argues, stands in stark contrast to the idea of God as an undifferentiated subject. If God is conceived as a solitary subject before the full diversity of the created world, God's absolute priority entails that "all temporal distinction would evaporate, and with that the quality of life itself."[118] This argument is similar to Dorner's claim that in the face of God's absolute or objective simplicity, the created world appears as an illusion.[119] But as triune, Pannenberg continues, the simultaneity of time in the eternality of God's being makes space for the temporal distinctions manifest in the economy of salvation, notably in the sequence of creation, incarnation, redemption. Pannenberg states, "the unity of the immanent and the economic Trinity secures these distinctions to be significant within in the eternal life of God."[120] The temporally distinguishable acts of God, along with time's distinctions, are grounded in God's eternity.[121] On the flip-side, the differentiated totality of the immanent Trinity, from which the divine acts originate, guarantees that such acts obtain the wholeness or fulfillment that God intends. For the character of the divine acts as a whole in the "eventual actuality" of the economy rests on the fact that they proceed from the wholeness of God's eternity.[122] In short, the trinitarian nature of God's eternity grounds God's temporally differentiated activity and ensures that it comes to completion.

4: The Trinitarian Mediated History God

In this chapter I have traced several themes in Pannenberg's theology, from his critical engagement with Barth's doctrine of God to his early conception of futurity and mature theological views on the triune God's relation to history. There is both doctrinal development in Pannenberg's work, as well as an explicit arrangement of topics in Pannenberg's *ST* that intends to show the interrelated nature of different theological loci. Divine eternity, for instance, resembles the theological function of the true Infinite (i.e., incorporating that which is distinct from itself) while serving to fill out the previously addressed idea of God's self-actualization in the world. For the critical analysis here, this presents the problem of addressing any one of Pannenberg's dogmatic

---

118. Pannenberg, "Eternity, Time, and the Trinitarian God," 70.

119. Dorner, *Divine Immutability*, 96.

120. Pannenberg, "Eternity, Time, and the Trinitarian God," 70; Pannenberg, *ST*, 1:405–6.

121. Pannenberg, *ST*, 2:7–9.

122. Pannenberg, "Eternity, Time, and the Trinitarian God," 67, 70.

concepts that bear on the understanding of God's relation to history on its own. The concepts addressed above need to be considered, at least in part, in light of their explicit and implicit connections and through the ways that these connections impact their constructive application.

Thus what follows contains fewer individual points of analysis than the previous chapter. Rather, my critical assessment of Pannenberg's theology unfolds in three groupings (sub-sections). The first two groupings are closely related. The first focuses mainly on Pannenberg's trinitarian theology, particularly his notion of the dependent monarchy of God, and his concepts of infinity, self-actualization, and the unity of deity and lordship. This sub-section shows how Pannenberg's trinitarian theology brings together a notion of the eternal Trinity with a concept of God's involvement in history that avoids the peril of a two-fold reality of God. The second grouping follows directly from the first and contains my constructive appropriation of Pannenberg's trinitarian theology. I argue for a notion of the vitality of God in the process of history based on Pannenberg's concept of dependent deity and his trinitarian construal of divine monarchy. The third grouping looks more closely at issues in the doctrinal development of Pannenberg's theology and his idea of eternity. This sub-section is meant to set up the engagement with the trinitarian theology of Robert W. Jenson in the following chapter. For, as I show, Pannenberg's concept of eternity lends itself to two partially conflicting interpretations. The two renderings I consider present distinct challenges for understanding the reality of God's relation to history, and neither satisfactorily takes into account the trinitarian idea of God. This raises problems not only for understanding God's presence in history but also for a trinitarian based account of divine transcendence, to which I turn in chapter 4.

The Trinity: Eternal and Historical

Pannenberg's trinitarian theology is characterized by the mutuality or reciprocal self-distinctions of the divine persons. Pannenberg arrives at this notion through an approach to trinitarian theology at least partially motivated by his criticism of Barth on the divine subjectivity. An unbiblical conception of subjectivity governs Barth's idea of God, as Pannenberg sees it. While many of the central claims in Pannenberg's critique are misguided, as I argued in the previous chapter, the way that Pannenberg's critical engagement with Barth's theology positions his own starting point for reflection on the being of God in Jesus' relation to the Father remains important. Accordingly, the mutuality through which Pannenberg conceives of

God's being derives from, or is simply identical to, the complex of relations evident in the Father's bestowal of authority on the Son, on one hand, and the Son's Spirit driven glorification of the Father, on the other. A key result of this is that Pannenberg's doctrine of God's being is more informed by the biblical witness, or the revealed relations of the divine persons, than Barth's conception of God's being prior to his account of election in *CD* II/2. This trinitarian idea of God, summarized in the notion of the reciprocal self-distinctions of the divine persons, informs both Pannenberg's formulation of the divine attributes and the related concepts he employs for understanding God's relation to history.

I begin with Pannenberg's notions of divine infinity and self-actualization. Both the notion of God's self-actualization and the true Infinite have the reciprocal self-distinctions of the divine persons as their underlying and essential content. A constraint, however, is placed on the notion of the true Infinite due to the ordering of Pannenberg's treatment of the divine attributes. The infinity of God's being contains the finite as a moment within itself, and so is not fundamentally at odds with the finite world of creation. But Pannenberg conceives of the God-world relation through this idea only in general terms. The idea of the true Infinite gives expression to the basic structural framework for the God-world relation, but ultimately gives way to the more revelation specific qualities of God in the attributes that fall under the divine loving. It therefore remains unclear whether the idea of the true Infinite can be further exploited in regards to the specific temporal relations between Jesus, the Father, and the Spirit. Pannenberg's brief description of the true Infinite in terms of the mutual indwelling of the transcendent Father and the temporally abiding Son and Spirit is suggestive, but he does not develop the idea.

Pannenberg's concept of divine self-actualization is more promising. Pannenberg situates this concept more firmly within the monarchical relations between the Father, Jesus, and the Spirit. In addition, his earlier exegetical findings on the mutual dependency and reciprocal self-distinctions of the divine persons more readily apply here. In divine action, the monarchy of the Father, contingent upon the Spirit driven faithfulness of the Son in establishing the Father's rule, comes to be in the world. Pannenberg makes two important moves in his treatment of God's self-actualization. First, Pannenberg roots God's worldly self-actualization in the eternal monarchy of God's being. The Son honors the Father's rule from eternity, which serves as the foundation in the divine lordship for the establishment of the kingdom of God among us. Thus, as Pannenberg puts it, the establishment of the divine rule is a "repetition or reiteration" of the lordship of God in time.[123] Pannenberg is resolute on the point, God does not become triune in time, specifically in the eschatological consummation. God already is triune, and it is precisely this triunity which makes the characteristic feature of God's activity among us the establishment of divine lordship.

But does not the notion of the 'repetition or reiteration' of the eternal Trinity in time bring us right back to the ambiguity of Barth's primal history, and with it, the problem of a two-fold history of God? Here is where it becomes important to consider Pannenberg's notion of the eternal monarchy alongside his commitment to the principle of the unity of deity and lordship. According to that principle the being of God hinges on the realization of the divine lordship among us, a realization that is not yet complete apart from the total triumph of God's kingdom over sin and death in the eschatological consummation. "The rule or kingdom of the Father is not so external to his deity that he might be God without his kingdom."[124] Likewise, the Son acts in time to establish the divine rule "by winning form for it in the life creatures."[125] The Son "prepares the way" for the Father's rule in his Spirit driven mission.[126] The divine rule rests on the success of the Son's temporal work, and subsequently on the ongoing activity of the Spirit to bring about the eschatological end. Pannenberg's principle invokes the historical nature of God's actualization in the world, or the way in which the divine lordship, while rooted in the immanent and unchanging Trinity of God's being, unfolds in time. God does not become triune in time, as stated above; but this does not mean that created history is so external to God's being as to have no constitutive significance for God. If there is created history, God, to be God, must be Lord over it. And since this is not (yet) the case—the overcoming of sin and all hostility to God is an eschatological reality—the being and lordship of God remain at stake until the ultimate end arrives.

Both points matter. God acts in revelation history through the eternal Trinity; God's being is at stake in this history. The first point indicates the unchanging source through which God acts among us, as well as the trinitarian relations that characterize and shape God's temporal acts. The second point indicates that while God's identity remains the same in time, revelatory history is not incidental for God; it is part of the divine life, and testifies to the truth of the divine presence. Extrapolating on this second point, the concern in the last chapter with Barth's formal doctrine of the

---

123. Pannenberg, *ST*, 1:389.

124. Pannenberg, *ST*, 1:313.

125. Pannenberg, *ST*, 1:389.

126. Pannenberg, *ST*, 1:389.

Trinity (*CD* I/1) was that a potential correspondence between the eternal Trinity and the being of God in revelation continues *in* revelation itself, so as to suggest an ulterior reality of God that mirrors God's revelatory history in eternity. Pannenberg also posits an eternal, antecedent Trinity. But, unlike Barth's, Pannenberg's account is not susceptible to the criticism of a two-fold history of God. For Pannenberg conceives of the divine history to bear on God's being through the ongoing establishment of the divine lordship among us. God takes this history into Godself, making it a focal point of the divine lordship and its execution. Anecdotally, we might not be able to say anything more than that God's being, if truly one with God's lordship, is at stake in history. For it seems equally true on biblical grounds, and likewise, through the riches of God's trinitarian being, that the end which God wills is a certainty. Nevertheless, if God's revelatory history is just that, a real history with others, than the claim from Pannenberg's principle must stand undiminished.

The Trinity in History

Thus Pannenberg, I have argued, rightly speaks of the trinitarian basis for God's activity in time through his concept of God's self-actualization in the world. Equally important, he shows that this history matters for God through his principle of deity and lordship. But there is something more that can be said here which is not clearly articulated in Pannenberg's trinitarian theology. Trinitarian theology allows us to conceive of God *within* history itself, in the very movement of time and historical reality. This is to say more than what Pannenberg's principle does insofar as that principle only (though, of course, importantly) demonstrates the truth that God exists in history itself, or that history matters for God.[127] It can be noted here that in Pannenberg's early theology the ontological side of his principle, alongside closely related concepts in the doctrine of God, plays a more extensive role in articulating God's relation to time. It funds his radical claim that 'God does not yet exist.' More importantly, it underwrites his early concept of transcendence as the futurity by which God straddles, and so intimately relates to, every momentary present from the future. In tandem with his futurity concept, it indicated how God might be understood to move in (or ahead of) history. But as I explore more in the next sub-section, the concept of futurity undergoes at least a modest, if not significant, modification in Pannenberg's later theology. While

---

127. When Pannenberg utilizes his principle to address God's movement in time, he refers mainly to its epistemological side. See Pannenberg, *ST*, 1:332.

still functional, futurity plays a secondary role to Pannenberg's notion of eternity as a simultaneous whole. As a result of this it becomes less clear how God exists and moves in history in Pannenberg's mature theology. The proposal that follows, in contrast, allows for an understanding of God in the movement of history that rests on God's triunity.

The insights of Pannenberg's trinitarian theology can be used to reflect on the way that God moves in history. I begin by restating Pannenberg's point that prior to the establishment of the divine lordship in time the Son acknowledges the monarchy of the Father from eternity. The love that the Father and Son share through the Spirit in time, they also possess before the world is created (John 17:24). The importance of this point lies in the way that it points to the fact that the triune God acts in time through the already existing fellowship or monarchy of God's being. The understanding of God's movement in history in what follows relies on this key point. Moreover, I also utilize classical trinitarianism's affirmation of the unity-in-distinctions of God's being. Based on this classical trinitarian observation, two points can be drawn from Pannenberg's formulations for understanding God in history and the process of time.

First, the divine unity. The monarchy of God's being expresses the divine unity. A theological account of the Trinity that begins with Jesus' relation to the Father, like Pannenberg's, is lush with references to the relational distinctions of the divine persons. However, these relational distinctions, as Pannenberg rightly maintains, are characterized by reciprocity and mutuality. The Father is the divine monarch, but only in relation to the Son upon whom his lordship depends. The internal relatedness of the Son and Spirit is also expressed through the eternal relations of origin, in the paternal acts of the Son's begetting and the Spirit's procession. The Father is Father only in relation to the Son and the Spirit. In terms of the divine monarchy, however, the underlying reciprocity is reinforced through the Son's obedient acknowledgement of the Father's lordship, empowered by the Spirit who glorifies the Son to honor the Father. No divine person can be conceived apart from the other two. To conceive of a divine person in God, at any level of depth, is to follow the track of their myriad self-deferrals into the living unity of the Godhead. The fellowship of the Trinity, here expressed in terms of the divine monarchy, underwrites the incomparable unity of God.

Divine unity secures the abiding identity of God in history. This point reiterates a key concern in Pannenberg's concept of divine self-actualization. God does not become triune in time. God does not, because the mutuality of the divine persons, a basic feature of God's being from eternity to eternity, entails that every divine act takes place through the self-deferring complex of the divine persons. In more traditional terms, the divine persons act through their appropriated roles and in accordance with their relational distinctions in God. The salvific and individual acts of Jesus' ministry simultaneously bring about the Father's lordship (Matt 12:27). Likewise, Jesus' life is encompassed by the Spirit, who acts to bring about his conception in Mary's womb and directs him in his mission to carry out the Father's will (Matt 4:1; Luke 1:26–28). Jesus breathes the Spirit upon his disciples, so that through the Spirit his work will continue in establishing the Father's rule in the interim period between the ascension and eschatological consummation (John 14:12–17; 20:22). A pattern emerges here in which the individuality of the divine persons points outwards, from one divine person to the web of relations and the underlying unity of the one God. As I show below, the distinctions of the divine persons are important for understanding God's movement among us. But the key point to note here is that the unity of the divine persons upholds God's unchanging being in time itself. Every distinct act of God in time, executed through a divine person, incorporates the persons of the Godhead as a whole.

And second, the divine distinctions. As just shown, the unity of the divine persons secures the divine immutability, in God and in the being of God in time. However, this unity is also the unity of the Father, Son, and Spirit in the totality of their relational differences. It includes the eternal acts of begetting and proceeding that distinguish the hypostatic identities in God while underwriting their unity (e.g., in the Father's begetting and the Son's being begotten). Expressed in terms of Pannenberg's theology, it is a unity that includes, and is manifest in, the Father's conferring of authority on the Son and the honor which the Son returns to the Father in the Spirit. In a word, it is unity-in-movement. The initial and basic observation to be made here follows the point above about the divine unity. Just as the divine unity holds together the abiding identity of God's being in time, the living nature of that unity, expressed through the relational distinctions of the divine persons, can be understood to animate the living history of God with others. The movement of the divine life enables God's movement in time. God lives in Godself, and acts among us accordingly.

We can, however, be more precise. God moves in history toward a goal: the eschatological end. The differences of the divine persons within their unity grounds God's activity in this eschatological history. How so? In elaborating upon, but also going beyond, Pannenberg's trinitarian formulations, the general answer I give here is that in relation to the inner-movements of the divine persons, God's being, so to speak, leans forward; it is eschatological in nature. God acts and moves in history through the eschatological being of God. This claim relies on a decisive point: the Father as the unoriginate origin in God depends for his monarchy upon the Son and the Spirit. He does not have it independently, but rather his deity and lordship depend on what (who) proceeds from him. The Father's deity depends on what comes—logically, not temporally—*after* him in God, the begetting of the Son and the Spirit's procession. The Father is the fount of deity in the Godhead, but that deity cannot be conceived apart from the Son's acknowledgement of the divine lordship upon which it rests. Nor is the Father's deity truly honored apart from the empowerment of the Son's relation to the Father in the Spirit. The Father is unoriginate origin in God *within* the teleological focal points, the divine ends, of the Son and the Spirit.

Accordingly, every act that the Father wills in time through the Son in the Spirit can be understood in two ways. In one way, it re-enacts the divine unity. The lordship of God's being, the divine monarchy, occurs in time in a way that reflects its antecedent reality in God's eternity. The triune God can act no other way, for God is Lord in Godself and so acts among us, acts as the one selfsame Lord God is, in kind. And yet, the divine action is not mere repetition; or, more accurately, divine action is not the re-playing of a prior reality closed off from the world that God creates. The second way God's action in history can be understood is through the out-playing or three-fold nature of the divine persons in their perfect mutuality and unity. This does not entail that God becomes God in history. Rather, it consists of the fact that every activity of God in history and the process of time follows the similar movement of God's being in its directionality *from* the primal monarchy of the Father *to* its instantaneous realization in the Spirit-enabled obedience of the Son. God moves this way in history and the process of time because already in God's being God moves eschatologically, toward the end of the Father's monarchy realized in the Son and the Spirit. The activity of God in time re-enacts the living unity of God's being, which makes this history a living history, the real eschatological movement of God among us. God moves in history and the process of time, always as the one selfsame God, because God is triune.

In sum, the divine nature of God's being does not change; God moves and lives a history with others. Both of these are true because, again, God is triune. The Trinity of God's being is the dialectic of the unity-in-distinctions and the distinctions-in-unity of the divine persons. Their implacable unity secures the divine immutability; their distinctions underwrite the internal movements of God's being and the being of God in history. But each one only in light of the other, or only insofar as the unity of God within the divine distinctions, and the distinctions of the divine persons within the unity of God, just are the truth of God's being.

Finally, using Pannenberg's concept of divine monarchy I have sought to establish the trinitarian possibility of God's being in the movement of history. The divine presence travels with Israel through the desert and acts in history in created flesh (Exod 33:14; John 1:14). But God, of course, is also not merely one agent among others who acts within finite history. The point of this sub-section is necessary: God really lives a history. And yet, "even heaven and the highest heaven cannot contain you" (1 Kgs 8:27). It remains essential, therefore, to ask how the triune God transcends the history God lives with others. I note this here in anticipation of the following chapter in which I address God's distinction from the world in Robert W. Jenson's trinitarian theology. The final sub-section on Pannenberg's doctrine of eternity sets up this engagement.

Remaining Ambiguities

Having offered a constructive appropriation of Pannenberg's trinitarian idea of God, I now return to a critical analysis of Pannenberg's claims on the God-world relation in his doctrine of eternity. I begin by considering two potentially competing concepts of eternity in Pannenberg's theology.

The dominant view of eternity in Pannenberg's mature theology reflects Plotinus' notion of the presence of the totality of life. For Pannenberg, God is eternal as comprehensively related to all of the dimensions of temporal existence. These dimensions are simultaneously present to God. On this view, the future is an important aspect of God's eternity, particularly, as Christiaan Mostert highlights, as the locale from which God acts in the world. But in contrast to Pannenberg's earlier theology, futurity does not constitute eternity, at least not decisively. It is closer to a part or a key aspect of God's more inclusive and temporally encompassing eternity. Mostert, who highlights this shift away from futurity in Pannenberg's mature theology, puts it this way: "God's eternity must have priority over God's futurity because God's being encompasses all the modes of time."[128] It would seem that Mostert is right. As Pannenberg claims, "all time is before the eyes of God as a whole."[129]

And yet, one cannot rule out the presence of the earlier view of eternity as futurity in Pannenberg's mature theology. On that view, God actualizes the present as the power of the future. God is, so to speak, just ahead of us, and before God no present slips into the past without having presence to God. This perspective also entails God's simultaneous presence to all dimensions of time, although differently from the more general Plotinus based view. I return to this point momentarily. Mostert is correct, I believe, in saying that

---

128. Mostert, *God and the Future*, 144.

129. Pannenberg, *ST*, 1:331. See Mostert, *God and the Future*, 144.

Pannenberg favors Plotinus' idea of eternity in his later theology. However, Pannenberg's continued references to the futurity of God make his actual understanding of eternity somewhat puzzling. As Pannenberg claims in his *ST*, God is "absolute future," and "the future of the world is the mode of time that stands closest to God's eternity."[130]

It seems that Pannenberg can be read in at least two different ways. As already indicated, on the Plotinus based view of eternity, what appears to be the essential futurity of God is only an element in God's more encompassing presence toward time as a whole. The future is significant here as the locale from which God acts, though it is not entirely clear how much weight this idea carries in light of the more central notion of God's simultaneous presence. Or, on the second view and in contrast to this, the simultaneous presence of God to time as a whole might simply be the fact that every momentary present proceeds from God as the power of the future, and thus all time has presence before God. In Pannenberg's descriptions of eternity, *both* are tenable interpretations. Unfortunately, Pannenberg's trinitarian theology does not help in delineating them. For when Pannenberg speaks of the internal differentiation of God's being as the grounds of the temporally distinct events of creation, incarnation, and consummation, or that this internal differentiation secures the meaning of temporally distinct events in the immanent Trinity, he favors the idea of eternity as God's all-encompassing presence.[131] "In virtue of trinitarian differentiation God's eternity includes the time of creatures in its full range, from the beginning of creation to its eschatological consummation."[132] However, in the context of his trinitarian based idea of divine self-actualization, Pannenberg implies a form of futurity and its priority to God: in "the coming of God into the world . . . the goal of its history, the kingdom of God, is already really present as the in-breaking of its consummation from the future."[133]

As they stand, however, neither of these views on eternity in Pannenberg fully satisfies. This takes us to the first of three points in the critical assessment of Pannenberg on eternity. The first point considers the more dominant idea in Pannenberg's later theology, the Plotinus based notion of eternity through which God encompasses time as a whole. Pannenberg refers to the trinitarian nature of God as the internal basis that grounds a notion of differentiation within his (Plotinus based) idea of eternity. Nevertheless, even though Pannenberg incorporates his trinitarian idea of God

130. Pannenberg, *ST*, 1:390, 409.

131. See Pannenberg, "Eternity, Time, and the Trinitarian God," 70.

132. Pannenberg, *ST*, 1:406.

133. Pannenberg, *ST*, 1:390.

into the notion of eternity in order to accentuate its complexity, the notion of eternity remains fairly abstract. For instance, while the sense of diversity that Pannenberg adds to his concept of eternity eschews a notion of eternity as an undifferentiated, timeless whole, it does little to clarify how the encompassing nature of God's eternity relates to the different dimensions of time. "All time is before the eyes of God as a whole."[134] This warrants asking questions such as whether the future has presence to God, even ontological presence. And if so, what does this entail for the reality of the future for creatures, and likewise, the truth of history itself? Eternity, understood as such, risks sweeping up history into its simultaneous structure so as to make the creaturely reality a mere tableau in the eyes of God. Pannenberg's Plotinus based view of eternity, as it stands, does not offer particularly helpful answers to these difficult questions.

Second, and perhaps more problematic, is the conceptual conflict that arises between the all-encompassing or Plotinus based notion of eternity that Pannenberg adapts and the futuristic sense of eternity. This becomes clear in Pannenberg's statement that the "eternal God does not have ahead of him any future that could be distinguished from his present."[135] Without any sense of distinction between present and future in the all-encompassing presence of time to God's eternity, what results is clear: a notion of sheer timeless eternity. Perhaps Pannenberg does not mean that all time is present to God identically, which he remarks on elsewhere.[136] Still, an inconsistency emerges here that at least suggests the possibility of a timeless idea of eternity. The problems with the timeless view of eternity have already been outlined, above all, its incompatibility with the reality of divine incarnation. Jenson presses Pannenberg on the point of timeless eternity from the just cited passage. However, Pannenberg's response does not bring much clarity. He states, "the presence of God is different," and then doubles down on the previous assertion, "since it is no other than his future."[137] Again, Pannenberg does not intend a timeless idea of eternity. But the claims noted here, and the ambiguity that arises from his Plotinus based notion of eternity while holding onto a semblance of God's futuristic presence, at least implies a notion of God's eternal presence without temporal distinction—the very stuff (i.e., time) that Pannenberg describes as "the quality of life itself."[138]

134. Pannenberg, *ST*, 1:331.

135. Pannenberg, *ST*, 1:410; Pannenberg, *Systematische Theologie*, 1:443. English translation slightly altered.

136. See Pannenberg, *ST*, 1:405.

137. Pannenberg, "Eternity, Time, and the Trinitarian God," 69. See Jenson, *Systematic Theology*, 1:218n61.

138. Pannenberg, "Eternity, Time, and the Trinitarian God," 70.

Third and lastly, this leaves us with the other conception of eternity, Pannenberg's more radical idea of divine futurity. Before I turn to the critical perspective on this notion, it is important to reiterate a point from section 2 of this chapter. Pannenberg's concept of futurity, particularly as conceived in his early theology, uniquely articulates a notion of transcendence from within the structures of time itself. That is to say, with the idea of futurity Pannenberg does not need to revert to a notion of divine reality closed off from the temporal world in order to speak of God's transcendence. As the one who generates every momentary, created present from the divine future, and thereby straddles the present and future divide, God transcends what is in the same way that God is present to all creation. This conception avoids the problematic idea of God transcending all things from an alternative reality above that runs strangely parallel to God in revelation below.

Pannenberg's early concept of futurity offers a promising idea of divine transcendence. However, it contains a notable shortcoming: What does it mean to relate to God as future? Even if God is different from future time itself, what does it mean to relate to divine futurity as the generative source of the present? The problem is not so much the abstract nature of the notion of futurity, but that it is too general to be the object of faith's devotion. Pannenberg, of course, evidences how this concept proceeds from the inner workings of the divine rule and Jesus' proclamation of the kingdom of God. But this primarily shows how the concept derives from the eschatological structure of revelation. More specific *content* around the nature of divine futurity is needed in order for it to be sufficiently intelligible and of practical use for faith. Pannenberg's later theology adds little if anything new to this concept, primarily due to the prominence of his Plotinus shaped idea of eternity.[139]

What was said of Pannenberg's concept of infinity can be said of his doctrine of eternity. His trinitarian understanding of God is not rigorously enough applied to his notion(s) of eternity. Regarding the understanding of the God-world relation, the stakes are high here, even more than in the concept of infinity. For Pannenberg's doctrine of eternity shapes the understanding of not only God's transcendence but also the specific contours of God's relation to created time. Despite the implications of eternal timelessness that I outlined above, Pannenberg takes the trinitarian being of God to express, and provide a foundation for, God's simultaneous presence to all of created time. Conversely, the wholeness of the triune God's eternity secures that God's

139. One possible exception being Pannenberg's eschatological remarks in the section on divine self-actualization, and the extent to which the trinitarian shape of this idea lends itself to reconceiving the content of what Pannenberg might mean by futurity.

acts in time come to a corresponding fulfillment in the world. This much, I believe, is right; but it nevertheless leaves much to be said. God's trinitarian being grounds God's simultaneous relation to time. But what does this mean for the actuality of God's relation to the created future? Does the future have ontological presence to God? Or if we consider the earlier and more radical view of eternity as futurity and the God-world relation, there is some trinitarian underlay that grounds God's differentiated relation to the dimensions of time. But, again, how so? Within the context of his mature trinitarian theology, Pannenberg does not develop the idea of futurity enough to provide an adequate answer to this question. Moreover, the more general Plotinus based idea of eternity as God's simultaneous presence to time as a whole, grounded in God's triunity, still does not tell us how God moves in time toward the created future. To make the latter point we had to incorporate other resources from Pannenberg's trinitarian ontology.

However, the promising note is that nearly all of the concepts in Pannenberg's doctrine(s) of eternity, the early radical idea of futurity and the later notion of God's encompassing presence, can be constructively employed, and the problems noted above can be avoided, when the trinitarian idea of God plays a more central role. A distinct notion of divine transcendence also becomes conceivable. While all of this may be possible through a reconfiguration of Pannenberg's trinitarian theology, I do not attempt such an undertaking here. Rather, I take up this task in outlining a trinitarian concept of transcendence based on Robert W. Jenson's temporal understanding of the Trinity in the next chapter.

Conclusion

In this chapter I have set out a notion of the vitality of God in history in view of the trinitarian theology of Wolfhart Pannenberg. The value of Pannenberg's trinitarian theology for an understanding of God's relation to history lies in his notion of the mutuality of the divine persons, or the dependent monarchy of God. Expressed in terms of the unity-in-distinctions of God's being, the mutuality that underlies the divine unity secures the abiding identity of God in time, while the movement of the divine relations, particularly the monarchical dependency of the Father on the Son and Spirit, enables God's activity *in* history and gives it its forward moving shape. The application of Pannenberg's principle on the unity of deity and lordship shows how the revelatory history matters not only for creatures but also for the being of God. The key idea of this chapter, the triune God's livingness in history, serves as the second essential point in the argument of this work, building on the sense of vitality that underlies the relation between pre-temporal eternity and God's history in Barth's doctrine of election from chapter 2.

I concluded the chapter with a more critical assessment of Pannenberg's doctrine of eternity. Pannenberg's construal of eternity leaves itself open to multiple renderings, which results in a set of ambiguities regarding God's relation to time as well as the connection between the eternality of God's being and divine futurity. I argued that these problems stem from the fact that Pannenberg does not adequately apply his trinitarian theology to the concept of divine eternity. Divine eternity is first and foremost *God's* eternity, the *triune* God's eternity. I carry on with this reflection on divine eternity, specifically God's transcendent relation to time, in the following chapter.

4

"Unboundedly Lively"

Trinity and History in the Theology of Robert W. Jenson

IN THIS FINAL CHAPTER on the trinitarian thought from a figure in contemporary theology I consider the work of Robert W. Jenson. Jenson, an American Lutheran theologian whose work spans from ecumenical projects to the theology of culture, belongs to a generation of scholars following after Karl Barth and influenced by his theological program. Like Wolfhart Pannenberg, Jenson picks up on the turn to eschatology in later twentieth century theology and sets forth a doctrine of God along eschatological lines. For Jenson, this eschatological understanding of God is imminently historical: "God is what happens to Jesus and the world."[1] In this chapter I reflect on the God-world relation in Jenson's trinitarian doctrine of God, focusing specifically on the theme of divine transcendence.

As indicated in the quote above, the emphasis in Jenson's understanding of the God-world relation falls on divine immanence. In a review of Jenson's *Systematic Theology*, Pannenberg claims that "in Jenson's presentation, the difference between the 'immanent' Trinity, the eternal communion of Father, Son, and Spirit, and the 'economic' Trinity almost vanishes."[2] I note this at the outset in order to clarify the purposes of my engagement with Jenson's trinitarian theology. I do not use Jenson's theology as a foil for an understanding of divine transcendence. Rather, in keeping where we left off in the last chapter, the purpose of what follows is to specify an account of divine transcendence in keeping with the concept of the triune God's movement in history and the process of time. Rather than a hindrance, Jenson's underlying concern with the being of God *for us* actually opens up a notion of divine transcendence that coheres with and complements a conception of the triune God who lives a history with others in time. The aim of this chapter is two-fold: (1) My central argument is that Jenson's temporal (divine) ontology is governed by a trinitarian idea of God that

---

1. Jenson, *Systematic Theology*, 1:221. Hereafter cited as *STh*.
2. Pannenberg, "Systematic Theology," 49–53.

allows for a conception of God's transcendence from within the strictures of time; God transcends time through the temporality of God's trinitarian being. (2) Moreover, I build on Jenson's concept of divine envelopment to show how God not only moves in history (chapter 3), but also how the Trinity of God's being can be understood to bring about eschatological fulfillment as the transcendent source of created history.

The chapter is divided into three sections: In section 1 I situate Jenson's theology in relation to the work of Barth and Pannenberg through Jenson's early theological engagements with these figures. I focus on Jenson's early criticisms of Barth in order to outline this chapter's primary aim of identifying a temporal understanding of divine transcendence. The comparison with Pannenberg leads into a final introductory sub-section on Jenson's notion of narrative identity. In section 2 I turn to Jenson's trinitarian theology and lay out some of the main features as they bear on his understanding of God's relation to history. I consider Jenson's eschatological concept of God and his doctrine of creation, giving special attention to Jenson's idea of eternity as temporal infinity and his pneumatology. The first two sections of this chapter set up the final section's constructive engagement with Jenson's theology in which I argue for the temporal understanding of divine transcendence and the trinitarian conception of God as both moving in and mover of created history.

This chapter therefore adds another layer to the understanding of God's relation to history outlined in this work. In review, I outlined the central problem of this study in conceiving of God's relation to history through the Trinity based on Isaak A. Dorner's treatment of the unity of divine immutability and the revealed vitality of God in chapter 1. In chapter 2, I turned to the trinitarian theology of Karl Barth. Tracing some of the doctrinal development in Barth's *CD*, I argued that the christology of Barth's doctrine of election helps demonstrate both how the pre-temporal Trinity and who God is among us are one and the same as well as the underlying vitality that exists in the relationship between the eternal Trinity and the being of God in time. Chapter 3 underscored the eschatological nature of the God-world relation in Wolfhart Pannenberg's trinitarian theology. I showed how Pannenberg's theology proffers a conception of the vitality of God in history and the process of time. The current chapter picks up on the eschatological side of the God-world relation with a focus on God's transcendent relation to history. If the accent in Barth's protological construal of God and history falls on the conformity of the Son to the divine will, and with Pannenberg, on the dependent rule of the Father in history, in Jenson's theology it belongs to the Spirit, the futurity of God, who enables the transcendent relationality of God in the world.

1: Eternity, Eschatological Transcendence, and Narrative Identity

In what follows I consider Jenson's early critiques of Barth on divine election and eternity and compare Jenson's and Pannenberg's respective views of eschatology (or futurity) and historical reality. The latter comparison sets up a short exposition of Jenson's concept of narrative identity as important background for his trinitarian idea of God that I consider in section 2. Furthermore, I attempt to situate Jenson's theology between Barth and Pannenberg and identify some of the main concerns in Jenson's construal of the God-world relation, particularly a temporal concept of transcendence, that I unpack further in section 2 and build on in the constructive assessment of Jenson's trinitarian theology in the final section of this chapter.

1.1: Beginnings with Barth

Jenson's thought is shaped by an enduring engagement with Barth's theology. Jenson undertook his doctoral studies at the University of Heidelberg in the 1950s. His dissertation under the supervision of Peter Brunner is one of the earliest treatments of Barth's doctrine of election.[3] In writing the dissertation, Jenson moved to Basel for a period of five months to be in closer proximity to Barth, whom he describes in an autobiographical sketch as an "informal advisor."[4] Jenson published a slightly condensed version of the dissertation entitled *Alpha and Omega* in 1963. In 1969 Jenson published his second work on Barth's theology, *God after God*, in which Jenson takes up Barth's doctrines of revelation and God in the context of debates around theodicy following World War II and the Death of God movement. Both works evidence the positive influence of Barth on Jenson's thought and, especially in the case of *God after God*, mark out some of the major trajectories in Jenson's theological work.

The critiques that Jenson levels against Barth's theology of election in *Alpha and Omega*, the more expository of Jenson's two works on Barth, are best understood as an attempt to carry out what Barth intends by this doctrine with greater consistency. Concerning the central doctrine of this work, Jenson lauds Barth's assertion that the "goal of history" for the electing God lies in the "life of Jesus Christ, as God's life with and for unworthy man."[5] As for Barth's handling of the question of how God rules history,

3. Jenson, "Cur Deus Homo?"
4. Jenson, "A Theological Autobiography," 49.
5. Jenson, *Alpha and Omega*, 168–69. See also Jenson, *STh*, 1:21.

concretely centered on the person of Jesus Christ, Jenson states, "we could not wish a more unequiocal answer."[6] In the more explicitly constructive book, *God after God*, Jenson writes that "everything is indeed there [in Barth's theology] for the creation of a *new* understanding of theological meaning . . . and we will use it."[7] The claim echoes a statement made years before in a letter that Jenson sent to Barth shortly after submitting his dissertation: "For me, it is not possible to do theology without the *Kirchliche Dogmatik*."[8] As will become clear, Jenson's work diverges from Barth's theology in significant ways. At a basic level, however, there is little doubt that Jenson remains indebted to it.

Before turning to the criticisms, a positive point in Jenson's reception of Barth's work in *Alpha and Omega* should be noted. Jenson states that "the most striking and true side of Barth's doctrine of God's rule of history is his insistence that the act of will by which God rules is identical with the history of Jesus Christ."[9] The essential importance of Barth's christocentric notion of God's rule for Jenson lies in the underlying link between the will of God and the work of God. "Jesus Christ *is* God ruling human history."[10] This rule, the activity of God in history, is based in the divine decision. As a self-determining decision, election means that what can be said about God's reality is identical to Jesus Christ. To conceive of God, divine activity, or creation is to reflect on the doctrine of reconciliation in which "God's work outside himself is one great uninterrupted act of rule, proceeding from His decision to reconcile sinful man to Himself in Jesus Christ."[11] This link between God's will and work gleaned from Barth's theology plays a foundational role in Jenson's theological reflections on God. In some ways, Jenson's theology can be understood as an attempt to carry out what Barth initiates in his insight on election as the divine decision to be God *for us*, to be God in history.

More critically, in his early theology Jenson often distances himself from Barth on the meaning of God's temporal history. In *Alpha and Omega* Jenson argues that for all the merits of Barth's doctrine of election, his account of God's pre-temporal life conflicts with the reality of God in history. Jenson writes,

6. Jenson, *Alpha and Omega*, 17–18, 169.

7. Jenson, *God after God*, 154–56.

8. Letter from Jenson to Barth, 18 February, 1960, Karl Barth-Archive, University of Basel, Switzerland. Translation mine.

9. Jenson, *Alpha and Omega*, 161.

10. Jenson, *Alpha and Omega*, 161.

11. Jenson, *Alpha and Omega*, 145.

Jesus Christ is the eternal decree of God before all time. Jesus Christ is the history in Palestine which reveals this decree. Barth does not separate these two; his concept of revelation and knowledge is far too rich. But we must still ask: Which is the prior definition? Barth defines the history in time as the revelation and analogy of eternal history and so gives his answer. And with this answer he puts himself in danger of removing reconciliation itself, the inner reality of Jesus' life, from our history.[12]

This claim, on Jenson's view, follows from assertions in Barth's theology such as, "the giving of the Son by the Father indicates a mystery" that Jesus reveals "in the necessary decision and achievement here below of what is decided and achieved by God Himself up above."[13] Jenson locates a kind of duality in perspective in Barth's theology, God above and God below, that comes into view more sharply in the criticisms from *God after God*. The point to note is that election, achieved in the inner life of God *and* in time, clashes with Barth's apparent intention to speak of election as an eternal decision actualized in time. Jenson's concern is similar to what we addressed in chapter 2: the concept of election as a *replaying* of the eternal or 'primal history' of God and Jesus Christ in time.[14]

In the second and more constructive book on Barth's theology, *God after God*, Jenson attends to Barth's doctrine of divine eternity. Here Jenson largely endorses the way in which Barth works to overcome a notion of eternity that smacks of timelessness. For Barth, eternity is not merely time's negation, but a duration in God which includes "beginning, succession and end."[15] Such distinctions are real in God's eternity, and yet distinguished from their worldly instantiations insofar as in God's perfect duration they are "free from all the fleetingness and the separations of what we call time."[16] Although the timeless concept of eternity is common in the theological tradition, it is hard to square with God's genuine involvement in the created order and the capacity of God to become (and be) incarnate. As Barth puts it, "the theological concept of eternity must be *freed* from the Babylonian captivity of an abstract opposition to the concept of time."[17] Or as Jenson insists, if God is ultimately

---

12. Jenson, *Alpha and Omega*, 162–63.
13. Barth, *CD* III/2:66, cited in Jenson, *Alpha and Omega*, 85–86.
14. Barth, *CD* II/2:8.
15. Barth, *CD* II/1:610.
16. Barth, *CD* II/1:615.
17. Barth, *CD* II/2:611, cited in Jenson, *God after God*, 72.

defined by what happens with Jesus Christ in time, then the existence and even the eternality of God must be historical.[18]

Also important for Jenson is Barth's proposal for a trinitarian based concept of eternity. Barth grounds the idea of a beginning and end in God's eternity, and other descriptions like the "whither and whence" or even "present, past and future" proper to divine eternity, in the trinitarian relations that include a principle of origin and the internal movement of one from another as issued by its source (e.g., the Father's begetting of the Son).[19] Trinity gives eternity its temporal-like structure. Barth turns more specifically to christology in order to fill out the content of God's relation to time in its pre-temporal, supra-temporal, and post-temporal dimensions.[20] In Christ, Barth writes, God "takes time to Himself" and makes it the "form of his eternity."[21] This in turn highlights the identity between the eternity of God and the covenant of grace, and consequently points to the decision of the triune God to be God among us in the person of Christ from eternity to eternity. As Barth states in the tag-line of his formal doctrine of the Trinity: "as Father, Son and Spirit God is, so to speak, ours in advance."[22]

Jenson responds to Barth's temporal understanding of eternity in two ways. The first way is positive. He notes that Barth's trinitarian-christological construction of eternity designates a view of God's reality with its own time. This, it appears, is the "radical temporality" of God in Jesus Christ that gives creaturely existence its "concrete temporal structure."[23] The second response is more critical. Jenson claims that Barth's concept of eternity can be read another way. In his notion of the "fulfilled time" that occurs in Jesus, Barth describes the time that God takes for creatures as the replacement "of our non-genuine and improper time."[24] Likewise, Barth accounts for the "eternal presence of God" in the resurrection event of Jesus as "a present without any future."[25] This results in a view of eternity not as uniquely temporal, but in terms of God's essential immunity to time and historical change; that is, an idea of divine timelessness. Jenson is aware that such a

---

18. Jenson, *God after God*, 72.

19. Barth, *CD* II/1:610–13, cited in Jenson, *God after God*, 128–29.

20. See Barth, *CD* II/1:615, 619–38.

21. Barth, *CD* II/1:616.

22. Barth, *CD* I/1:384. See also Jenson, *God after God*, 108.

23. Jenson, *God after God*, 151, 153.

24. Barth, *CD* I/2:66.

25. Barth, *CD* I/2:114. Similarly, "the fact that Christ had risen actually points to a time, a real part of human time amid so many other portions of time, which, as it cannot become past, neither needs any future, a time purely present because of the pure presence of God among men." Barth, *CD* II/1:114.

reading conflicts with Barth's intentions. "When we read [Barth's] theology
so we are reading it wrongly." He continues, "but there is something that
compels us to read it wrongly in this way."[26]

What compels this reading? The answer has to do with Barth's use of
analogy. Barth, Jenson claims, retains a notion of "God in himself distinct
from God-for-us."[27] To avoid an idea of God different from God's self-disclosure, this reality of God apart from creatures is taken to be "the prototype
of God-in-his-revelation."[28] This holds for the relation between eternity and
time. But if God's eternity only resembles time, there remains a potentially
radical rendering of it. Not radical in the sense of the divine temporality that
structures creaturely time, as noted before, but radical in the sense of utterly
without time.[29] "It all depends on which way you look at it."[30] Jenson adds
to this. Barth sets forth a temporally inclusive view of eternity. However, he
does not "sustain the dialectic [of eternity and time] to the end as a *temporal*
dialectic." Barth wants to say that God "is and is not in Jesus," but he fails to
provide a way of describing God as what happens with Jesus *and* God as free
over against this happening at the same time.[31] In other words, Barth does not
have a notion of "God's transcendence within the terms of time itself."[32] This
results in the possibility of speculation into the timeless idea of eternity that
ultimately undermines a notion of Jesus' history as God's own.

I turn now to an assessment of these criticisms. The common concern in Jenson's critiques of Barth's theology is the tendency to conceive
of God's eternal life in a way that evades the historicity of God. My sym-
pathies with Jenson's criticism of Barth on election will be expected. In
chapter 2 I argued that Barth's account of election can be construed both
as the happening below of a more ultimate reality above *and* as an eternal
decision to be enacted in time. Problematically, a good case can be made
for both interpretations. Jenson's criticism differs from my own in that
he finds Barth's use of analogy to favor, and so prioritize, Christ's reality
in the divine decree over God's revealed history; whereas I highlight the
conceptual difficulty that arises from multiple viable renderings of Barth's

26. Jenson, *God after God*, 152.

27. Jenson, *God after God*, 153. For another comparison of Jenson's and Barth's
theology on the relation between the eternality of God and time, see Langdon, *God the
Eternal Contemporary*, 22–26.

28. Jenson, *God after God*, 153.

29. Jenson, *Alpha and Omega*, 86–93.

30. Jenson, *God after God*, 152–53.

31. Jenson, *God after God*, 154.

32. Jenson, *God after God*, 155.

account. The outcome is relatively the same: election should be understood as the *temporal* enactment of God's eternal decision.

Barth's doctrine of election plays an important but largely background role in Jenson's later theology. Jenson mostly assumes the core of Barth's doctrine of election, and proceeds to conceive of God's reality taking shape *with us*—the focal point or telos of election.[33] The other focal point in Jenson's criticism of Barth's thought plays a more visible role in Jenson's theology. The concept of eternal timelessness is arguably the main foe in Jenson's theology. Timeless eternity, according to Jenson, is the God of conventional religion, or what creaturely beings posit to secure themselves against the inescapable reality of death. The mode of the eternally timeless God's life is "the *nunc simul*, the all-already-now-at-once of eternity."[34] For Jenson, God without a semblance of time is, to borrow Pannenberg's phrase, God without "the quality of life itself."[35] Equally important to this criticism is the constructive theological suggestion that follows in Jenson's analysis: the need for a temporal notion of transcendence. In Jenson's later theology he pulls back, at least in degree, on the charge of timelessness in Barth's doctrine of eternity. However, he pushes ahead in working out temporal concepts of both transcendence and deity. Jenson works out these concepts, as we explore later, through his trinitarian theology.

My agreement with Jenson on the need for a temporal notion of divine transcendence should be evident following my assessment of Pannenberg's doctrine of eternity from chapter 3. For Pannenberg, eternity is inclusive of time. This is based, at least in part, on his trinitarian theology. But the governing concept in Pannenberg's doctrine of eternity is God's comprehensive relation to time as a whole, or time's simultaneous presence to God. There is merit to this idea. God is the everlasting one, and does not stand in a simple one-to-one relation with created time, even as God indwells it. But Pannenberg, I argued, does not adequately specify the eternity-time relation. This results in confusing conceptions of God's relation to the temporal process, particularly created future time and its (ontological) presence to God. Or in the case of Pannenberg's claim that God has no "future that could be distinguished from his present," a timeless concept of eternity emerges.[36] Importantly, this also means that it is not clear how the eternal God transcends time from within it. This shows that Jenson's charge against Barth

33. See Jenson, *STh*, 1:59, 73, 140.

34. Jenson, "God, Space, and Architecture," 11.

35. Pannenberg, "Eternity, Time, and the Trinitarian God," 70.

36. Pannenberg, *ST*, 1:410; Pannenberg, *Systematische Theologie*, 1:443. English translation slightly altered.

applies to Pannenberg as well. Jenson is right, I believe, to call for a more robustly *temporal* notion of transcendence. In other words, a temporal idea of transcendence, rooted in a concept of the triune God's eternity, is needed to solve the recurring problems in the relation between divine eternity and time identified in this work, whether in the form of an eternal timelessness at odds with God's revealed history or a notion of eternity that hinders an understanding of God's presence and movement in time.

1.2: *Beginnings with Pannenberg*

I turn now to a short comparison of Jenson's and Pannenberg's early theology. The previous section identified the need for a temporal notion of transcendence. This section highlights a problem from chapter 3, namely, how to conceive of transcendence as God's futurity. Here I address the issue and only hint at a way to resolve it in Jenson's theology, which, as the central problem of this chapter, I return to later. I begin, though, by pointing out a general way that Jenson distinguishes his theology from Pannenberg's theological approach.

Jenson claims that the basic notion which guides Pannenberg's thinking is "the postulate of a totality of history."[37] It is the sense of the whole, or the full scope of history, that logically functions to unite reality, including the creature's understanding of God. As Pannenberg asserts, "an individual event can say something about the one God only when it has in view the totality of reality."[38] Even Pannenberg's eschatological focus, Jenson claims, is consequent upon the concept of the whole in his theology.[39] In contrast, Jenson asserts that the fundamental concept for understanding reality is "the contradiction of death and life." And this not in the abstract, but in "the suffering unity of the crucified and future one as the very being of God."[40] Jenson's theo-centric vision of reality takes the form of a theology of the cross (*theologia crucis*). In his adaptation of Barth's doctrines of God and election, Jenson puts it this way: God is "a particular event, the active

---

37. Jenson, *God after God*, 178.

38. Pannenberg, *Jesus—God and Man*, 185.

39. It is not decisive for our purposes here, but one could certainly argue that concepts of totality and eschatology are both basic to Pannenberg's theology and mutually implicating: while the eschatological future presupposes the whole, the whole, not experienced as such, invokes anticipation of the ultimate future. See Pannenberg's earliest exegesis on the biblical revelation of God as dually concerned with totality and eschatology, or the revelation of God at the *end* of history as a *whole*. Pannenberg, "Dogmatic Theses," 125–35.

40. Jenson, *God after God*, 179.

relation of the triune persons, the event in which we are involved in that the crucifixion and resurrection occur among us."[41]

The actual difference between Pannenberg and Jenson here is one of emphasis. Pannenberg's conception of the resurrection is consonant with his idea of the whole, and especially in his later theology Pannenberg conceives of the dependency of the Father's monarchy, the Father's eschatological rule, as connected to the death of Jesus and his victory. Conversely, Jenson understands the whole or totality of reality in relation to the activity of God in history.[42] Still, difference in emphasis matters. Here we can simply note one implication: the centrality of Jesus' death and resurrection in Jenson's theology, or Jenson's resolve to conceive of God's being *in* these events, results in a more temporally determined notion of divine being than we find in Pannenberg's theology. Whether this helps or hinders for understanding God's relation to time, specifically God's transcendence of time, remains to be seen. As noted in the previous chapter, Pannenberg's inclusion of time in the eternality of God's being does not preclude certain difficulties in conceiving of the God-time relation, or even the implication of eternity as timelessness. A great deal hinges on the temporal nature of God and the way this is structured in light of God's trinitarian being. I return to the foundations of Jenson's temporal idea of God in the next sub-section on narrative identity.

The central motifs or guiding concepts for understanding God's being in Jenson's and Pannenberg's theology differ to a significant degree. However, there are other areas in which greater overlap exists, such as eschatology. In order to conceive of a notion of transcendence that stems from the eternity of God as triune, Jenson proposes the following: "we will understand God's freedom over against what he is for and with us as his *futurity* to what he already is with and for us."[43] The framework for this notion follows from the above, a concept of transcendence over created reality that is identical to the structure of the divine immanence. The content of this notion, or how Jenson conceives of God's transcendence and immanence in a single idea—divine futurity—echoes the early Pannenberg, particularly Pannenberg's conception of God who straddles the present from the generative point of the (divine) future. Jenson describes Pannenberg as a pioneer in the constructive thinking about God's relation to time in terms of futurity. In *God after God* Jenson outlines Pannenberg's idea of history as a whole in

41. Jenson, *STh*, 1:221.

42. See Jenson's comments on his connection to Pannenberg's theology in Jenson, "A Theological Autobiography," 49.

43. Jenson, *God after God*, 155.

light of the latter's understanding of Christ as "the end of history."[44] Jenson also highlights the connections between Pannenberg's eschatological view of history, his idea of God, and the unity of deity and lordship. Jenson notes how these concepts line up with his own theological vision. He quotes Pannenberg approvingly: God is "the power of the future."[45]

In the turn to eschatology, particularly the concept of divine futurity, there is overlap between the early theology of Jenson and Pannenberg. I registered a criticism of this concept in Pannenberg's theology in the last chapter. The notion of divine futurity, as Pannenberg articulates it, derives from the eschatological orientation of the scriptural narrative, such as Jesus' proclamation of God's kingdom. But it leaves much to be desired in terms of actual content and consequently in its function as the object of faith. Later in this chapter, following a fuller explication of Jenson's doctrine of God, I consider whether Jenson's invocation of futurity is susceptible to the same critique. The question is important, for while the concept of futurity helpfully provides a temporally structured idea of transcendence, it must also conform to the specific contours of the biblical God's identity in order to be serviceable for faith. In his earliest construction of a divine ontology in *God after God*, Jenson makes recourse to the concept of futurity within the immediate context of a theology of God as Father, Son, and Spirit. Therefore if Jenson's eschatological concept of God is able to provide a solution to the problems of both conceiving of God's transcendence of time from within it as well as the potentially vacuous idea of futurity, it will be on trinitarian grounds.

1.3: Narrative Identity

In the previous section I utilized comparisons of Jenson's theology with Barth's and Pannenberg's to identify the key problems of this chapter: the need for a temporal notion of transcendence and the question of whether the concept of futurity can be salvaged within a trinitarian framework. In this final introductory section I lay out the basic framework for Jenson's narrative understanding of God. Jenson's narrative idea of God means not only that God is identified in time but that God's being is temporal. The goal of this sub-section is to provide the exegetical and conceptual background for Jenson's narrative-temporal concept of the Trinity.

---

44. Jenson, *God after God*, 176.

45. Pannenberg, *Grundfragen systematischer Theologie*, 292, cited in Jenson, *God after God*, 166.

The "chief theological task," Jenson holds, is the identification of God.[46] In this way theology provides churchly discourse with answers to the fundamental question of faith: Who is God? Insofar as the central genre of Scripture is narrative, this identification takes shape in a similar way; God is identified through a story. "The Bible on its face tells a history running from its first verses to its last, from Creation to creation's End—to be sure, with detours, subplots, and incorporated stories; memoirs of the prophetic word by which in Israel's understanding God drives history; and pauses for prayer and for lament or celebration of major turnings."[47] In one of Jenson's favored expressions, "the world God creates is not a thing, a 'cosmos,' but rather is a history," including pilgrimage through the desert, exile, and the Spirit driven mission of God's people.[48] God is identified by the narrative movements of Scripture's story.

At a deeper level, the narrative identity of God follows from God's self-identification in Scripture, specifically in the Old Testament.[49] The influence of Jenson's former teacher, Old Testament exegete Gerhard von Rad, is evident here. The story of God and Israel is "a history of promise, of the leapfrogging succession of promise, fulfilling—or penultimately un-fulfilling—event, and new promise."[50] For instance, in Isaiah 40–45 God is depicted by recounting promises of old, and makes them anew in light of the exilic predicament. "See, the former things have come to pass, and new things I now declare; before they spring forth, I tell you of them" (42:9). The biblical narrative links the divine faithfulness to the contingencies of history.[51] At the fulfillment of the promises, all *will* know that "I am the Lord" (Isa 45:5). In this way, Jenson writes, "the Lord explicitly puts his self-identity at narrative risk," for the identity of the Lord as Lord hinges on the establishment of divine promises, made and brought to completion in time.[52] In light of the divine sovereignty, it is in a sense certain that the divine promises will come to fruition. But even the manifestation of God's sovereignty takes place among us. It occurs in the midst of the contingencies of this world, and therefore it includes the narrative-temporal character of God's faithfulness.[53]

46. Jenson, "Three Identities of One Action," 1.

47. Jenson, "Choose Ye This Day," 14.

48. Jenson, *Systematic Theology*, 2:14.

49. See Jenson, *STh*, 1:42–44, 63–74; Jenson, *Christian Dogmatics*, 2:109–21. On two recent works that attend to this theme in Jenson's theology, see Lee, *Trinitarian Ontology and Israel in Robert W. Jenson's Theology*; Nicol, *Exodus and Resurrection*.

50. Jenson, *STh*, 2:13.

51. Jenson, *STh*, 1:65.

52. Jenson, *STh*, 1:65.

53. Jenson, *STh*, 1:48, 65. The parallel to Pannenberg's principle is evident here.

Or to borrow a line from Willie James Jennings, "God has entered the life of the creature and joined the storytelling that is history."[54]

Anticipated in the example above from Isaiah, Jenson takes the step from identifying God by the narrative aspects and events of Scripture to ascribing narrative to God's being. In his words, God is not only identified "*by* events in time," but also "*with* the particular plotted sequence of events that make the narrative of Israel and her Christ."[55] Jenson is aware of the aberrant nature of this claim. In much of Greek and conventional religion, God is not "conditioned by the relations that exist between things in space." This idea of God derives from the variations in space.[56] Jenson refers to Aristotle's belief that susceptibility to the contingencies of history is an ontological defect. But why? Jenson asks. "Why should commitment in a history not be . . . an ontological *perfection*?"[57] We must be careful to note, however, that Jenson's historical ontology is not primarily motivated by perceived faults in the Greek understanding of being. Nor is it simply due to the fact that Scripture identifies God through a narrative genre.[58] Rather, his ontology is rooted in the self-commitment of God to this world as told in Scripture, specifically to the temporal nature of the scriptural events. "God's story is committed as a story *with* creatures."[59] Accordingly, the will of God is "invested in the reality of this world."[60] In the scriptural story God's involvement in history and the process of time is simply a given; it holds the story together. In it God is disposed to repeatedly become a character in the dramatic interplay of the life of the people of God with God. Moreover, as Jenson conceives this, God so invests in the story of creatures as to be committed without remainder. God binds Godself so deeply to the creaturely history that God "can have no identity except as he meets the temporal end which creatures live," death.[61] This brings us to the final point on narrative identity and Christ's passion.

Jenson's construal of Christ's death and resurrection brings together several of the points above. The passion accounts are the climax of the four gospel narratives, and so play a basic role in the narrative identification of God. Even

---

54. Jennings, *Acts*, 2.

55. Jenson, *STh*, 1:59–60. Latter emphasis mine.

56. Jenson, "God, Space, and Architecture," 11.

57. Jenson, *STh*, 1:64.

58. Francesca Aran Murphy overlooks Jenson's recourse to the nature of the scriptural events themselves when she claims that, according to Jenson, "because God is identified by a narrative, God is a narrative," and leaves it at that. Murphy, *God Is Not a Story*, 268.

59. Jenson, *STh*, 1:65. Emphasis mine.

60. Jenson, *STh*, 1:69.

61. Jenson, *STh*, 1:65.

more, Jenson considers their implied narrative *ontology*. The death of Christ forces a question: if God is *one*, and God is revealed to us in and as Christ, how does the personhood of God hang together at the cross? Jenson claims, at the cross of Christ the being of God as a "self-identical personal reality" is at stake; for either there, in Jesus' cry of God-abandonment and subsequent death, God is and remains the one God as Father, Son, and Spirit, or is simply three gods, a "mutually betraying pantheon," and not a tri*unity* of persons.[62] The key point is this: if God maintains the divine unity in the occurrence of Jesus' death, which Jenson assumes, then the identity of God must take place in and through the events of the cross and Jesus' victory. Given that no ontological rift between the Son and Father occurs in the crucifixion, then the abandonment and death of Jesus must be incorporated into the Father-Son relation.[63] The God of the Bible is not only known by the events of Christ's death and resurrection, but is constituted, quite literally, *through* them. Temporal events belong to God's deity. Or as Jenson puts it, "God is what happens between Jesus and his Father in their Spirit."[64]

I have highlighted some of the basic reasons that support Jenson's narrative ontology. God makes promises in which the divine self-identity is at stake in time. God acts in time so as to assimilate historic events, particularly Christ's way through death, into God's being. For Jenson, God happens; God is an event; God is both temporally identified and temporal being. What all of this shows, however, is only that God's being is structured along narrative and temporal lines. It does not say *how* God is temporal. And so we are led to ask, what are the conditions in God that enable or constitute God as temporal being? In the next section I consider how Jenson's narrative idea of God has a sort of lodging place within the strictures of God's being. For this we turn to Jenson's trinitarian theology.

2: The History of the Trinitarian God

Having situated Jenson's theology in relation to the work of Barth and Pannenberg and briefly treated his concept of narrative identity, I now consider Jenson's doctrine of the triune God. What follows is divided into three sub-sections that engage a set of related concepts in Jenson's theology: Jenson's trinitarian idea of God, with a focus on his doctrine of the Spirit; the temporal infinity of God (or divine eternity); and divine envelopment. Elaborated, section 2 of this chapter shows how Jenson's narrative-temporal

62. Jenson, *STh*, 1:65.

63. Jenson, *STh*, 1:65.

64. Jenson, *STh*, 1:221. See also Jenson, "Three Identities of One Action," 2.

concept of God is rooted in his trinitarian thought, while giving special attention to different aspects of the God-world relation in his theology. In sub-section 1 I lay out the basic features of Jenson's trinitarian theology. I use Jenson's doctrine of the Spirit as a way into his broader trinitarian reflections, and demonstrate how Jenson conceives of God's distinction from created reality through his pneumatology and a qualified notion of divine aseity. In sub-sections 2 and 3 I consider two theological concepts that direct our attention more closely to the particularities of the relationship between God and time in Jenson's theology. I draw from this overview in the final section of the chapter in order to address the need for a temporal notion of divine transcendence.

Before proceeding I note Jenson's use of the term "identity" in place of the more traditional nomenclature of a divine person or *hypostasis*. Jenson's use of identity is an attempt to put the Cappadocian notion of *hypostasis* into modern idiom.[65] He notes three concerns in using this alternative term: First, an identity is distinguishable by name and identifying description (e.g., the Holy Spirit, the breath of God). Second, an identity can be repeatedly identified. The being of God, as triune, is thrice-repeated, and thus has a three-fold identity more basic to God than a fixed set of characteristics such as timelessness or omnipotence. And third, and closely related to the second concern, identity captures a sentiment in the modern notion of personal existence as posited over the course of time. While the three-fold being of God is not straightforwardly sequential (we will return to this), Jenson likens personal identity in time to the concept of God's self-repeated being: "God does God, and over again, and yet over gain."[66] In accordance with Jenson's theology, I will use the term identity for a divine person in the exposition that follows.

2.1: The Trinity and the Spirit of God

In this sub-section I consider the dynamic of the Spirit in Jenson's trinitarian theology. Jenson's doctrine of the Spirit, alongside his accompanying temporal idea of God, buttresses his conception of what distinguishes God from created reality in a notion of God's self-sufficiency or aseity. I again return periodically to Pannenberg's eschatological idea of God as a point of comparison with Jenson's doctrine of the Trinity in this sub-section. These comparisons with

65. Jenson, *STh*, 1:105–06.

66. Jenson, *The Triune Identity*, 109–11. Jenson is aware that the last point is something that only "struggled for expression . . . in the Cappadocians." Jenson, *The Triune Identity*, 110. See also Jenson, "Three Identities of One Action," 6–8. On self-repetition in God, see Barth, *CD* I/1:350.

Pannenberg's thought provide a backdrop that illuminates Jenson's theology. A more constructive and critical comparison between Jenson's and Pannenberg's theology awaits in section 3 of this chapter.

I begin with the way that Jenson's doctrine of the Spirit picks up on the creedal era formulations of God's being (i.e., Nicaea-Constantinople). In the traditional schematic, the eternal relations of God's being flow primarily one way, in a linear direction that proceeds from the Father to the Son and the Spirit. Jenson does not object to this, and as we will see below, in important ways he draws from this conception for understanding creation and the God-world relation. It is more apt to say that Jenson's trinitarian theology seeks to fill out the traditional schematic rather than rework it from the ground up.[67] With its focus on origins, Jenson argues, creedal era trinitarian theology left largely untouched the significance of Scripture's eschatological dimensions for understanding the divine being.[68] Like Pannenberg, Jenson takes up the question of the eschatological reality of God's eternal being as triune. Jenson describes this as a "pneumatological deficit" in the tradition, and his trinitarian theology is an attempt to remedy it.[69]

Somewhat unexpectedly, one way in which the eschatological reality of God comes into view for Jenson is through a consideration of the Spirit's originating role in God, distinct from the Father's unique identity as the unoriginate origin or *arche* of the Godhead. This is connected to Jenson's related concern to distinguish the Spirit's personhood in God. The traditional conception of the Spirit as the bond of love between the Father and Son, according to Jenson, all too easily lends itself to an I-Thou trinitarianism that underwrites much theology in the west.[70] The Spirit is not only the bond of love in the Godhead, but as the Spirit of the Father who rests on the Son, and the Spirit of the Son who animates all that the Son does, the Spirit distinctly frees them for one another.[71] The Spirit of God, as Jenson puts it, "liberates Father and Son to love each other," and so frees God to be God. In other words, the Spirit frees God *to be*—eschatologically—at one and the same time the love that God *is*; the Spirit binds Father and Son unto one another, and is simultaneously the loving result of their unity. Most relevant for our purposes, however, is Jenson's understanding of the Spirit's eschatological identity and its theological implications.

67. See esp. Jenson's summary of the trinitarian relations. Jenson, *STh*, 1:161.

68. Jenson, *STh*, 1:108.

69. Jenson, *STh*, 1:157.

70. Jenson, *STh*, 1:155, 157–59. Jenson points to Augustine, Hegel, and Barth as exemplary here. See Augustine, *De Trinitate*, 5.12. With reference to Barth, see Jenson, "You Wonder Where the Spirit Went," 296–304.

71. Jenson, *STh*, 1:155–56, 158.

Jenson describes the Spirit as the transcendent force of God. Reflective of the Spirit's presence in creation, in the Exodus event the Spirit (*ruach*) resists Israel's oppressors and opens a path for the chosen people through the waters (Exod 15:8–10). The presence of the Spirit among the prophets can be seen to both create a future for the people of God and, at the same time, to be itself the content of that future: "I am going to open your graves . . . I will put my spirit within you and you shall live" (Ezek 37:4, 12–14).[72] Post-exilic Israel attributes its remote origins in Egypt, its liberation from slavery, and its way into the unknown future to the presence of God in the Spirit (Isa 63:10–14).[73] The Spirit of God rests on the people Israel, encompassing its history and driving it forward.

In the New Testament Jesus appears as the bearer of God's Spirit (Mark 1:9–11). The Spirit is responsible for his conception in Mary's womb (Luke 1:35). At the outset of Jesus' ministry, the Spirit uniquely descends on him at the river Jordan (Matt 3:16).[74] The acts of Jesus' ministry, performed in the Spirit, "means that they are done from the pressing futurity of the Kingdom" (12:28).[75] Moreover, the Spirit is variously described as the life-giving principle of God. The Spirit makes alive the once lifeless flesh of Jesus in the event of the resurrection, and, likewise, is the power that inhabits God's people as the temple of God and who enables their faithfulness (Rom 1:4; 1 Cor 3:16–17; 1 Pet 3:18; 4:6).[76] Finally, specifically eschatological cues coincide with the Spirit's presence. This is demonstrated not only in the resurrection of Christ, "the first fruits of those who have fallen asleep" (1 Cor 15:20), but also in the dialectic between the law of the Spirit and the law of sin and death that Paul employs in Romans 8 as well as the longing for a future redemption of the body that accompanies the Spirit's presence here and now (1–13, 23). A similar eschatological directive marks the giving of the Spirit in the Lukan-Acts account of the mission of the early Christian community (Acts 2:17, 32–33 [Joel 2:28]; 3:19–21).[77]

Based on the Spirit's identity in Scripture, Jenson describes the Spirit in specifically eschatological ways. Several of Jenson's descriptions for the Spirit align with Pannenberg's early theology. The Spirit is God "from and toward the End."[78] The Spirit "*is* the End of all God's ways," he writes, as well as "God

72. See also Isaiah 32:15–16; Jenson, *On the Inspiration of Scripture*, 10.

73. Jenson, *Christian Dogmatics*, 2:110–13.

74. Jenson, *STh*, 1:88; Jenson, *Christian Dogmatics*, 2:114–15.

75. Jenson, *STh*, 1:143.

76. Jenson, *Christian Dogmatics*, 2:116.

77. Jenson, *Christian Dogmatics*, 2:114–15, 118–19.

78. Jenson, *STh*, 1:89.

coming to us from the last future."[79] In striking similarity to Pannenberg's concept of futurity as that which straddles the present from the future, Jenson asserts that "the Spirit is God coming from the future to break the present open to himself."[80] However, Jenson develops the concept of God's futurity more systematically than Pannenberg. Pannenberg describes his early ventures into the idea of God as the power of the future as a "first sketch," and continues to use this notion in his *Systematic Theology* to address the temporal structure of God's activity in the Spirit within his doctrine of creation.[81] However, the overall place of God's futurity in Pannenberg's mature doctrine of God, as highlighted before, remains ambiguous. In contrast, Jenson fleshes out the notion of futurity through his trinitarian idea of God. As I show below, this enables Jenson to better conceive of not only God's being but also God's relation to history and the way that God transcends the temporal world from within the strictures of time itself. Functionally, Jenson's concept of futurity is more analogous to Pannenberg's notion of the Father's dependent deity than Pannenberg's pneumatology. For Jenson's concept of the Spirit as God's futurity, like Pannenberg's idea of the Father's dependent deity, designates a principle in God that animates the historical involvement or movement of God in history and the process of time.

The eschatological understanding of the Spirit in Jenson's theology applies not only to the worldly activity of God. The Spirit is also the eschatological reality of God's being *ad intra*. "The Spirit," writes Jenson, "is God as the Power of God's *own* and our future."[82] We come to Jenson's reappraisal of the traditional relations of origin here, though as noted before his conceptual reframing of these relations functions more so to complement rather than alter the traditional perspective. The Father breathes forth the Spirit in God, and the result (following the begetting of the Son) is that the Spirit exists as the Goal of the Godhead. The traditional language of the eternal relations points this way, in this direction: "God 'Begets,' and is 'Begotten,' and is the Outcome—'Proceeds from' this relation."[83] Likewise, Jenson writes, "in himself, God confronts his own future; he confronts that Spirit who is the

---

79. Jenson, *STh*, 1:157, 219. See also Jenson, *STh*, 2:121; Jenson, "On the Doctrine of Atonement," 133; Chalamet, "God's 'Liveliness' in Robert W. Jenson's Trinitarian Thought," 147. The earliest invoking of God the Spirit as the "power of the future" by Jenson that I am aware of is a quotation from Pannenberg's 1967 volume, *Grundfragen systematischer Theologie* (292), in Jenson, *God after God* (166).

80. Jenson, "Does God Have Time?," 194.

81. Pannenberg, *ST*, 2:95–112, esp. 98.

82. Jenson, *STh*, 1:160.

83. Jenson, *Story and Promise*, 126.

Spirit 'of' the Father."[84] By means of the Spirit the divine life "is ordered by an Outcome that is [God's] own, and so in a freedom that is more than abstract aseity."[85] Through the Spirit a sense of future belongs to God's being. How this sense of divine futurity relates to the future of creaturely time in Jenson's theology is examined below. First, however, we consider the broader portrayal of Jenson's trinitarian idea of God and how the divine relations factor more explicitly into his temporal ontology.

Through the notion of the Spirit as the futurity of God's being, Jenson builds on the structure of Barth's trinitarian based idea of eternity. For Barth, eternity includes "beginning, succession and end," as well as "past" and "future," "a before and an after."[86] What marks off these qualities in God's being from their analogues in creaturely reality lies in the fact that in God they remain perfectly united in their differences. As noted in section 1, Barth grounds this point in the divine unity. Specifically, Barth bases the temporal structure and internal differentiations of eternity in the trinitarian nature of God, or the unity-in-distinctions of God's being.[87] Jenson continues to make use of Barth's account of eternity in his later theology. He becomes less critical of the slips into a timeless conception of God identified in his early work on Barth's theology, although at least an allusion to this criticism remains.[88] More important, a key difference between Jenson and Barth on eternity lies in that Jenson appropriates specific dimensions of eternity to the identities of God as Father, Son, and Holy Spirit. Particularly, he appropriates the distinct dimensions of time—past, present, and future—and notions of whence and whither in God to the divine identities.

How does Jenson coordinate these dimensions to the divine persons? The Father is the *arche* of God, the unoriginate origin of the Godhead. Jenson thus identifies the Father with the whence of God's being. As noted above, in the procession of the Spirit from the Father there is a Goal proper to God's being. In time the being of the Spirit is most closely related to the eschatological activity of God. Accordingly, Jenson identifies the Spirit with the whither or Outcome of God. It follows that the Son plays a mediating role in the divine life. The Father intends the Son from the beginning of all God's ways, on one hand; the Spirit frees the Son for the Father, to obey the Father's will from eternity and to bind them together, on the other. Hence the Son

84. Jenson, *STh*, 1:160.

85. Jenson, *STh*, 1:160.

86. Barth, *CD* II/1:610–15.

87. See esp. Barth, *CD* II/1:615.

88. See Jenson, *STh*, 1:216–18.

mediates the two, the Origin and Outcome as the one God.[89] Herein lies Jenson's narrative ontology in creedal perspective. God's being includes whence and whither, Origin and Outcome. While unique to the absolute unity of the one God, Father, Son, and Spirit exhibit a narratively coordinated identity based on their inner-relations. Jenson builds on this point:

> This narrative structure (in God) is enabled by a difference between whence and whither, which one cannot finally refrain from calling 'past' and 'future,' and which is identical with the distinction between the Father and the Spirit. This difference is not measurable; nothing in God *recedes* into the past or *approaches* from the future. But the difference is also absolute: there are whence and whither in God that are not like right and left or up and down, that do not reverse with the point of view.[90]

The qualitative descriptions are followed by temporal ones. In God, the Father is Past, the Spirit is Future, and the Son is the specious Present, which makes him the "present Possibility of God's reality for us."[91] More specifically, the Son is the present actuality of all that the Father wills from eternity past in the power of the Spirit, God's creative future.[92]

The block quote above requires unpacking. First, it is important to note that Jenson applies these temporal ascriptions to God (i.e., the Father with Past) through their similarity to created time.[93] The ascriptions are analogous to created time—or as I show in a sub-section below, created time is analogous to the temporal life of God—insofar as temporal succession does not apply to God straightforwardly. As Jenson notes elsewhere, what God *anticipates*, namely, the Spirit as the Outcome in God, God uniquely *possesses*.[94] Hence the statement in the quote above: the difference of whence and whither in God 'is not measurable.' And yet, insofar as the originating being of the Father and the procession of the Spirit are essential to God, the difference of whence and whither in God 'is also absolute.' Jenson does not aim to work out perfect conceptual congruity between temporal distinction and wholeness in God. Rather, the controlling factor is the structural nature of the trinitarian relations as depicted by the creedal affirmations. When this

---

89. Jenson, "Does God Have Time?," 194–95. Jenson works out the basic structure of this organizational pattern in God in several ways. See Jenson, *Story and Promise*, 113–28; Jenson, *The Triune Identity*, 138–48.

90. Jenson, *STh*, 2:35. See also Jenson, *STh*, 1:218.

91. Jenson, *Triune Identity*, 24; Jenson, *Story and Promise*, 126.

92. Jenson, *STh*, 1:219–20.

93. Jenson, *STh*, 2:35.

94. Jenson, *Ezekiel*, 87.

point is missed, the temporal ascriptions in God become liable to myriad misunderstandings, not only regarding God's identity but also in relation to the nature of God's eternity and the God-world relation.[95] The deity of the Son, for example, is constituted in his being begotten by the Father. He is as such "God *from* God." Jenson states, here is a clear "before and after" proper to God's being, and yet one that cannot be plotted on a timeline in any simple way.[96] It cannot, because this begetting, or real act of *being from* in God, also belongs to the divine unity and the eternality of the Son in relation to the Father. There was never a time when he was not.

The point here is the dialectic. Temporal movement and difference underlie the relations of the divine persons; but simultaneously, so does the divine unity and a form of mutual indwelling such that Father, Son, and Spirit perfectly coincide. The *Father, Son,* and *Spirit* are the *one* God. "Only a trinitarian concept of God can contain this dialectic within itself."[97] What does this mean for understanding the Spirit in relation to the being of God? As the eschatological reality of God, the Spirit is God's future.[98] This future is as real to God as is the distinctiveness of the Spirit's personhood. That God possesses God's future, writes Jenson, is not "equivalent to his having *no* future distinct from his present."[99] Jenson locates this distinction, as indicated in the block quote above, within the narrative framework of the divine persons' inner-relations. "There is difference between Father and Spirit and so between beginning and goal."[100] Likewise, Jenson conceives of the distinction of the Spirit's futurity in God in terms of the unity of the divine identities. "For God and in God, the future is not the present, yet it has presence."[101] Unique to God alone, the future does not approach God from the outside. Jenson writes, "there is future in God, but not so as to transcend God: God *anticipates* his future and so possesses it."[102] To summarize this temporal dialectic, on one hand, the distinct futurity of the Spirit's identity makes God's being timely; on the other, the self-possession of the Spirit's futurity by the Father and the Son makes this future unique

---

95. I address several of Jenson's readers on these points in Rice, "Timely, Transcendent, and Alive," 253–66.

96. Jenson, "*Ipse Pater Non Est Impassibilis*," 102–3.

97. Jenson, *God after God*, 171.

98. Jenson, "The Hidden and Triune God," 11.

99. Jenson, *STh*, 1:218n61.

100. Jenson, *Ezekiel*, 87.

101. Jenson, *Ezekiel*, 87.

102. Jenson, *STh*, 2:121.

to God alone. The dialectic of the trinitarian unity-in-distinctions governs Jenson's temporal idea of God.

One final point remains to note here. The temporality of God's being distinguishes God from the world. The central claim for Jenson is that insofar as God is Spirit, and therefore uniquely "his own future," God "is *unboundedly* lively."[103] For creatures, the future is always beyond our grasp. Not so with God. Because God is Spirit, God is God's own future, and therefore ensures a future identical to the self-contained goodness of God, the trinitarian life of Father, Son, and Spirit. Herein lies a notion of God's freedom, Jenson says, that "is more than abstract aseity," though it is still akin to the classical concept of God's self-animated life.[104] Jenson writes, "the Spirit is God's *freedom*," and "has this role *first* in God himself."[105] What stands out in Jenson's concept of aseity and its theological function lies in its trinitarian shape. Aseity, as God's uniquely self-grounded being, distinguishes God from all else. But this type of aseity does not mean merely that the uniqueness that underlies God's alterity lies in God's sheer difference from what is not God, or only in terms of the self-derivation of God's being (itself not derived) that stands in sharp contrast to all else. The difference between God and creation for Jenson has a temporal valance to it, and accords with the limitless nature of God. As Jenson puts it, in the person of the Holy Spirit God "*is* himself only eschatologically." God is with us and yet always beyond or ahead of us. Triune aseity as such does not entail strict or absolute alterity. Rather, it means that God's being is "unsurpassable."[106]

2.2: *The Temporal Infinity of God*

The unique temporality of God's being includes God's difference from us. God's temporality, however, also indicates that the unsurpassability of God is to be understood in a historical way. Jenson is specific about this: God is unsurpassable in the events of Christ's life, death, and resurrection. I consider this side of Jenson's doctrine of God and his concept of temporal infinity in this sub-section. I begin with his general concept of temporal infinity and then turn to its concrete expressions in the life of Christ and the triunity of God's being.

Jenson derives the concept of temporal infinity from Gregory of Nyssa. It is Gregory who famously deployed the concept of infinity for

103. Jenson, *STh*, 1:143.

104. Jenson, *STh*, 1:160.

105. Jenson, *On the Inspiration of Scripture*, 33. Latter emphasis mine.

106. Jenson, *The Triune Identity*, 169.

the nature of God. Jenson likens this to what Thomas Aquinas calls the most appropriate name for God as 'He who is,' for "God's act of being is constrained by no form other than itself."[107] A very brief comparison with Pannenberg is helpful in showing how Jenson uses this concept. For Pannenberg, following Hegel, the infinity of God narrows in on the *inclusion* of that which is distinct from itself, the finite, while remaining other in its infinity. There is significant overlap between Pannenberg's employment of this category and Jenson's concept of creation as divine accommodation that I explore in the next sub-section. The difference in focus between Pannenberg's and Jenson's use of the concept of infinity surfaces in Jenson's more explicit engagement with Gregory's notion. In Jenson's articulation of Gregory's theology the idea of the infinite has to do with the limitless nature of God. More specifically, God is not endless extension but infinite in the capacity to *surpass* every conceivable obstacle; God does not lack boundaries, but overcomes them.[108] Moreover, Jenson states that Gregory's deity is the kind of being that "keeps things moving."[109] Jenson cites Gregory: "The transcendent and blessed Life has neither interior nor exterior measure; no temporal process can keep pace with it." The infinity of God therefore extends over time, both past and future.[110] Jenson gives Gregory's concept a futuristic slant: "to be God," he writes, "is always to be open to and always to open a future, transgressing all past-imposed conditions."[111]

Jenson points to Barth's account of eternity as capturing the movement and temporal dimensions of God's infinity. I referenced Barth's formulation of eternity above as inclusive of beginning, middle, and end in God, or temporal past and future, which are grounded in the trinitarian distinctions and perfectly cohere through the unity of God's being.[112] I also showed how Jenson diverges from Barth by identifying these distinctions, such as past, present, and future in God, with the trinitarian persons. He goes beyond Barth in another way. The notion of pure duration in Barth's idea of eternity can have a temporal quality to it, Jenson argues, only if source and goal are not merely present to God but are "asymmetrical in

107. Jenson, *STh*, 1:215. See Aquinas, *Summa Theologica*, 1.13.11.

108. The difference between Pannenberg and Jenson on the infinite is, from another perspective, about starting points. For Pannenberg the starting point involves bridging what is separate, the infinite and the finite; for Jenson it has to do with transcendence, the uncontainable presence of the infinite in the finite. It is possible to map these conceptions onto their methodological (epistemological) starting points as well.

109. Jenson, *STh*, 1:216.

110. Gregory of Nyssa, *Against Eunomius*, 1:366, 1:666–72, in Jenson, *STh*, 1:216.

111. Jenson, *STh*, 1:216.

112. See Barth, *CD* II/1:610, 611, 615; Jenson, *STh*, 1:217.

him."[113] Or, likewise, "God is not a presence possessing his past and future in himself; he is a future possessing his past in himself and therefore always present."[114] If source and goal are not asymmetrical in God, the whole schematic, it seems, is susceptible to falling back onto itself into a circular and thus timeless notion of eternity. Notably, Barth is willing to speak of "a direction that is irreversible" in the beginning, middle, and end of God's eternity.[115] But Barth, unlike Jenson, does not hold that God "is *primally* future to himself and only thereupon past and present for himself."[116] Jenson has God the Spirit in view here. The Spirit is God's future, the Goal of God's ways. God is eternal "not in that he perfectly persists, but in that he perfectly anticipates."[117] Oriented to a future that is God's own, the eternity of God is a *temporal* infinity and thus eschews timelessness.

The notion of temporal infinity shapes Jenson's doctrine of eternity. However, Jenson intends something more particular and historical here. Divine eternity, he writes, is identical to God's "faithfulness." God is not eternal as immune to time and the vagaries of creaturely life, but rather eternal in that God is "faithful to the death and then yet again faithful."[118] Trinity provides the essential link between the notion of temporal infinity outlined in the paragraphs above and the temporal or this-worldly concept of eternity that Jenson references in the just quoted passage on divine faithfulness. Jenson writes,

> The Father is the "whence" of God's life; the Spirit is the "whither" of God's life; and we may even say that the Son is that life's specious present. If, then, whence and whither do not fall apart in God's life, so that his duration is without loss, it is because origin and goal, whence and whither, are indomitably reconciled in the *action* and *suffering* of the Son. . . . The way in which the whence and the whither of the divine life are one, the way in which the triune God is *eternal*, is by the events of Jesus' death and resurrection.[119]

God is eternal through temporal events. The passage here recalls the thematic claim from the sub-section on Jenson's narrative ontology: God is not only

113. Jenson, *STh*, 1:217.

114. Jenson, *God after God*, 171.

115. Barth, *CD* II/1:639.

116. Jenson, *STh*, 1:217. Emphasis mine.

117. Jenson, *STh*, 1:217; *The Triune Identity*, 141.

118. Jenson, *STh*, 1:217.

119. Jenson, *STh*, 1:218–19. Emphases mine.

identified "*by* events in time," but "*with* those events."[120] I unpack the block quote above in two ways: first in terms of the relational structure of Jesus' ministry, or the whence and whither of God as reconciled in the 'action' of the Son; and second, in terms of Jesus' cross and resurrection, or the whence and whither of God as reconciled in the 'suffering' of the Son.

First, the whence (Father) and whither (Spirit) of God's being are united in the life of Christ. I consider this claim from both sides of the Son's relation to the Father and the Spirit, and then in view of the Trinity as a whole. The Father's will is made concrete in the Son. The Father, as Jenson puts it, "intends himself in the Son."[121] Sent from the Father, the Son hears the Father's word in order to convey it to others (John 12:49). The Father is the "enabling word" of Jesus' ministry, the reason that Jesus the Son "does not cling to what he is or has," but "lives utterly for his mission, that is, for the Father."[122] Jesus' ministry is also driven by his relation to the Spirit. "In the Bible generally," Jenson writes, "the 'Spirit' is God as the power of the future to overturn what already is, and just so to fulfill it."[123] In the action of Christ this occurs as the Spirit dwells in the Son and divulges the eschatological future, or as Jenson articulates the meaning of Matthew 12:28, "in Jesus' proclamation the power of the Spirit and the pressing immanence of the Kingdom are the same thing."[124] Moreover, the Spirit plays a definitive role in the divine unity. The Spirit of the Father rests on the Son while enabling his obedience to the Father (Isa 11:2; 61:1–2; Luke 4:14). Likewise, the Spirit mediates the Father-Son relation, as seen in the events of Jesus' baptism and his conception in the womb of Mary (Matt 3:16–17; Luke 1:35).[125]

And second, the whence and whither of God, the Father and Spirit, are one. What the Father wills the Spirit brings to pass. But what the Father wills, or rather, who he wills, is Jesus the Son, whom the Spirit frees to carry out the Father's plans. Therefore whence and whither are one in God insofar as they have their content—the content of the Father's will—and their actuality—the Spirit's execution of the Father's will—in Jesus.[126] It is worth noting that Jenson's formulation is not new. It is patterned after the Cappadocian principle in which every singular act of the triune God is three-fold: the divine activity *ad extra* proceeds from the Father,

120. Jenson, *STh*, 1:59.

121. Jenson, *STh*, 1:219.

122. Jenson, *STh*, 1:220.

123. Jenson, *The Triune Identity*, 23.

124. Jenson, *STh*, 1:157.

125. Jenson, "Conceptus . . . De Spiritu Sancto," 105–6.

126. Jenson, *STh*, 2:27.

is actualized by the Son, and is perfected by the Spirit. I return to Jenson's use of this principle in the next sub-section. The main point here is that the identities of the Trinity, specifically the Father as the principle of origin in God and the Spirit as the divine end, are one, a perfect harmony, in the three-fold nature of the divine activity manifest in the life of Christ. However, as the block quote above indicates, this point comes to definitive expression in the events of Christ's suffering.

"The triune God is eternal . . . by the events of Jesus' death and resurrection."[127] There are at least two reasons for the special place of the passion, death, and resurrection of Christ in Jenson's theology. Jenson's idea of God and his concept of eternity hinge on God's temporal involvement. Recall the claim from section 1 of this chapter on Jenson's idea of narrative identity: "God's story is committed as a story with creatures. And so he too, as it is, can have no identity except as he meets the temporal end toward which creatures live."[128] Death settles the question of God's identity—*who* God is. To at least some degree therefore Christ's death impacts the eternal-ity of God as well. We also touched on the second reason for the centrality of Christ's passion and resurrection in section 1. Jenson largely assumes Barth's concept of election as an eternal decision enacted in time.[129] At the heart of this decision is what happens with God in the freely willed suffering and victory of Christ. This decision, for both Barth and Jenson, constitutes God's being. Jenson, however, is more adamant than Barth on the temporal side of election. Election, Jenson writes, is "God's will—its eternity undi-minished—as an event in history . . . an event which occurred in time at the Cross."[130] One does not find talk of a primal history in Jenson's theology, but greater stress on God *as* a history. "God is an *event*; history occurs not only in him but as his being."[131] The election of God, as a self-constituting decision, has Christ in his sufferings and his resurrection as its focal points. Accordingly, these temporal events define God's eternity.

Temporal events belong to God's eternity. How, though, are the whence and whither of divine eternity reconciled through Christ's passion, death, and resurrection? For Jenson, the answer lies in the divine activity that surrounds Jesus' resurrection, but the narrative lead-up to Christ's

127. Jenson, *STh*, 1:219.

128. Jenson, *STh*, 1:65.

129. Jenson, *STh*, 1:72–73, 140. One difference lies in Jenson's concept of Christ's post-existence. See Rice, "Timely, Transcendent, and Alive."

130. Jenson, *Alpha and Omega*, 163, 165. See also Jenson, "Jesus in the Trinity," 317; Jenson, *STh*, 2:175–78.

131. Jenson, *STh*, 1:221. However, Jenson does speak of an inner-trinitarian history. See Jenson, "The Great Transformation," 41.

victory is also significant. Jesus' life as a whole, Jenson states, is "selfless obedience to the Father's mission." The obedience of Jesus culminates in the sacrificial prayer of his dying: "My God, my God, why have you forsaken me?" (Matt 27:46).[132] As noted previously, the moment of Christ's cry of dereliction and subsequent death raises the question of whether God subsists as the *one* God or turns into a "mutually betraying pantheon."[133] Given that Christ's death does not undermine the truth of God's oneness, the abiding unity of God in the death of Christ can be attributed to the Spirit as the mediating principle of the Father-Son relation. Jenson conceives of the Son's undertaking of death this way, or his state in-between the moment of his final breath and resurrection. In Jenson's words, "the unity of the crucified Son with the risen Son is posited in the essential unity between this Father and this Spirit."[134] The Spirit, as the power by which God raises the Son, "already rested on the Son," evident throughout his ministry and, tellingly, in the anticipatory way that the Spirit precedes and enables the Son's birth to Mary.[135] From conception to death and to new life again, the Spirit abides in and with the Son, and so—again, given that the divine unity holds—it can be said that the Spirit rests on the Son *through* the temporal events of death and resurrection.

Christ's life and death are marked by the triune activity of God. The resurrection, however, has special importance in Jenson's understanding of the way that the whence and whither of God's eternity are united. In order to demonstrate this I show how the notion of the divine whence and whither's unity applies to the content and actuality of God's will, here specified in terms of the self-determining act of God in time.

Recall that for Jenson the whence of God stands in for the divine Father, and the whither of God for the Holy Spirit. Whence and whither are "indomitably reconciled" in Christ's resurrection insofar as in this event two movements in God coincide: the divine willing and its temporal realization.[136] First, what the Father "eternally initiates" from the beginning is Christ.[137] The Father wills Jesus, victorious over sin and death. Jenson iterates, "death is time's ultimate act."[138] Death is the fate of all creaturely things, and, as stated above, the threat that God also faces in the crucifixion of Jesus. But for Jesus

132. Jenson, *STh*, 1:192.

133. Jenson, *STh*, 1:65.

134. Jenson, *STh*, 1:200.

135. Jenson, *STh*, 1:200; Jenson, "Conceptus . . . De Spiritu Sancto," 105–6.

136. Jenson, *STh*, 1:219.

137. Jenson, *STh*, 2:27.

138. Jenson, *STh*, 1:219.

death is not the ultimate end of the Father's will. Rather, in Christ's cry of dereliction and his entry into death the unity of God holds. The divine life remains intact because, now turning to the second movement, the Spirit brings the Father's willing to perfection. As the goal of the Father's will, the Spirit actualizes the Father's intentions in liberating Jesus from death.[139] Put another way, the Spirit raises Jesus into "a future that, because death is past ... must be unlimited." But since "only God's future is unlimited," Jesus' being raised is also described as his "entry into God."[140]

These two movements hang together in Jesus, the content of the Father's will and the actuality of the Spirit's dynamism.[141] Or, adapted to the concepts of whence and whither from above: what the Father wills as the whence of God's eternity, and what the Spirit as the whither of God's eternity brings forth from the Father's will to be reality, is Jesus, risen from the dead. The whence and whither of God, the end points of God's eternity, are thus reconciled in this temporal event. God is eternal in an imminently historical way.

2.3: Divine Envelopment

For Jenson, the temporality of God's being is unique to God. God possesses God's future, as well as God's past, in a way that creatures do not. Nothing in created reality is identical to it. And yet, God's identity is wrapped up in time and temporal events, specifically Christ's death and resurrection. There is both identity and distinction between God and the creaturely reality of time. I return to the pressing issues on this relation in the concluding analysis of Jenson's theology in section 3, for one of the outstanding questions is how God actually transcends the world given the deeply constitutive nature of the crucifixion and resurrection, *as* temporal events, for God's being. In this sub-section I treat a few other related questions: How does Jenson understand God's relation to time more generally? Jenson ascribes time to God's being. What does this mean for time as a created thing? And does God move in the process of time itself? The answer to these questions lie in Jenson's doctrine of creation and his trinitarian conception of God's envelopment of time.

I begin with Jenson's theory on the relation between eternity and the nature of religion that reaches back to some of his earliest works.[142] Not all of

139. Jenson, *STh*, 2:27.
140. Jenson, *STh*, 1:143.
141. Jenson, *STh*, 2:26–27.
142. See esp. Jenson, *A Religion against Itself.*

Jenson's theory is relevant to the questions we are addressing above on God's relation time. I start with it here insofar as it offers some initial perspective on the relation between eternity and time in Jenson's theology, specifically regarding Jenson's temporal understanding of God's being.

According to Jenson, to be human is to posit eternity. There are multiple forms of eternity. "There are as many eternities," Jenson claims, "as there are styles of life, as there are cultures and faiths with each its way of living in the present between past and future."[143] The reason for this, Jenson argues, lies primarily in the time-bound nature of creaturely existence. Whether the concrete past will somehow align with the openness of the future is a source of creaturely anxiety. Eternity, from the creaturely point of view, serves to unite past and future. Eternity is the overarching reality that cuts through temporal life and gives it a greater sense of purpose, a sense that something (or someone) unites the whole.

Eternity makes the stories that give life meaning possible, at least the grand stories that make the world in which we live, as Jenson often describes this, dramatically coherent.[144] Jenson enumerates different versions of eternity. At the top of his list is Plato's eternity "of the *nunc stans*, the 'still now-moment.'" Jenson categorizes Plato's concept as the "eternity of persistence: it is the time*less*ness in which past and future cohere because there really is no future, the stasis in which all things already are everything that they ever will be."[145] As expected, Jenson sets this perspective against the biblical conception. It is evident on the pages of Scripture that God is not eternal as somehow immune to time. God is deeply involved in the temporal proceedings of the world. God's eternity is not timeless. Rather, it is the gift of freedom for all things in time, just as they are, "for what they are not yet." God's eternity is "triumphant temporality" that gives time—a future—to others.[146] This temporal conception of eternity hinges on God's trinitarian being. As Jenson states, "the specificity of the triune God is not that he is three, but that he occupies each pole of time as a *persona dramatis*."[147] God relates to time, and opens up a future for creatures in time, by enveloping temporal creation.

To articulate this notion of divine envelopment Jenson relies on two concepts from classical trinitarian theology. The first has already been

143. Jenson, *Story and Promise*, 105.

144. Jenson, *STh*, 1:55.

145. Jenson, *Story and Promise*, 106.

146. Jenson, *Story and Promise*, 107.

147. Jenson, *STh*, 1:89. Timo Tavast looks at Jenson's notion of eternity in religion as a form of negative natural theology. "The Identification of the Triune God," 155–63, esp. 157, 162.

noted. This is the Cappadocian principle in which the divine acts *ad extra* are at once singular acts of God and three-fold according to their trinitarian structure: God acts from the Father, through the Son, in the Spirit. Jenson adapts the Cappadocian principle into his own idiom to describe God's creating activity: "God the Father is the sheer given of creation; God the Spirit is the perfecting Freedom that animates creation; God the Son is the mediator of creation."[148] To this Jenson adds Thomas Aquinas' doctrine of subsistent relations. According to this doctrine the relations between the divine persons are not accidental features of a more basic and essential divine nature. Rather, as subsisting relations in the divine nature they are identical to the divine essence.[149] Together, the classical concepts indicate both the three-fold and encompassing activity of God in creation as well as the unitary nature of God's acts *ad extra*. I return to Jenson's invocation of these classical concepts and their implications for understanding God's relation to time in the concluding part of this chapter. For now, the key point to note is that God's bracketing of created reality, as the one God, leads Jenson to posit a notion of creation as situated *within* the divine life.

In a sort of riff on the Lutheran understanding of Christ's real presence in the sacrament, God encompasses created reality, at once, as behind, with, and ahead of it. Jenson describes this embracing presence in terms of an "accommodation" for what is other than God in the very being of God itself. "In himself, [God] *opens room*, and that act is the event of creation."[150] As is clear, accommodation introduces a spatial conception into Jenson's primarily temporal idea of God and the God-world relation. The temporal space within the divine bracketing of creation is the room that God makes for creatures. In God we "live and move and have our being" (Acts 17:28). That the creature is both included and yet remains a creature and not God in the self-accommodation of God for others is ensured by the reality of the Spirit. The Spirit, on one hand, "draws to and into the triune converse those for whom the Trinity makes room."[151] The Spirit brings the creature into God. On the other, the Spirit is the condition of the creature's abiding alterity in and from God. By means of the Spirit, as the future of God, there is difference in God, although not other than Godself. As noted before, the Spirit is God's future: "God *anticipates* his future and so possesses it."[152] This internal

---

148. Jenson, *STh*, 2:25. Jenson's articulation is influenced by John of Damascus' inflection of the Cappadocian principle.

149. See Aquinas, *Summa Theologica*, 1.29.

150. Jenson, *STh*, 2:25.

151. Jenson, *STh*, 2:26.

152. Jenson, *STh*, 2:121.

differentiation within God's being is the grounds by which the creature, and with it, all creation, can be assumed at once into the divine life without being subsumed by the sheer singularity of God's being.[153] Difference in God enables the creature's participation in God *as* creature. Jenson thus gives a spatial and temporally stylized conception of the Spirit's relation to the Father and Son akin to what other theologians conceive as the place for others in God as grounded in the Father-Son relation.[154]

Jenson continues in this way of specifying God's relation to creation along trinitarian lines. Expanding on his previous application of the Cappadocian principle, Jenson identifies the Father as the sheer given of creation and the *arche* of God's being. The Father is "the absolute Antecedent of all possible other reality."[155] The Father as such posits all being. Jenson uses a hypothetical articulation to identify the Spirit's creative role. If the Father is the principle of being in God, then the Spirit "frees the Father from retaining all being with himself, and so frees what the Father initiates from being the mere emanation it would have been were the Father God by himself."[156] The Spirit bears a heavy load here. For the Spirit does this as the principle of alterity in God, who both makes it possible for creation to derive from God alone, creation *ex nihilo*, and enables creation to be accommodation for others in the life of God. Importantly, as God's future the Spirit brings the Father's will to its rightful end. The Spirit's animating power and the Father's will have their dynamism and content in the second person of the Trinity. Specifically, they have their dynamism and content in Jesus as a figure in time and space.[157] All of the divine ways *ad extra* have his history with us as a kind of anchoring point in identifying God. The importance of the divine Son's historical identification will become clear momentarily. Once more, the roles of the divine identities result in temporal appropriations: the Father with time past as the will before all things; the Spirit with time future as the carrier and fulfillment of the Father's will; and the Son with time present, in whom the Father's will and the Spirit's power come to fruition. These temporal appropriations instance the converse side of creation's accommodation in the divine life: God *envelops* temporal creation.

A final point of clarification is helpful here. I have referenced Jenson's notion that "the Son mediates the Father's originating and the Spirit's

153. Jenson, *STh*, 2:26.

154. E.g., Balthasar, *Theo-Drama*, 323–24; Pannenberg, *ST*, 2:27–30. See also Eugene R. Schlesinger's way of situating Jenson's theology in relation to the tradition on this point. Schlesinger, "Trinity," 199–201.

155. Jenson, *STh*, 2:25.

156. Jenson, *STh*, 2:26.

157. Jenson, *STh*, 2:26–27.

liberating." Similarly, Jesus is the content of the Father's will and the means by which the Spirit is actual among us.[158] There is directionality in God, a movement of God toward us, expressed in the divine envelopment of creation. However, while Jenson intends this envelopment to rest on a trinitarian thought pattern—the Father before, the Son in, and the Spirit as the future of temporal creation—created reality does not fit within the divine being in a straightforward way. Specifically, there is no literal partitioning of the Father before and the Spirit ahead of creation. There are two reasons for this. The first lies in the identity of the Son. The divine Son, writes Jenson, "has his own individual entity *within* created time, in that he is himself one of those among whom and upon whom creatures' participation in God's story is being 'worked out.'"[159] Insofar as God's identity hinges on the Son, for he is the content of the Father's will and the actuality of the Spirit's dynamism, God's way of enveloping temporal creation gets intertwined with the desired movements of God in the world. Jesus is distinctly the divine Son, but his being *in time* includes also the presence of the Father and the Spirit (Luke 3:22; John 14:11). The second reason gives further expression to the first and can be put quite simply. If God is one, God must envelop created time in the process of time itself. Jenson expresses this idea in the succinct claim: "The envelopment of our time by God is itself accomplished *in* the course of our time."[160]

How then for Jenson does God relate to the movement of time? The Trinity of God's being requires two answers to be given. First and more straightforwardly, through the Son God exists *in* time. This is true for Jesus, a figure in time and space. And as just described, it pertains also to the Father and Spirit in their living unity with the Son as the one God. Of course, more could be said here regarding the gift of the Spirit at Pentecost and the Spirit's presence in the church. Second and more complex, time is contingent on God. Time, as Augustine stated, is a created thing. It is therefore at the disposal of the creator. Jenson's trinitarian theology adds a layer of depth to this. His trinitarian formulations are not simple borrowings of temporality as a useful category for identifying God. It works the other way around, or at least it can. And herein lies the key point: time has its basis in the inner-trinitarian relations of God. God's being is "the archetype of all times."[161] "What we know as time is located within and enabled by [the

158. Jenson, *STh*, 2:27.

159. Jenson, *STh*, 2:27.

160. Jenson, *STh*, 2:27. Emphasis mine.

161. Jenson, "*Ipse Pater Non Est Impassibilis*," 124. Related to this is Jenson's rejection of simple linear and circular conceptions of time. Jenson proposes a concept of narrative time based in the complex of the inner-trinitarian relations. 121–24.

narrative] structure" of God's triunity.[162] For this reason time is an accommodation in the life of God. How then does God relate to time? To the first affirmation of God's movement in time (through the Son), there must be paired a second affirmation of time's movement in and through God. And this because God envelops time—albeit from within time itself—as Father, Son, and Spirit. Both answers are present in Jenson's short statement: "God takes time in his time for us."[163] God *has* time, the temporality proper to the personal relations of the Trinity; and God *takes* time, the created time that God envelops and makes God's own through the Son.

3: Trinity, Temporal Transcendence, and Eternity

In this chapter I have laid out Robert W. Jenson's narrative ontology of the Trinity and his understanding of the God-world relation. Jenson conceives of God in a radically temporal way. "God is an *event*," he writes, "history occurs not only in him but as his being."[164] I noted at the outset that the goal of this chapter was to glean a conception of divine transcendence in keeping with the Pannenberg inspired description of the triune God's movement in history and the process of time from the previous chapter. Neither Jenson's temporal ontology nor the way that he conceives of certain temporal events as constitutive of God's being preclude such a concept of transcendence. Rather, as I show, the radical historicism of Jenson's distinct understanding of God enables it. For the very resolve of Jenson to fixate on God in relation to us proffers a comprehensively temporal notion of transcendence. The key to this notion of transcendence, situated within the context of God with us, lies in Jenson's trinitarianism.

The constructive analysis that follows is divided into three sub-sections. In the first sub-section I argue for the central thesis of this chapter, the temporal understanding of divine transcendence. This is done by building on the critical assessment of Barth's theory of correspondence and, more prominently, Pannenberg's concept of futurity from the previous chapter and section 1 above. In the second sub-section I consider the relevance of this temporal understanding of transcendence in relation to some of the main arguments of this work. The final sub-section fills out the Pannenberg inspired account of God's relation to history from chapter 3. There, with the understanding of temporal transcendence in place, I show how Jenson's idea of envelopment adds a necessary and complementary

162. Jenson, *STh*, 2:35.

163. Jenson, *STh*, 2:35.

164. Jenson, *STh*, 1:221.

point to the understanding of God's movement in the process of time. The triune God is also the transcendent source of created history's movement through the Father's initiating will, the Spirit as the bringer of eschatological fulfillment, and their unity in Jesus the Son.

Temporal Transcendence

How is the triune God transcendent? Specifically, how does the Trinity transcend the revelatory history of God with others without suggesting a two-fold history of God, one in eternity above and another here below? How do we avoid the perception of two trinities? We have yet to find a fully satisfactory answer to these questions. In chapter 2 I showed how Karl Barth's theory of divine correspondence between the antecedent Trinity and the being of God in revelation risks positing a kind of ongoing correspondence *in* revelation itself, and so two distinct histories of God. On this view the triune God would transcend history by not really abiding in it at all. Of course, Barth does not say this. Rather, it is a potential implication of his theory of correspondence that results from a lack of reflection on the significance of configuring the eternal Trinity and the God-world relation in light of Christ's concrete history. I went on to argue that Barth rectifies the problem of conceiving of the eternal Trinity through the incarnation of the Son in his doctrine of election. God assumes Christ's history into the eternal life of God in such a way as to eliminate the notion of a two-fold history of God. Elsewhere in Barth's doctrine of election, however, another issue surfaces. Barth resorts to a "primal history" of God in order to describe the divine decision. Moreover, Barth claims that this decision "occurs in the very midst of time *no less than* in the far distant pre-temporal eternity."[165] Admittedly, there is more than one way to explicate Barth's claims around the primal history of God and the actuality of divine election in eternity and in time. Unfortunately, Barth's formulations do not rule out the view that pits the eternity of God, specifically the pre-temporality of God's electing, against the actualization of election in time. Again, the transcendent reality of God can appear to lie in an ulterior domain of God, a kind of divine history that either occurs before or that runs strangely parallel to God's history with us.

Similar problems emerge in Pannenberg's theology. I draw attention to one of the pertinent examples here. In his mature theology Pannenberg endorses the Plotinus based view of time's simultaneous presence to God. "All time is before the eyes of God as a whole."[166] Pannenberg uses the doctrine

---

165. Barth, *CD* II/2:8, 185–86. Emphasis mine.
166. Pannenberg, *ST*, 1:331.

of the Trinity, specifically the diversity of relations of the divine persons, as the basis for time's simultaneous presence to God in its different dimensions, from creation to the future eschatological consummation. But it seems that Pannenberg does not carry out this application of Trinity to the eternal God's relation to time far enough. Pannenberg's claim that the "eternal God does not have ahead of him any future that could be distinguished from his present" denotes a sense of eternity as divine timelessness.[167] However, Pannenberg's mature theology contains a series of claims on the theme of divine futurity, a notion that was even more prominent in his earlier work, that would render a different (i.e., not a timeless) view of eternity possible, namely, God's activity from the eschatological future. But Pannenberg does not develop this line of thought substantially in his mature theology. The Plotinus based view of God's presence to time as a whole stands front and center. And on that view the problem of a lack of temporal distinction in God is significant. For if all time is present to God without differentiation, what meaning does the process as well as the individual moments of the Son's incarnation in time have for God? Or, to take a step back, what is the possibility in God's being, in God's eternity, for *becoming* temporally incarnate? Adapting the foundational question of this study inspired by Isaak A. Dorner's theology from chapter 1, we can ask: How do we square a concept of timeless eternity with the temporal vitality of God in revelation? More to the point here, on the timeless view of eternity God clearly transcends temporal reality. But it is a concept of transcendent divine reality that is fraught with problems around negating the significance of the temporal movements of God in revelation history.

In section 1 of this chapter I argued that a *temporal* concept of transcendence is needed. Pannenberg gets us moving in the right direction here. His early concept of futurity is a radical take on divine transcendence insofar as it works to conceive of divine alterity as God's abiding relation to the present movement of time. God straddles the present from the future as the generative source of every momentary happening. God is the power of the future. My criticisms of this notion were two-fold: conceptually, Pannenberg does not develop his early notion of futurity and as a result it remains too closely identified with an abstract concept of future time. This becomes most problematic, however, in Pannenberg's later theology and his inclusion of the just noted Plotinus based concept of eternity alongside his continued references to God's futurity. For in this way abstract divine futurity, present to time as a whole, risks denoting a concept of eternity by which the future

---

167. Pannenberg, *ST*, 1:410; Pannenberg, *Systematische Theologie*, 1:443. English translation slightly altered.

is not merely known to God but is already real. On this view the future has a kind of literal ontological presence to God that undermines the authenticity of temporal history. Second and practically, the abstract nature of Pannenberg's idea of radical futurity prevents it from serving as the object of faith. Still, the basic structure of Pannenberg's concept of futurity for conceiving transcendence is right and should be emulated: God transcends temporal reality from within the contours of time itself.

We are in need of a more carefully defined concept of temporal transcendence. Jenson's theology shows itself as an obvious candidate for this. As he states in his early work, *God after God*, God's "transcendence is his futurity to what already is."[168] The claim, of course, could have just as easily been made by the early Pannenberg. But what gives Jenson's theology an edge over Pannenberg's in this case lies in Jenson's more robust application of the doctrine of the Trinity to the categories of transcendence, eternity, and his conception of the God-world relation as a whole. Trinity is the controlling concept of Jenson's theology. What difference this makes becomes clear in what follows. Gathering together the points from the explication of Jenson's theology in sections 1 and 2 of this chapter, I show below how Jenson's trinitarian theology enables a notion of temporal transcendence in three steps: first, in terms of Jenson's temporal idea of God; second, in terms of the directionality of God's temporal being; and third, in terms of God's transcendence in (or by) temporal events. At each step it is the idea of God as triune that secures a notion of God's eternality and historical being as one and the same—that is, the temporal notion of transcendence that we are seeking.

From the early criticisms of Barth's and Pannenberg's theology to his doctrine of creation, Jenson advocates a temporal idea of deity. Based on the eschatological orientation of God's involvement in revelation history, Jenson posits a temporal ontology in which the being of God dramatically coheres. God's being as such is not only oriented toward the future, but in the death and resurrection events of Christ the being of God is constituted by and through temporal events. I focus on this last point in step three below. Jenson's temporal ontology, however, ultimately rests on his ascriptions of the dimensions of time to the divine identities; the divine past of the Father, the divine future of the Spirit, and the divine present of the Son. For Jenson, these ascriptions follow from the revealed activity of the divine persons as well as the traditional understanding of the eternal relations of origin (inclusive of divine ends). At the most basic level, the positing of temporalities among the divine persons highlights the analogy between the Trinity of God's being and the temporal world. God is both

168. Jenson, *God after God*, 159.

triune and the supreme creator. It thus makes sense to say that God is "the archetype of all times."[169] To invoke the idiom of Dorner's question once more, the eternity of God is (doctrinally) reconciled with the temporal vitality of God among us insofar as the eternality of God's being is temporal. Eternity and time are compatible.

There remains, however, a basic distinction between the temporal eternity of God and the reality of creaturely time. The difference is grounded in the configuration of time within the divine life. The temporality of God's eternal being is God's own. This is the time between the divine persons: based on the Father and Son's relation to the Spirit, "God *anticipates* his future and so possesses it."[170] God is the source of God's future. This self-possessed future distinguishes the temporality of God's being from the way in which creatures anticipate a future in time separate from themselves. The self-possessed futurity of God, or the Father and Son's unity with the Spirit, is the temporal form that is distinctly proper to God's being. Two notions are therefore at play here: On one hand, created time is grounded in the Trinity of God's being. The time of creatures, based on the divine prerogative, is founded in the temporality of God. And yet, on the other, in light of God's self-possessed future, the time of God's being is unique to God. Unlike God, no creature possesses its future within itself. *Both* the compatibility as well as the distinction of God's temporal eternity and created time hold based on a single reality: the triunity of God's being. Trinity funds the dialectical reality of God's relation to and difference from the creaturely reality of time. By means of the Spirit God is temporal and transcendent being. Thus God is in time yet "no temporal process can keep pace with him."[171] This first step establishes the basic point that God's triunity entails both a sense of identity with and distinction from created time.

But this is only a first step. A second must be taken if we are to avoid the problem identified in Barth's theory of divine correspondence from chapter 2. For while the above opens up the notion of God's compatibility with temporality, it does not fully secure against the temptation to conceive, even if only implicitly, of the eternality of God over against the being of God in time, God with us. In fact, the very uniqueness of divine temporality, God's self-possessed futurity, when emphasized and set in contrast to created time, may actually serve to reinforce the two-fold or bifurcated idea of God in eternity above and God in time below. What is required then is attention to the way in which God assumes God's history with others

169. Jenson, "*Ipse Pater Non Est Impassibilis*," 124.

170. Jenson, *STh*, 2:121.

171. Jenson, *STh*, 1:216.

into the divine being. In other words, it is important to understand how revelation history is part of God's identity. To reference again Kathryn Tanner's important statement from chapter 2: "Even if the very same [triune] relations are simply being extended into the mission they undertake for us, when they incorporate the human in a situation of sin and death through the Word's incarnation, the relations that the members of the trinity have with one another come to reflect that fact."[172]

This point comes to the fore in Jenson's theology through his consistent identification of the second person of the Trinity with Jesus. Absent from Jenson's theology, and even explicitly rejected, is an abstract concept of the *Logos asarkos*.[173] The divine Son "has his own individual entity *within* created time."[174] For our purposes this means that there can be no real conception of the eternal Trinity and the configuration of God's unique time—the Father with the divine past, the Spirit with the divine future, and the Son as their specious present—that understands the Son and his present existence apart from his being as God for us and with us *in* time. The eternal Trinity, in the very uniqueness of the divine temporality, includes Jesus' temporal identity. There can be no real conception of a bifurcated notion of God in eternity above and God in time below, the image of two trinities, because the economic history of the divine Son is assumed into God's being. It gets assumed into God's being insofar as the identity of the second person of the Trinity is Jesus, a figure in time and space. There is no other Son, only Jesus. Put another way, there is a kind of directionality to God's being, the historic movement of God *with* us in the Son that gets taken up into the divine life.

Of course, this raises critical questions. Before moving to the third step, I first consider the objection of Pannenberg noted at the beginning of this chapter. In a review of Jenson's *Systematic Theology* Pannenberg states that "in Jenson's presentation, the difference between the 'immanent' Trinity, the eternal communion of Father, Son, and Spirit, and the 'economic' Trinity almost vanishes." He continues, "without that distinction, the reality of the one God tends to be dissolved into the process of the world."[175] Regarding

---

172. Tanner, *Christ the Key*, 180.

173. See Jenson, "Once More the *Logos Asarkos*," 130–33.

174. Jenson, *STh*, 2:27.

175. Pannenberg, "Systematic Theology," 49–53. Thomas G. Weinandy goes so far as to say that "for Jenson, God comes to be who he is by acting in a triune manner within the course of history and so becomes trinitarian." Weinandy, "God and Human Suffering," 102. For Jenson's response to Weinandy see Jenson, "*Ipse Pater Non Est Impassibilis*," 118–19. The passages I go on to reference from Jenson in addressing Pannenberg's claim sufficiently refute Weinandy's charge of a trinitarian self-discovery of God in time.

the difference between the immanent and the economic Trinity, Pannenberg is right in at least one sense. Jenson does not freely conceive of an immanent Trinity apart from the being of God with us. This point requires some unpacking. Jenson does affirm that God would still be triune if God had not decided upon being in relation to us, though more than this we cannot say.[176] Moreover, Jenson acknowledges a notion of the immanent Trinity and its priority in relation to the economic Trinity. As noted before, Jenson asserts that "the Spirit is God's *freedom*," and the Spirit "has this role *first* in God himself."[177] Perhaps most importantly for Jenson, the immanent structure of God's being determines God's acts *ad extra*. Stated clearly, "there is a birth of the *Logos* as God," the eternal generation of the divine Son, that "enables and therefore must be somehow antecedent to his birth as man."[178] But although Jenson admits of the place of the antecedent or immanent Trinity, the more urgent consideration here is whether his insistence on a conception of God in relation to us results in anything like the tendency that Pannenberg notes of a collapse of God into the world process.

I do not think so. One reason for the permanent distinction between the eternal Trinity and the world process has to do with the unique temporality proper to the abiding triunity of God's being that distinguishes God from created time. But we can also consider Jenson's trinitarian notion of divine envelopment. Jenson latches onto the Son's revealed identity as the man Jesus. There is no *Logos asarkos* capable of being identified as other than him. And yet, Jesus is also the second member of the Godhead. As the second member of the Trinity the Son is one with the Father and the Holy Spirit. The Father is the unoriginate origin of all things, and the Spirit is the power of creation's future. The Son is thus present in time as one with the creative origin and end of all things. One with the creative Father and Spirit, the whole of temporal reality, a created thing, is at the disposal of the Trinity. There can be therefore no sheer collapse of the eternal Trinity into the world process insofar as all things remain at the mercy of God's creative and sustaining grace. To be sure, through the Son the triune God makes an accommodation for created reality in the divine life. God envelops creation. But because God is triune this envelopment also entails the free and sovereign transcendence of God over all that God has made. Even as God exists in time, God's creative agency holds through the unity of the divine persons.

---

176. Jenson, *STh*, 1:221. But see also Jenson, "Once More the *Logos Asarkos*," 130–32.

177. Jenson, *On the Inspiration of Scripture*, 33. Latter emphasis mine. See also Jenson, *STh*, 1:215.

178. Jenson, *STh*, 1:141.

A third and final step toward a notion of temporal transcendence concerns the relationship between God and specific events in time. If the second step involved locating divine transcendence within the context of the divine appropriation of the Son's temporal identity, along with his temporal life, the third step intensifies this problematic by means of the triune God's identification *with* temporal events. As Jenson poignantly puts this, "the way in which the whence and whither of the divine life are one, the way in which the triune God is eternal, is by the events of Jesus' death and resurrection."[179] In this third step I show how God's identification with temporal events includes the mode of God's transcendence. The trinitarian logic that underlies Jenson's theology can be applied to any act of God *ad extra*. I focus on the definitive events in the quote above, namely, the transcendent nature of God in the death and resurrection of Jesus. More specifically, I argue that Jenson's understanding of the resurrection, conveyed along trinitarian lines, reveals how God is temporal and transcendent at the same time.

The movement from Jesus' suffering and death to his resurrection, in Jenson's account, shows how temporal events are included within the divine life. From Jesus' cry of God-abandonment to his victory over death, God is either the one God or a "mutually betraying pantheon."[180] The unity of God remains intact because of God's triunity; the Spirit maintains the Father-Son relation. To include these events in the divine life, as God does, is to include them in, or even equate them, with God's eternity. In the exposition from section 2 of this chapter I showed how this fits within Jenson's understanding of eternity as that which brackets finite reality from its temporal ends (past and future). In terms of Jenson's temporal appropriations in God, whence (Father) and whither (Spirit) are one in Jesus' death and resurrection insofar as what the Father eternally initiates, on one end, and what the Spirit liberates as the goal of all things, on the other, are one and the same: Christ, triumphant over sin and death. God's eternity includes, even hinges upon, a temporal event. However, does this reduce eternity to temporality, or at least an entirely temporal schematic? What remains of eternity? The answer to these questions, as well as the transcendent nature of divine eternity, come into view by considering more closely the relationship between the resurrection and the trinitarian structure of God's being.

Jenson describes the resurrection as Jesus' "entry into God."[181] We have already shown how for Jenson God does not become triune in time. Nor is this sense of Jesus' entry into the divine life a form of adoptionism, given

179. Jenson, *STh*, 1:219.
180. Jenson, *STh*, 1:65.
181. Jenson, *STh*, 1:143.

Jenson's strong identification of the eternal Son with the man Jesus and his assertion on the eternal Son's generation from the Father as what enables the birth of the divine *Logos* to Mary in time.[182] This entryway into God can be described in two different ways. First, the Son is sent by the Father for the sake of his divine mission in the world. His resurrection brings his mission to completion whereby he returns to sit at the Father's right hand. This movement in the divine life, Jesus' return or entry into God, does not designate a point of worldly absence on the part of the Son. Just as his unity with the Father holds in being sent *from* the Father, so too does his return to God include his abiding presence among us (John 10:30; Matt 28:20). Again, we recall that God's space is not merely set over against the world; God envelops created reality. Second, Jenson characterizes the resurrection as entry into God because of what it demarcates in time. For the risen Jesus, death is now a thing of the past. And with death behind him, Jesus lives unconstrained; he lives by means of the futurity that belongs to God alone.[183] Risen from the dead, Jesus possesses unlimited life. Resurrection, as Jenson puts it, is Christ's "life in the future."[184] There is a key point of alignment here. The language of futurity that Jenson invokes around the resurrection of Jesus as his entry into God is infused with his description of the Spirit's identity and role in the Godhead. The Spirit is the futurity of God that rests on Christ in his mission. Moreover, by means of the Spirit "God *anticipates* his future and so possesses it."[185] This claim for Jenson does not indicate an abstract futurity in God. Rather, it has to do with the internal nature of God's transcendence in the Spirit, the power by which God's being—in itself and among us—is *"unboundedly* lively."[186]

Raised by the Father into the futurity of God the Spirit, the resurrection of Jesus is a trinitarian act. It is therefore also a transcendent act of God in time. Insofar as God assumes the events of the passion and resurrection into God's being, God is eternal in a temporal way. God's eternity takes shape in the manifestation and outplaying of the inner-relations of the Trinity in temporal events. And yet, the temporal inclusion of Christ's death and resurrection into the being of God does *not* reduce divine eternity to the confines of creaturely time and events. Nor, going back to Pannenberg, does the near conflation of the immanent Trinity with the divine economy in Jenson's theology dissolve the eternal Trinity into the world

---

182. Jenson, *STh*, 1:141.

183. Jenson, "A Christological Answer," 41; Jenson, *STh*, 1:143.

184. Jenson, *STh*, 1:143.

185. Jenson, *STh*, 2:121.

186. Jenson, *STh*, 1:143; Jenson, *STh*, 2:121.

process. Neither is the case because the manifestation and outplaying of the inner-relations of the Trinity in temporal events *include* the basic mode of God's transcendence—the transcendent life of the Trinity itself. While this involves the members of the Trinity as a whole, the focal point here falls on the Spirit. Through the Spirit as the self-possessed futurity of God's being God is unbounded life. Therefore when God acts in time, and even structures divine eternity around the events of Christ's death and resurrection, God acts from and through the transcendent vitality that God is. God can act in time, can assume temporal events into God's being, without loss to the transcendent nature of God's eternity. God can, because God's triunity is not only the means by which God acts in time and assumes temporal events into the divine life, but because God's triunity is also the means of God's transcendence. Through the triunity of God's being God acts among us and transcends what is at one and the same time.

Herein lies the temporal notion of divine transcendence sought after in this chapter. The key is the doctrine of the Trinity. As described in step one, in Jenson's theology the trinitarian nature of God is convertible with a temporal understanding of God's being. Consequently, the trinitarian being of God, while distinct from all that is through its unique temporality, is compatible with the world of creaturely time. Detailed in step two, this compatibility precludes the idea of two divine histories, God above and God below. For Jenson's focus on God with us entails that God assumes the economic reality of Jesus the Son into the very depths of God's being. At the same time, this conception can be paired with Jenson's idea of divine envelopment to show how God's being does not become part and parcel of the world process, for God transcends the world that God indwells through the mutuality of the divine persons. Similarly, as laid out in step three, God's identification with the temporal events of Christ's cross and resurrection do not result in a conflation of God and the world. For these events, as the self-enactment of the triune God among us, are characterized by the unbounded vitality of the inner-trinitarian relations of God. At each step, the vitality of God's real and transcendent relation to history is predicated on the Trinity of God's being. Because God is triune God transcends time from within the strictures of time itself.

Critical Comparisons

I began the previous sub-section with an outline of some of the major criticisms of this work around Barth's and Pannenberg's theology that illuminate the need for a temporal conception of divine transcendence. Having set forth the notion of temporal transcendence in Jenson's theology, we can now ask how this concept directly relates to some of the main arguments of this work. The first point was directed toward Barth's theory of correspondence and the idea of a primal history of God, with the implication of an ulterior history of God that runs parallel to, and hence undermines, the reality of God's history with us. The temporal concept of divine transcendence from Jenson's theology addresses this point in a fairly straightforward way. The key idea in Jenson's notion of transcendence is that the way in which God lies beyond the world *includes* God's indwelling of it, not as two separate realities but as a single truth of God's being. For Jenson's temporal ontology has to do with God's relation to and difference from created reality as grounded in the selfsame nature of God's trinitarian being. In the same way, God acts in time, and even takes temporal events into the eternality of God's being, without succumbing to the world process.

The other critical points focused on Pannenberg's theology. First, the notion of eternity in Jenson's theology avoids the slip into timelessness that comes to the fore in Pannenberg's statement, the "eternal God does not have ahead of him any future that could be distinguished from his present."[187] Jenson's notion of eternity does not fall prey to a notion of divine timelessness insofar as temporality remains essential to God's eternity through the trinitarian pattern of God's being as a unity-in-distinctions. Specifically, the Spirit as the divine future can be distinguished from God's present (and past)—for the Spirit is neither the Son nor the Father—and yet the Holy Spirit exists in eternal union with God's present (and past)— for the Spirit, Son, and Father are the one God. Put another way, the temporality of God's being is, again, unique to God alone; the self-possessed futurity of God's being, the divine unity, marks God as wholly distinct from creaturely reality. And yet the Spirit's distinction from the Father and the Son also marks the abiding sense of futurity's reality in God, the truth of the Spirit as the goal and telos of the divine relations. There is time in God because of the Spirit who proceeds in God's being. In short, Jenson avoids the problem of timeless being by conceiving of God's eternity at its greatest depth through the trinitarian idea of God.

The second criticism pertained to the problem of understanding the concept of futurity. Pannenberg's early concept of futurity appeals because of its dynamic notion of transcendence in time, or at least from the boundary point at which the future gives way to the present. However, without further developing this notion it is unclear in Pannenberg's theology how

---

187. Pannenberg, *ST*, 1:410; Pannenberg, *Systematische Theologie*, 1:443. English translation slightly altered.

this futurity connects to the character of God. An ambiguous notion of God as divine futurity cannot serve as the object of faith. The solution to this problem in Jenson's theology requires little explanation at this point. Futurity is not an abstract dimension of God's being. Rather, it is identified with the third person of the Trinity, the Holy Spirit. Faith in the future of God is to trust in the power by which God is present and transcends, trust in the power through which God makes all things new. Faith in the future of God is to trust in a person.

The third and final critical point is related to the connection between divine futurity and the future of created time. This follows in part from the second problem above. An underdeveloped notion of divine futurity risks being identified with the created future in a crassly literal way. On this view the future has a kind of ontological presence in divine eternity, turning the future into something that is present for God, proper to God's eternal now, or even something past in the divine life insofar as it is already real within God's eternity. The future as already played out in relation to God, a claim that goes beyond even the assertion of God's exhaustive foreknowledge of future events, would undermine the reality of the creaturely present, for God and creatures alike.

How does Jenson's theology enable a response to this problem? The key idea lies in Jenson's primary identification of futurity with the life of God in the Spirit. Above all, the future's presence to God is its presence as the Holy Spirit. This includes the Spirit's procession as the goal of the divine life and the way in which the Father and Son anticipate and thus possess their shared future in the Spirit. This opens up a distinct way to speak of the Spirit as creation's future. This secondary way of identifying the Spirit as futurity is not the same as the future of created time, but rather how the Spirit serves as the goal of the created order. The Spirit is the vitality of God's being who both animates the Father-Son relation and exists as the love that they share. The goal of creaturely beings is to participate in this relation. Therefore as the Spirit both frees the Father and Son for one another and exists *as* the endpoint of this relation, the divine love itself, the Spirit is likewise what creaturely beings long for in time, their future full inclusion in the divine loving. The Holy Spirit is the "first fruits" of the eschatological future (Rom 8:23). In sum, beginning with the trinitarian idea of God, and not with an abstract notion of temporality's place in divine eternity, allows for an alternative conception of the relation between divine reality and the future of created time. Divine futurity is not the created future as something already played out in the far reaches of God's eternity. Rather, in a shift of focus, futurity is firstly the eternal identity of God in the Spirit who stands in relation to creaturely reality as drawing all things to their rightful end in the presence of God.

Moving (in) History

I conclude this chapter with a brief addendum on what Jenson's idea of divine envelopment adds to the Pannenberg inspired conception of the triune God's movement *in* history from the previous chapter. I first review this notion and then turn to the way that Jenson's trinitarian theology allows for an understanding of the triune God as the *transcendent source* of history's movement. I then show the relevance of this point in relation to one of the major criticisms that Pannenberg levies against Barth's trinitarian theology in chapters 2 and 3.

My constructive appropriation of Pannenberg's trinitarian theology from chapter 3 centered on his concept of the dependent monarchy of God's being. The monarchy of God's being is already actualized in the eternal relations of God through the Son's acknowledgement of the Father's lordship in the Spirit. This pattern of relations precedes and grounds God's activity *ad extra*. Alongside the concept of the eternal actualization of the divine monarchy of God's being stands a second point, gleaned from Pannenberg's trinitarian formulations but also going beyond him. The divine monarchy exemplifies the movement of God's being. The critical point here is that the lordship of the Father, the unoriginate origin in God, rests on what derives from him: the Son and the Spirit. There is thus a telos, or even teloi, in God, not merely movement but a specific eschatological direction that underlies the divine monarchy of God's being. I argued that the nature of God's activity in time follows this pattern: God acts as the living God in history through the living fellowship of the divine persons. God's activity in history advances toward the eschatological end based on the eschatological nature of the Father, Son, and Spirit's fellowship. In a word, the triune God moves in history and the process of time.

This Pannenberg inspired conception describes the eschatological mode of God's existence *in* history. It provides a conceptual basis for scriptural claims like Deuteronomy 33:14: "My presence will go with you, and I will give you rest." Above all, it coheres with the dynamics of the incarnation and the activity of the Spirit in time. The basic aim of this chapter has been to uncover a notion of divine transcendence that aligns with this understanding of the triune God's presence and movement among us. The presence of the Lord God moves in history. In what follows I add on to the Pannenberg inspired account of God's movement in history by means of Jenson's idea of divine envelopment. God is present and active in history, but as Solomon's prayer at the dedication of the temple indicates, it is also true that "even heaven and the highest heaven cannot contain you" (1 Kgs 8:27).[188] At one and the same time, God both moves in history and transcends it. How God transcends history, however, allows us to specify God's relation to history as a whole and God's movement in history itself. Here I fill out one of the key implications of Jenson's doctrine of divine envelopment.

In the main features of Jenson's notion of envelopment the triune God brackets created reality, giving it its basic theological coordinates, through the divine unity. The Father is associated (but not exclusively) with the beginnings of created history, not simply once and for all but as he continually puts things into motion through his creative willing shaped by Jesus the Son. The Spirit is associated (not exclusively) with the future of created history, for the Spirit who perfects the Father's will draws created history toward its proper end, participation of creaturely beings in the Father-Son relation. The Son mediates the Father's primal beginnings and the eschatological thrust of the Spirit's activity as a figure in space and time. Consequently, God both exists in time and, as the creative source and goal of all temporal things, transcends time; time, as a created thing, remains at the disposal of the triune God.

Like the constructive appropriation of Pannenberg's trinitarian theology from chapter 3, Jenson's idea of divine envelopment supports a notion of the movement of God in history and the process of time. But Jenson's notion of divine envelopment allows us to say something more: the triune God also exists as the transcendent source of the movement of history itself. God moves history through God's trinitarian being insofar as God exists in time while simultaneously bracketing created history as its primal beginnings in the Father and the power that draws it toward its eschatological end in the Spirit. Or slightly tweaked, as the creative origin (Father) and telos of history (Spirit), and as the one who mediates these ends *in* time (Son), the movements of history, in the most basic sense of what history as God's creation is, namely, its theological sense, follow upon the eternal relations of God's being. As argued before in response to Pannenberg's criticism of Jenson on the immanent-economic Trinity relation, God is not one and the same as the process of history. However, the relation between God and created history, grounded in the self-determining life of the triune God, is nevertheless marked by a resolute sense of intimacy and commitment on the part of God to be God in relation to us. In God "we live and move and have our being" (Acts 17:28). To borrow an

---

188. Cf. Isaiah 66:1.

expression of Katherine Sonderegger, the triune God acts in the world and "creaturely time is bent."[189] God acts in the world and gives created history both its ultimate endpoints as well as the imminent, christological means by which it is sustained through God's own trinitarian life.

The central idea here is also relevant to another criticism made by Pannenberg in this work, namely, his charge that Barth's notion of divine subjectivity, or the sheer singularity of God's being (the divine I), results in a heteronomous understanding of the God-world relation. The sense of deity behind Barth's trinitarian idea of God from *CD* I/1, Pannenberg argues, risks being conceived as the transcendent correlate of the world. While I argued that Pannenberg overstates the case in Barth's doctrine of the Trinity, the key point is that, unlike the notion of God's sheer singularity, the inherent relationality of the divine being precludes the idea of God from being pitted against the world in its complexity and diversity. Jenson's trinitarian notion of envelopment takes Pannenberg's argument, specifically Pannenberg's positive vision of the God-world relation, a step further.

With both Pannenberg and Barth, Jenson's trinitarianism entails that God cannot be understood as the transcendent correlate of the world. Jenson's theology also allows us to add this point, however: God is not at a remove from created history because the being of God is a history unto itself; a history not in the ambiguous sense of Barth's primal history, potentially above (before) and beyond all else, but rather the history that occurs between the Father, Jesus the Son, and the Spirit in taking our created time into the unique temporality of the divine life. "The way in which the triune God is eternal," Jenson writes, "is by the events of Jesus' death and resurrection."[190] Similarly, "God is an *event*; history occurs not only in him but as his being."[191] As already demonstrated, Jenson's notion of divine envelopment shows that these passages do not entail that God succumbs to the world process. To be sure, Jenson fixates on the movement and identity of the eternal Son in time. But the Son exists in time in unity with the sovereign polarity of the Father and Spirit, the creative origin and future of all things. And it is in this reality, in the totality of the trinitarian relations as they intimately encompass temporal creation, that the triune God transcends history from within, and even through, the process of time itself. Enveloping created reality through the originating activity of the Father, the eschatological power of the Spirit, and the temporal identity of the Son,

189. Sonderegger, *The Doctrine of God*, 297.
190. Jenson, *STh*, 1:218–19.
191. Jenson, *STh*, 1:221.

the being of the triune God is a history unto itself, the divine history that enables our creaturely history with God.

This point adds a layer of depth to Pannenberg's vision of the God-world relation. Insofar as God is triune, or the divine relations are basic to God's being, God is not the transcendent correlate of the world. But this is not merely because God's relationality is compatible with the complexity of the created world, and vice versa. More concretely, it is because God indwells history through the self-transcendent life of God's triune being. And, with the precautions against Barth's idea of a primal history in view, we may go so far as to say that God is not the transcendent correlate of the world insofar God abides with us through the history of God's being, the inherent transcendence that God *is* as Father, Son, and Spirit. Thus when the inner-relations of the divine persons extend beyond Godself and toward us, into our created history so as to give us a share in the divine life, God is really here, present among us in history, and not confined to a static duality that keeps God at a distance from created life. And yet in relating to us, in the absolute immanence afforded to God through God's triunity, God lives among us in the only way God can, transcendently. Once more, God not only moves in history but exists as the transcendent source of history itself. The two points are inseparable, a single reality of the one God viewed from different perspectives, because God is triune.

Conclusion

In this chapter I have set forth a temporal understanding of divine transcendence based on the trinitarian theology of Robert W. Jenson. Jenson's theology lends itself to a useful conception of divine transcendence insofar as the trinitarian dialectics he employs, grounded in the unity-in-distinctions of God's being, provide a way to conceive of God as both beyond and within temporal reality simultaneously. The use of Trinity to secure a concept of God's transcendence from within the strictures of time avoids the common pitfalls we have encountered in this study, namely, divine timelessness and the subtle implication of an ulterior history of God running parallel to ours. Lastly, I supplemented the Pannenberg inspired conception of God's trinitarian movement in history from the previous chapter with Jenson's notion of divine envelopment. Through the Trinity of God's being God not only moves in history but exists as the transcendent source of history itself.

Conclusion: The Triune History

THE DOCTRINE OF THE Trinity is a gift to Christian faith and theology alike. In this study I have made use of this classical doctrine in order to address the problem of reconciling the eternality of God's being with the revealed vitality of God in history. On the flip side, the trinitarian idea of God provides the means for understanding God's abiding transcendence over created reality. And what is more, Trinity uniquely allows for a way to conceive of both these realities, the divine immanence and transcendence, without falling prey to a divided perception of God's being, or a notion of God with us here below, present in time, and an ulterior history of God in eternity above. The triune God transcends history from within time itself.

In this concluding chapter I offer an overview of the work as a whole. Following the overview I return to the central problem of this work in order to address two additional topics concerning the question of how the eternal God relates to history through the triunity of God's being. This will not be a complete theological statement on God's relation to history. Rather, drawing from some of the central findings of this study, I make the case for (1) a specific methodological approach in conceiving of the eternal relations of God in light of the divine missions and (2) set forth an eschatological understanding of the immanent Trinity for understanding the God-world relation.

1: Overview

I introduced the problem of this study in chapter 1 through Isaak A. Dorner's essay on the immutability of God. My use of Dorner's essay focused on the lucid way that Dorner treats the question of reconciling divine immutability with the revealed vitality of God in history. Furthermore, I started with Dorner's essay to explore the possibilities that his trinitarian solution to this problem raises in further examining the question of the relation between the eternity of God and the being of God in history. Dorner conceives of divine immutability in terms of the Spirit's actualization of God's ethically necessary and free being; he associates ethical necessity in God with the Father and freedom with the Son. This conception both allows for a dynamic understanding of the Trinity capable of reconciling the immutability of God's being with the revealed vitality of God in history as well as a notion of God's being as the foundation for God's activity *ad extra*. However, Dorner does not evenly apply this doctrine to God's living relation to history, seen in the way that Trinity moves to the background when he accounts for God's activity in history in terms of God's involvement with ethically independent creatures. Consequently, one of the key unanswered questions in Dorner's immutability essay is how the idea of God as triune can be understood as not only the grounds for God's activity *ad extra*, but as the way in which Father, Son, and Spirit indwell created reality and live out a history with others. I also brought attention to an inconsistency between Dorner's understanding of God's essential, trinitarian based immutability and what Dorner describes as a higher form of God's unchanging being in his account of the divine love for creatures that I return to in the following chapter.

In chapter 2 I addressed Karl Barth's trinitarian understanding of God's relation to history. In the first part of this chapter I looked at Barth's early notion of God in revelation and his trinitarian theology in *CD* I/1 and *CD* II/1. Barth points to a foundation for God's activity in history in *CD* I/1 in what he calls the antecedent being of God or the idea of God as "ours in advance."[1] The antecedent Trinity grounds God's sovereign self-disclosure in revelation and salvific history with creatures. In the initial assessment of this chapter I drew on Eberhard Jüngel's observation concerning the relational structure of Barth's foundational trinitarian assertion, "God reveals himself as the Lord," in order to defend Barth's theology against Pannenberg's charge that Barth's concept of divine subjectivity leads to a heteronomous notion of the God-world relation.[2] However, I sided with Pannenberg in his critique that Barth moves too quickly in formulating a doctrine of the Trinity from revelation. Passing over the scriptural witness to the eschatological nature of revelation history, Barth does not adequately identify the grounds in God by which God can be said to abide and move in an eschatologically oriented history with others. As a result, Barth makes only little of an advance on Dorner's use of Trinity to conceive of God's living history in the material treated in *CD* I/1 and *CD* II/1. Further, in considering Barth's theory of correspondence, the relation between the eternal Trinity and God with us, I argued that Barth's trinitarian formulations leave open the unwanted possibility of a two-track history of God, or parallel

1. Barth, *CD* I/1:383.
2. Barth, *CD* I/1:306.

running histories, one above and one below. Based on a key claim from Kathryn Tanner's theology, I pointed to the need to conceive of the Trinity through God's personal involvement in revelation history and the way that it bears on God's eternal identity. Despite the significance of Christ's person in Barth's adherence to revelation, it appears that many of these problems result from the limited role that the concrete history of Jesus plays in Barth's understanding of God's eternal being.

In the second part of this chapter on Barth's account of divine election in *CD* II/2, I traced a line of doctrinal development in Barth's theology regarding the understanding of Jesus Christ in the Godhead. In his treatment of election Barth characterizes the Son's relation to the Father in terms of obedience based on the New Testament witness to the eternal Son's identity with the man Jesus. This adds a layer of depth to his previous formulations on the eternal Trinity, and consequently solves several dilemmas. Barth's doctrine of election overcomes the inconsistency in Dorner's essay that separates the essential immutability of God's ethical being from God's expressed love to creatures. For in Barth's account the idea of divine election, specifically as a self-determining decision basic to God's being, opens up an understanding of divine immutability rooted in the eternal fellowship of the divine persons that *simultaneously* includes the unwavering faithfulness of God to reconcile fallen creatures in time. I also made the case that by incorporating the notion of Jesus' conformity to the Father's will into the eternal life of the Trinity, and thus demonstrating that God, in the eternal depths of God's being, wills to be God *for us*, Barth largely staves off the potential problem of a two-track history of God that accompanies his theory of correspondence from *CD* I/1. I note that he 'largely' but not entirely achieves this point based on his description of election as the primal history (*Urgeschichte*) of God. A critical appropriation of Barth's account of election, I argued, requires us to make a more careful distinction than Barth does between pre-temporal election and its enactment in time. However, the central point of this chapter lies in the positive connection between God's pre-temporal eternity and time. The Spirit driven obedience of Jesus to the Father in time is grounded in, is even the natural expression of, the eternal conformity of the divine Son to the loving will of the Father. The point comes full circle: Barth's account of election allows for a better understanding of how the triune God is truly 'ours in advance.'

I turned to the work of Wolfhart Pannenberg and the topic of the trinitarian mediated history of God in chapter 3. I began by revisiting Pannenberg's criticism of Barth on the divine subjectivity, which comes into sharper focus through a similar assessment of Barth's trinitarian theology by Jürgen Moltmann, in order to shed light on Pannenberg's turn to the themes of eschatology and the reciprocity of the divine persons that charac-terize both his doctrine of the Trinity and understanding of the God-world relation. I then considered the basic features in Pannenberg's early views of God, revelation, history, and futurity, as well as his mature doctrine of the Trinity alongside some of the divine attributes. In his trinitarian construal of God, which is at least partially motivated by the critique of Barth above, Pannenberg sets forth a notion of mutuality basic to the relations of the divine persons, or what he calls their reciprocal self-distinctions. Pannen-berg conceives of this notion through the dependent rule or monarchy of the Father in relation to the divine Son and the Holy Spirit. The Father's dependency on the other persons of the Trinity applies to both the eternal relationality of the Godhead and the establishment of the divine lordship, the kingdom of God, through the Son in time.

I then used Pannenberg's trinitarian theology and his notions of de-pendent monarchy and divine self-actualization to make the case for an understanding of the movement of God in time and the process of history. I based this conception on the inner-relational movement of the Father, Son, and Spirit in God. Specifically, I argued that the eschatological orientation of the divine persons—the goal of the Father's monarchy in the Son's Spirit driven conformity to the Father—serves as the grounds for the forward moving activity of God in the world. I also showed how the abiding trinitar-ian structure of God's being, encapsulated by the divine unity, provides a way to understand how both the immutability of God and the dynamism of God in history hold at one and the same time. The governing norm in this conception of the God-world relation is the unity-in-distinctions of God's being. I affirmed the vital place of Pannenberg's principle—the unity of God's deity and lordship—as a means for understanding how God assumes the revelatory history of God into the divine life, thus avoiding the above mentioned problem of a two-fold history of God.

More critically, I concluded the chapter on Pannenberg's theology with an assessment of his doctrine of eternity. I highlighted two plausible render-ings of Pannenberg on eternity as either divine futurity or the Plotinus based view of the simultaneous presence of time to God as a whole. The idea of futurity is promising insofar as it incorporates the immanent temporality of God within a notion of divine transcendence. However, this concept is not sufficiently worked out in view of Pannenberg's later trinitarian theology. The second and more prominent rendering of eternity, the Plotinus based idea of the simultaneous presence of God to time as a whole, verges on a notion of timeless eternity, specifically when Pannenberg claims that God has no "future that could be distinguished from his present."[3] Perhaps Pannenberg means something different than all time as present to God in the same way, which he indicates elsewhere. The overarching problem, I believe, is not just inconsistency, but that Pannenberg does not adequately apply his trinitarian theology to the doctrine of eternity. While I noted that a fix to these problems is likely possible within the resources of Pannenberg's trinitarian theology, which might also yield a distinct notion of divine transcendence, I left these conceptual tasks for the following chapter.

I considered the trinitarian theology of Robert W. Jenson in chapter 4. The stated aim of this chapter was to uncover a temporally structured concept of divine transcendence. I identified the need for this concept through Jenson's early engagement with Barth's theology, particularly Barth's idea of analogy. Jenson's use of Trinity to conceive of themes related to transcendence, such as the doctrines of (temporal) infinity and eternity, was introduced through brief comparisons of Jenson's and Pannenberg's early theological views of history (the theology of the cross) and futurity as well as Jenson's notion of narrative identity. My reading of Jenson's later theology gave special attention to the trinitarian patterns that underlie his doctrine of God, including Jenson's temporal ontology, his articulation of eternity through the event of Jesus' resurrection, and his concept of divine envelopment.

In the constructive assessment of this chapter I laid out three key components for a temporal notion of divine transcendence based on Jenson's theology. First, I addressed how Jenson posits temporalities among the persons of the Trinity in a way that shows both the identity and difference between the being of God and time. Second, to avoid the problematic idea of a two-fold history of God, I turned to Jenson's understanding of how the identity of God reflects the history God lives with us and incorporates into God's being. I also addressed Pannenberg's criticism on the near absence of an immanent Trinity in Jenson's theology and the ensuing tendency to conflate God and the world process. I showed how the immanent Trinity continues to function in Jenson's theology and drew on his idea of divine envelopment to articulate the first of two conceptions for how God can be understood to simultaneously transcend the history God lives with others. Thirdly, I rounded out this construal with Jenson's notion of the transcendence internal to God's being, the divine triunity, specifically through the Spirit as the site of unlimited life in God. This enables the second understanding by which God acts in time—in and through events that become constitutive of God's eternity—and transcends time at once. I also showed

---

3. Pannenberg, *ST*, 1:410; Pannenberg, *Systematische Theologie*, 1:443. English translation slightly altered.

how Jenson's idea of futurity *as* the Holy Spirit improves on the more abstract notion of futurity in Pannenberg's theology, and can therefore better serve as the object of faith. I concluded this assessment by building on the previous chapter (Pannenberg) through an articulation of the way that God not only moves in history but also exists as the transcendent source of history's movement through the trinitarian nature of God's being.

My engagements with the theology of Dorner, Barth, Pannenberg, and Jenson in this study offer a set of interpretations and adaptive renderings of God's living relation to history. At a general level, I have articulated the God-world relation in two ways. First, I have shown how in the divine decision of election, God's *pre*-temporal reality, God enacts a history with us, centered on Jesus Christ, grounded in the trinitarian nature of God's being. Likewise, God acts *in* history through the mutuality of the trinitarian relations of God. Moreover, the trinitarian nature of God's being enables God to assume temporal events into God's eternity while God remains transcendent through the inner-vitality of God's being, otherwise described as God's *futurity*. This, in sum, is to show how the adaptive renderings of Barth's, Pannenberg's, and Jenson's trinitarian theology in particular can be used to articulate God's living relation to history in pre-temporal, inner-historical, and eschatological perspective. The second way makes the same point in terms of the appropriated activities of the divine persons. The concrete history of Jesus the *Son* in time flows from his conformity to the eternal will of God. The dependency of the *Father's* monarchy sets in motion the mutuality in God that makes God's activity *ad extra* a living history. And the futurity or unsurpassable being of God in the *Spirit* makes God's activity *ad extra* at once historical and transcendent. In either formulation, it is clear that the eternal God relates to history in a living way through the Trinity of God's being.

2: Trinity and History

The doctrine of the Trinity is the key for understanding God's relation to the world. As Pannenberg reminded us, the trinitarian idea of God "formulates the relationship of God to history in general" insofar as it summarizes God's revealed identity.[4] Likewise, it also provides the conceptual means for understanding how God relates to history through the trinitarian relationality of God's being. Divine relationality, the dialectic of the unity-in-distinctions of the one God as Father, Son, and Spirit, evidences the internal vitality of God's being and the self-grounded means of God's

4. Pannenberg, "Der Gott der Geschichte," 122. Translation mine.

living relation to history. Through the fellowship of the divine persons, God establishes and renews the divine fellowship with us. Or to take an example from this study, the inner-movements of God as Father, Son, and Spirit, particularly in the forward moving direction of these relations— from the Father through the Son to the Spirit—allows for an understanding of the eschatological movement of God among us in time. In short, the resources of trinitarian doctrine offer a grounded response to the *how* of the various relations between God and the world revealed to us in Christ.[5] Trinitarian based reflection on the God-world relation is therefore, as noted above, a work of faith seeking understanding.

There also exists another central reason for my engagement with the doctrine of the Trinity for understanding the God-world relation that I have not put at the forefront of this study. Trinity aids in understanding God's relation to history insofar as this concept uniquely captures the connection between the perfection and relatedness of God's being. Because God is triune, God is perfect in fellowship, in power, and in love—in each as they are exemplified first and foremost in the inner-life of God as Father, Son, and Spirit. An example from Jenson is helpful here. The divine Son is eternally begotten by the Father. Thus "to be God is not only to give being," but for the second person of the Trinity "it is also to receive being."[6] There is as such a basis in God's being for the steep involvement of God in the life of creatures in which God both gives and receives, speaks and listens to the prayers of God's children. And while the full spectrum of the biblical narrative does not allow this relationship to be reduced to one of pure mutuality, a simple give-and-take between creatures and the living God, it is evidently true that God hears, and all importantly, *responds* to our petitions. And this, trinitarian doctrine teaches us, not because of a lack or insufficiency on the part of God, but because the Trinity of God's being includes a prior and perfect receptivity in itself. God is perfectly related, first in Godself and consequently in the way that God relates to the world.

The possibilities for applying the trinitarian idea of God to the understanding of the God-world relation here cannot be exhausted. Given the question of how the doctrine of the Trinity is conceived in view of God's revealed acts; given the difficulties as well as the possibilities for conceiving of the transcendence and freedom of God as triune in relation to history; given, above all, the complexity and riches of the inner-relations of the divine persons, it is little surprise that trinitarian theology is an ongoing

5. For a similar formulation, see Papanikolaou, "The Necessity for *Theologia*," 122.

6. Jenson, *The Triune Identity*, 85.

task. In what follows I continue to consider the central question of how the Trinity of God's being serves as the grounds for a conception of God's living relation to history in two ways. In response to this question I make the case for (1) a methodological approach to conceiving of the eternal relations of God in light of their historical ends and (2) offer my own proposal on the immanent Trinity as the eschatological Trinity. I draw from my engagements with the figures of this study (and others) and my constructive appropriations of their work in order to outline some ways forward for trinitarian reflection on the God-world relation.

Eternal Trinity, Temporal Ends

In this first methodological proposal for understanding the God-world relation through the trinitarian idea of God, I suggest that the eternal relations of God must be conceived in light of their historical ends (the divine missions). This proposal can be understood as the positive response to the problem I highlighted in Barth's theory of correspondence. In the latter view, the externally directed activity of God in history "corresponds to what God in His own being is antecedently in Himself."[7] Barth is right to conceptualize the eternal Trinity of God as the ordering principle of God's activity *ad extra*. The triune life of God is the means by which God acts in and transcends historical reality. The potential problem lies in the general idea of a correspondence between the eternal Trinity of God's being and the being of God in time. To conceive of the revealed being of God in history, on one side, and the corresponding reality of the eternal Trinity, on the other, leaves open, or at least risks suggesting, a nebulous space between the two. One of my key objections to Barth's theory of correspondence was that he does not adequately specify the relation between the two sides, evident in the ambiguous meaning of Christ's concrete history for understanding God's eternal identity pre-*CD* II/2. Moreover, although it is not Barth's intent, the idea of a corresponding reality of God, particularly when the bulk of the emphasis is placed on the antecedent reality of God, threatens to situate the real locus point of God's activity outside of God's revealed history with us, and even denotes a kind of higher, ulterior reality of God that runs strangely parallel to our own.

How then do we specify the relation between the eternal Trinity and the being of God in time so as to preclude these undesirable outcomes? Or positively, how do we maintain a vision in which the history God lives with others is in fact the history of the eternal Trinity in time—God *with us*? A

7. Barth, *CD* I/1:425.

theological description of the eternal relations, I argue, must have in view not only a point of reference to the eternality of God's being, the inner-relations of God as triune, but also to the revelatory history of God with others. God's revelatory history, as I show, must be included, in a fixed and even determinative way, within the conception of the eternal relations of the Trinity. The God of the Bible is depicted as sovereign Lord. "I work and who can hinder it?" (Isa 43:13). Unlike the creature who comes from and returns to the dust, God always is. "From everlasting to everlasting you are God" (Ps 90:2). God is unbound. "Even heaven and the highest heaven cannot contain you" (1 Kgs 8:27). At yet, at the very the same time, but *not* in contrast to the aforementioned points, the particular identity of this God—sovereign, everlasting, and unbound—is given to us almost exclusively in terms of the history God has with Israel, the church, and the nations. Moreover, in the incarnation God makes the human situation God's own by becoming flesh and dwelling among us (John 1:14). More still, it is telling that in conceiving of the most fundamental relations by which the eternal being of God is, namely, the Father's begetting of the Son and the Spirit's procession, the tradition takes its cues from the revealed, temporal relations of God's history in time (John 1:18; 3:16; 15:26). What we have is this story—God, in the transcendent sovereignty of the divine life, *with us*.

The point is that the divine relations of the Father, Son, and Spirit have historical ends. This is what a theological formulation of the eternal relations must keep in view. Barth's early theory of correspondence in *CD* I/1 safeguards a notion of divine freedom. Likewise, his idea of a divine correspondence to the antecedent lordship, alterity, and fellowship in God highlight the true grounds for God's activity in history. However, his use of this theory nevertheless casts a shadow over the notion of God's living presence *in* revelation history. A corresponding relation between the antecedent Trinity and the being of God in time must say more than that the being of God in revelation manifests or confirms the antecedent reality of God in time. For if it does not, or without indicating the way in which God assumes the revelatory history into God's being, a quality like the divine lordship becomes liable to an abstract misunderstanding. The divine lordship is not only an eternal reality grounded in the perfection of God's being, but an enacted, historical reality of God—the lordship of God as gained with Israel and the church. A concept that takes its cue for the eternal relations in God from the revealed history of God cannot make extensive use of a theory of correspondence like this; it is too general.

For this reason I think that Pannenberg's and Jenson's respective conceptions of the eternal relations in terms of the dependent monarchy of the Father and the liberating power of the Spirit more successfully relate the eternality of God's being with the revealed history of God. They are more successful insofar as they conceive of the eternal relations in God to have a historical telos. The dependency of the Father's deity on the divine Son, and likewise, the liberating power of the Spirit toward an end, are not only eternal realities of God. Indeed, they are this. But what can be said in regards to the eternal relations of God can also be said, in a *new*, temporal way, of what God does in history. (For, again, what we have is God's revealed history with us, and the understanding of God's eternal being *through* that history.) The eternal relations extend into the revealed history of God. The eternal dependency of the Father on the Son for his lordship is not only an eternal truth of God's being, but, in the divine design, a historical reality as well. Its eternal basis and grounding in the eternal Trinity of God's being ensures the coming to fruition of the Father's lordship among us. This must be affirmed. It is affirmed, however, alongside—and not over against—the fact that it does this, the coming to fruition of the Father's monarchy among us, without loss to the real history of God. Similarly, the Spirit's liberating power or futurity is the inner-transcendence of God's being, which makes God transcendent being in time. The Spirit's being as such ensures the triumph of God over any finite obstacle. And again, it does this without loss to the real history of God. The key point is that the eternal relations of God extend themselves toward us and our creaturely history. The triune God moves from eternity into history as God assumes this history into the divine life. The eternal relations have a historical telos.

What is gained here? First, understanding the eternal relations of God to have a historical telos avoids the problematic notion of a two-fold history of God. There can be no suggestion that the revealed history of God mirrors a higher, divine history above insofar as God's revealed history is the aim of the eternal Trinity and is brought into the very life of God. Second, the historical ends of the eternal relations means that the eternal being of God not only grounds God's free activity *ad extra* but also enables the history God lives with others. This construal of the divine relations does greater justice to the understanding of the divine capacity to indwell and live out a history with creatures, the kind of history that God in Scripture is revealed to have. The temporal trajectory of the divine relations animates God's *living relation* to history.

The idea posed here approximates Thomas Aquinas' understanding of the eternal relations or processions of the divine persons as containing the temporal missions of the Son and Spirit. Mission, Thomas writes, "includes the eternal procession, with the addition of a temporal effect." The procession of a divine person is a "twin procession" that contains "a double term, temporal and eternal."[8] The only difference, if it is a difference at all, is that in my proposal the temporal missions get taken up into the eternal processions to such an extent that the processions—the inner-relations of the eternal Trinity—bear the identifying markers that derive from the work of God in the temporal missions. For they *must* bear these markers if we are to hold to the fact that the immanent Trinity is the economic Trinity; that is, if the eternal Trinity is the subject of God's living history with us.

Thomas' distinction between the end or the term of the eternal processions and the temporal missions (the 'double term') remains useful insofar as it indicates a fundamental difference between God and us. It need not indicate two different trinitarian histories. Rather, it can be taken to denote the inner-relations of the divine persons through which God acts among us, the eternal processions, on one hand, and the beloved creatures and creaturely history that God assumes into the divine life through the temporal missions, on the other. The eternal processions have theological priority, but, all importantly, not priority in the sense of remaining untouched by God's revealed history with us. For it is precisely the temporal missions that get taken up into the divine life, the eternal processions. Put another way, it is precisely the eternal Trinity, the Son and Spirit in their eternal processions from the Father, who enters into creaturely life, the temporal missions, in order to make this history God's own. The eternal God wills an end in revelation history. The apocalypse of John depicts this in terms of the victory of God who dwells with the faithful in the redeemed order of the new creation, a celebration of the slain lamb that lives and now reigns (Rev 5:6–8; 21:22). Ezekiel's apocalyptic imagery is also telling. In the midst of the prophet's detailing of the measurements of the eschatological temple, Ezekiel notes that the gate through which the Lord enters to be with the people remains shut. "The Lord said to me . . . it shall not be opened" (44:2). God has a telos, a point of fulfillment with us. "Mortal, this is the place of my throne and the place for the soles of my feet, where I will reside among the people of Israel forever" (43:7).

The Eschatological Trinity

The first proposal on the historical telos of the eternal relations rules out the idea of a two-fold history of God. In the second proposal I show how it is possible to conceive of the Trinity of God's being as the grounds for God's living relation to history when the immanent Trinity is understood as the eschatological Trinity.

8. Aquinas, *Summa Theologica*, 1.43.3.

Both Jenson and Pannenberg affirm versions of the immanent-economic Trinity relation along these lines.[9] However, neither develops their trinitarian theology or their understanding of the God-world relation by explicitly unfolding its meaning. For this reason Andrew W. Nicol can claim that for Jenson the immanent Trinity, in its "futurist [eschatological] dominion," is conceived so as to ensure "that God's telos is not severed from God's becoming. . . . The relations between the persons of the God of Israel enact the occasion of God's being."[10] It is not clear whether Nicol is suggesting that the enactment of the divine persons in time for Jenson means that the economic Trinity arrives at a final point of alignment with the immanent Trinity in the eschatological end, a strong notion of divine becoming in time, or whether there is a definitive and abiding sense of unity between the immanent-eschatological Trinity and the being of God as enacted in history. Similar debates accompany Pannenberg's understanding of the immanent-economic Trinity relation.[11]

In this study I have staked an interpretive claim on how I understand Jenson and Pannenberg on the God-world relation. In relation to Jenson's theology, my view is closer to the second of the two possible understandings of Nicol's claim above, the strict sense of unity between the immanent Trinity and the historical enactment of God. Things are more complicated in my interpretation of Pannenberg's theology, given that I detect an inconsistency between the foundational claims of his trinitarian theology and his doctrine of eternity as open to different, and sometimes contradictory, renderings. The point to be made here, however, is that neither Pannenberg nor Jenson sufficiently unpack the meaning of their respective formulations of the immanent-economic Trinity relation. In what follows I return to some of the key points of engagement with Pannenberg's and Jenson's trinitarian theology, both through rehearsing and building on the findings of this study, in order to provide greater clarity on the statement that the immanent Trinity is the eschatological Trinity. Along the way I show how this concept of the immanent Trinity affords an understanding of the trinitarian being of God as the grounds for God's living relation to history.

One way of understanding the immanent Trinity as the eschatological Trinity can be ruled out immediately. The idea that the immanent Trinity is the eschatological Trinity does not mean that the economic Trinity is truly itself, that the Trinity achieves itself in time, in the eschatological end. While also a rather unwieldily conception of divine becoming in

---

9. Jenson, *The Triune Identity*, 140–41; Pannenberg, *ST*, 1:330–36.

10. Nicol, *Exodus and Resurrection*, 200.

11. See, e.g., Eilers, *Faithful to Save*, 41.

history, the notion is problematic for reasons already noted. For the idea of an economic Trinity on its way to a self-constituting end, through which it becomes one with the immanent-eschatological Trinity, implies a notion of the immanent Trinity so ahead of temporal reality, so to speak, as to be different from the being of God who lives a history with others. The stark (ontological) contrast of the economic Trinity and the immanent-eschatological Trinity here raises the problem of a self-contained concept of God in a new way, in this case a notion of God who lies enclosed in Godself at history's end, beyond and apart from God with us in time. There are not two trinities, we must insist, but only one. An account of the relation between the immanent and the economic Trinity must take care to show how this is so. The immanent Trinity as the eschatological Trinity need not suggest a bifurcation in the reality of God, either in terms of God above the history God lives with us or ahead of it.

The view of the immanent Trinity as the eschatological Trinity that I set forth in what follows intends something more straightforward than the problematic notions above. The immanent Trinity is eschatological in view of the diverse set of relational ends in the Godhead. These relations belong to the triune God from eternity to eternity, and can be understood as the means through which God acts in time.

I begin with reference to Pannenberg's concept of the divine monarchy outlined in chapter 3. The special merit of this idea for our purposes lies in the way that it draws out the eschatological character of the first person of the Trinity. Pannenberg's concept of the divine monarchy is underwritten by the connection between the Father-Son relation and the coming reign of God. The Father is the God of Israel who stands alone as the unique Lord of all things and to whom all created things belong (Deut 6:4; 1 Kgs 8:23; Job 41:11). The deity of the Father is identical to his sovereign lordship. The Father relates to the Son by sending him into the world and handing over all things to the Son, including all authority (John 3:35; 17:2). In return, the Spirit empowered Son works to establish the Father's reign among us in his perfect obedience to the Father's will; "I always do what is pleasing to him" (John 8:29). The rule of the Father, and with it, the divine lordship over all creation, hinges on the success of the Son's mission and his victory over the powers of sin and death. The resurrection is the initial triumph of the Son's mission and the proleptic sign of the coming lordship of the Father in the world. This work continues in the ongoing activity of the Spirit until the arrival of the Father's kingdom in the eschatological consummation of all things.

This, in short form, is the heart of the exegetical foundation for Pannenberg's doctrine of God. The key point lies in the way that it illuminates the personhood and lordship of the Father. The Greek patristic tradition rightly describes the Father as the divine monarch and the unoriginate origin in God. Pannenberg's trinitarian theology can be used to accent these terms in a new way. From the economic activity of the divine persons we learn that the monarchy of the Father in God, the divine lordship itself, is realized by another, the divine Son, as well as the Spirit who empowers the Son to glorify the Father. Accordingly, there are movements that undergird the Father's monarchy. It is actualized by the Son's Spirit driven return of glory to the Father from whom he comes. Logically prior to that, however, the movement begins in the other direction. The Father gives the Son the gift of deity, and with it, the divine lordship, in a movement that proceeds ecstatically from the unoriginate origin of God's being toward the begotten Son. This gifting, the movement from the Father to the Son, denotes the eschatological directionality of God's being. For it originates with the Father as the *arche* of God's being and is realized in what flows *from* the Father and *to* the Son in the Spirit. Put another way, the Son and the Holy Spirit can be understood as divine ends in God insofar as they proceed from the Father. In relation to the Father, the Son and the Spirit are the twin goals of God's being. The Father's monarchy therefore moves toward, and is realized by means of, divine ends. The monarchy of God is eschatological because there is a telos, or teloi, proper to God's being.

The immanent Trinity is the eschatological Trinity. Like the constructive appropriation of Pannenberg's theology from chapter 3, I have taken Pannenberg's exegetical foundation and the concept of the divine monarchy and set it more explicitly within the traditional understanding of the eternal relations of origin. For the schematic of the eternal relations of origin is not only compatible with Pannenberg's account—both are based in God's revealed history—but it also brings to the fore the eschatological nature of the Father's lordship insofar as it rests on the divine persons who proceed from him.[12] This conception of the divine monarchy illuminates an understanding of how the eternal Trinity grounds the eschatological activity of God in time. Here we move from the activity of God gleaned from the revealed history and the creedal affirmations to the reverse procedure of understanding how, based on these gleanings and the subsequent construction of the divine relations, God relates to the world through the immanent Trinity. I now bring this procedure to bear on a connection between the movement of God in time and a previously articulated concept of immutability.

---

12. On the connection between Pannenberg's trinitarian idea of God and the traditional conception of the eternal relations of origin, see Pannenberg, *ST*, 1:320.

First, the fact that the divine monarchy has its antecedent basis in God's being, prior to its enactment among us, secures a notion of divine immutability. I articulated this in chapter 3 in terms of the self-deferring complex of the divine persons in their living, dynamic unity. From eternity, Father, Son, and Spirit are the one God in the eternal realization of the divine monarchy. God is immutable being. At one and the same time, the inner-relationality of God's immutable being, the movements between the Father in his dependence on the Son and the Son's affirmation of the Father's lordship through the Spirit, is foundational for the revealed vitality that characterizes God's history with us. God is living being. More specific to our concerns here, however, the nature of the Father's monarchy provides a basis for understanding how God moves in time. The activity of God in time follows the movements of God's being. Every act of God in time proceeds *from* the self-donated lordship of the Father *toward* its simultaneous actualization in the Son and Spirit. In time, this takes shape in terms of the Father's gift of all things to the Son, who responds to the Father's gift in his perfect obedience to the Father's will. When the Son acts in time he sets in motion the realization of the Father's lordship anew, in history as he knows it beforehand from eternity. The Spirit brings the realized lordship of the Father in the Son to perfection. At each step, which can be broken down one-by-one, but nevertheless remains simultaneous or a whole due to the divine unity manifest in the perfect obedience of the Son in response to the Father's gift and the Spirit's ongoing work, God acts among us in accordance with the pattern of God's trinitarian being. This is to say, God acts eschatologically. God moves in time and the process of history through the monarchy of the Father and the way in which his lordship is realized through the divine persons (the teloi) who proceed from him.

It is worth noting that this need not suggest two trinities. In keeping with the methodology outlined above, the establishment of the divine lordship among us is, based on the self-determining decision of God, the historical end of the eternal monarchy of God's being. The eternal relations of God have a historical telos; the eternal processions in God include the divine missions. If we speak of God's activity in time as a repetition of God's being from eternity, it is critical to note that this repetition of the divine lordship among us contains something new: the reenactment of the divine relations in a new sphere, in time and history, which are taken up into the eternal life of God.

The eschatological conception of the immanent Trinity, and the way that this notion figures into the God-world relation, can also be understood in view of the person of the Spirit. The most relevant part of this study for an eschatological understanding of the third person of the Trinity comes from

Jenson's conception of the Spirit as the futurity of God's being in chapter 4. I utilized Jenson's pneumatology to specify a notion of God's transcendent being in time. That account relied on the understanding of the Spirit's futurity based primarily on the trinitarian logic of the divine processions, or the Spirit as the divine, temporally unique goal of God's being, and the eschatological activity of the Spirit in Jesus' resurrection. There is plentiful material here for filling out a notion of the immanent Trinity as the eschatological Trinity. In what follows, though, I treat a less considered aspect of the Spirit's role in God that supports this thesis, albeit a role that is convertible with the eschatological idea of the Spirit based on the just noted trinitarian logic and understanding of Jesus' resurrection in Jenson's theology. The Spirit as God's futurity is manifest in the idea of the Spirit as divine love.

The association between the Spirit and the divine love was famously expressed by Augustine. Augustine finds the link between the Holy Spirit and the divine love in his rendering of Romans 5:5 ("God's love has been poured into our hearts through the Holy Spirit that has been given to us") and the role of the Spirit as the one who gives us the power to love.[13] "Why is the Spirit distinctively called gift? Only because of the love without which the man who has not got it, though he speak with the tongues of men and of angels, is booming bronze and a clashing cymbal." Likewise, without the divinely imparted gift of the Spirit that enables one to love God and neighbor, she "cannot transfer from the left hand to the right."[14] Augustine concludes, "so the love which is from God and is God is distinctivley the Holy Spirit; through him the charity of God is poured in our hearts, and through it the whole triad dwells in us."[15]

The Spirit is thus understood as the bond of love between the Father and the Son. This point, however, requires some unpacking. As we have seen, Pannenberg and Jenson raise valid concerns around a simple conception of the Spirit as the unity of Father and Son. For Pannenberg, to typify the Spirit as the mutual love of the Father and Son reduces the Spirit to an impersonal 'we' of the Godhead.[16] Mutual love does not adequately specify the Spirit's identity in God. Jenson detects something along these lines in Barth's theology and characterizes it as "'I-Thou' trinitarianism." Pushed to its limit, it means the eternal communion of God belongs properly to the Father and the Son. "The Spirit is not party to this converse."[17] What is the solution to this

---

13. See also Luke 11:13; Gal 5:6; 1 John 4:12–23.

14. Augustine, *De Trinitate*, XV.32.

15. Augustine, *De Trinitate*, XV.32.

16. See Pannenberg, *ST*, 1:315–17, 358.

17. Jenson, *STh*, 1:155.

problem? For both Pannenberg and Jenson, though the point is conveyed with greater emphasis in Jenson's theology, it lies in the liberating activity of the Spirit and the Spirit's enabling role in God.

John's gospel describes the Father as the source of self-giving life bestowed on the Son (John 5:25). This gift, however, can be understood to come by way of the Spirit's mediation. The two touchstone events that bracket the life of the incarnate Son stand out here. Jesus is both conceived in Mary's womb by the Spirit, and in an analogous movement that denotes the power of God to create *ex nihilio*, the Father raises Jesus from the dead through the Spirit's power (Luke 1:35; Rom 8:11).[18] The Father's relation to the Son is mediated through the Spirit; the Son relates to the Father in kind. Moreover, Jesus is led by the Spirit into the desert, wherein he undergoes the temptations of the enemy. Luke's gospel specifies the Spirit's role here. After the trail in the desert Jesus proceeds to prophesy the renewal of the Jubilee year and the coming of God's kingdom. In both cases, in his obedience to the Father's commands and the ministry he undertakes for others, he is described as "filled" with the Spirit and the Spirit's power (Luke 4:1, 14). Notably, in the immediate context of Luke 4, Jesus' self-identification with the subject from second Isaiah makes the Spirit's descent upon himself intrinsic to his divinely appointed mission. "The Spirit of the Lord is upon me, because he anointed me to preach the gospel to the poor" (Luke 4:18; Isa 61:1).

What does this mean? The Spirit is the bond of love between the Father and Son, yes. But the Spirit is also more. The Spirit plays an active role in the love that the Father and Son share and which is identical to the Spirit himself. One side of this relation is nicely captured by Kathryn Tanner: "The Spirit is the love or power of the Father by which the Son is drawn out of the Father to be the perfect manifestation of all that the Father is."[19] From the other side, we can add that the Spirit is the love or power of the Father by which the Son is drawn to the Father, and by which the Son perfectly conforms to the Father's will, in order to establish and manifest the kingdom of God among us. The Spirit is the mutual love of the Father and Son; but as is also evident here, the Spirit is this love as the divine person who enables the love that God is. At one and the same time, the Spirit is the love of God and the condition of its possibility. Jenson gets at both of the Spirit's essential roles in one claim: "The immediate objects of [the Spirit's] intention, the

---

18. Cf. Matt 3:16–17.

19. Tanner, *Christ the Key*, 193.

Father and the Son, love each other, with a love that is identical with the Spirit's gift of himself to each of them."[20]

What has been said here can now be put into eschatological perspective. This does not require any additional moves, but only to see how the divine loving is convertible with the futurity of the Spirit in God. The object of the Father's love is the Son; the object of the Son's love is the Father. They are in this way the twin goals or endpoints of the divine love. The Spirit is the futurity of God as the power who brings about the divine ends. The Spirit enables the Father to love the Son, and the Son to love the Father. The Spirit thus delivers on the ends of the divine loving in God, and can accordingly be described as the eschatological power of God's love. The Spirit is eschatological as mediator of the divine love.

But the Spirit is also eschatological as the divine love itself. The Father has an end in the love of the Son, and the Son in the love of the Father. The Spirit is identical to this love, and so is the goal of the Father and Son's mutual love. This does not displace Father and Son as the object of one another's love, but rather highlights the fact that the Spirit, from eternity to eternity, is the Spirit *of* the Father and the Son. The Spirit indwells the first and second persons of the Trinity, and as the divine love, we can say, makes them lovely and therefore the objects of one another's love (which brings us full circle to the Spirit as the power that enables the divine love, or in this case, that draws them to one another). In short, the Spirit is eschatological as both the mediator of the Father and Son's love and as the divine love itself, the goal or future that the Father and Son share in the Godhead.

Like the Father's monarchy, the Spirit as the divine love underwrites the eschatological nature of the immanent Trinity. And like the Father's monarchy, the Spirit's role in God illuminates an understanding of the God-world relation. I briefly apply this conception below to the idea of the Spirit as the possibility of God's history and draw out some of the particular eschatological content of the Spirit as the divine loving.

First, the addition of the Spirit's mediating role in God in order to identify, and maintain, the Spirit's individuality sheds light on the way in which God acts in history. In God, the Spirit mediates divine life, freeing the Father and Son for one another. The Spirit does the same in time, for we recall the methodological point on the historical telos of the divine relations. However, in time, the Spirit's activity takes on new form and character. The Spirit continues to liberate the Father for the Son, and the Son for the Father, to be the mutual ends of one another's affection. The Spirit persists as the bond of love between them. What is new, however, are those involved: the

---

20. Jenson, *STh*, 1:158.

Spirit draws Israel and the church into this relationship through union with the second person of the Trinity. Put another way, what the Spirit mediates as the bond of love in God becomes in time the mediation of a *history*: the history of the Father's love for the Son, on one hand, which includes the world that the Father loves and creates through the Son in the Spirit's power; on the other, this is the history of the Son's love for the Father and his Spirit empowered acts which restore to the Father a world that has lost its way. Taken together, the two sides of this relation give history its ultimate meaning and goal, the transformation of all creaturely things through deliverance into the family of God. In Romans 8 Paul identifies this change with the Spirit's activity. "When we cry 'Abba! Father!' it is that very Spirit bearing witness with our spirit that we are children of God, and if children, then heirs of God and joint heirs with Christ" (15–17). As the mediating love of the Father and Son, the Spirit enables God's relation to the world. The Spirit is the possibility of God's revelatory history.

I conclude this section by connecting the findings above, the eschatological nature of the Father's monarchy and the Spirit as the mediator and divine goal of the Father and Son's mutual love, with a key concept of this study. In chapter 3 I offered a critical endorsement of Pannenberg's principle on the unity of deity and lordship. As Pannenberg puts it in one of his early writings, "God's being and existence cannot be conceived apart from his rule."[21] Or as said in a later work, "the rule or kingdom of the Father is not so external to his deity that he might be God without his kingdom."[22] While there are different plausible readings of the meaning of this principle in Pannenberg's theology, based mainly on ambiguities in the concept of divine eternity, I use the principle here in order to highlight the future over the present as the locus point of God's ultimate revelation. The realities of sin and death, though held fatally in check by the resurrection of Jesus, stand in opposition to the reign of God and the express manifestation of God's lordship among us. Not until the future, the total victory of God over sin and death, is God known in full, for with that victory comes the revelation of the divine lordship over all things. The principle has clear epistemological significance. But it is the ontological side of this principle that concerns me here. The unity of God's deity and lordship, and the truth that God's lordship over all things is as yet incomplete, entails that the truth of God's being is at stake in history. God's being hinges on the triumph of God's coming lordship, however certain that outcome is, based on the proleptic victory of God over death in Christ's resurrection. God's activity in time, characterized

---

21. Pannenberg, *Theology and the Kingdom of God*, 55.

22. Pannenberg, *ST*, 1:313.

by the establishment of the divine rule among us, is thus oriented to the future. Divine activity is eschatological.

The eschatological nature of the Father's monarchy and the mediating role of the Spirit in God connect to this principle in different yet complementary ways. I address the connection to the divine monarchy first. The concept of the Father's lordship as realized in the Son and Spirit adds the important insight that prior to the eschatological consummation, the divine monarchy is already actualized within the Godhead. It is true that God's being is at stake in history until the divine victory over sin and death are complete. However, this does not imply ontological lack or deficiency in God. On the contrary, *because of* the Father's monarchy, the specific movements that characterize the lordship of God's being, both divine perfection and the real history God lives with others, the history in which the being of God is at stake, coincide. The plenitude of divine being holds both in the Godhead and in every activity of God *ad extra* insofar as the dependent monarchy of the Father is perennially realized through the Spirit driven obedience of the Son. The Son's conformity to the Father's will is perfect.[23] Accordingly, the kingdom of God is not only a future reality but is present in the trinitarian history of God with us. God establishes the divine rule among us through the trinitarian lordship of God's being.

The eternal Trinity's connection to God's living history can be expressed another way. Just as God's being has the divine lordship as its proper end, so does God's temporal activity aim at the establishment of the divine rule among us. In this way the trinitarian activity of God follows upon the eschatological contours of God's being: God's activity proceeds from the Father in the Son toward the Spirit. This three-fold activity of God results in the realization of the divine lordship. This is also to say, the triune God's activity in time pushes toward an end. In accordance with the eschatological structure of the divine relations, God acts in and with the movement of time and history (and as argued in chapter 4, transcendently *moves* it). It is important to note, however, that the realization of the divine lordship among us is not the mere repetition of God's being—though language of repetition need not be rejected. The problematic conception to avoid here is akin to what we saw in the ambiguous use of Barth's concept of an *Urgeschichte*, a primal history of God that risks overshadowing the truth of God's history with us. In contrast to this, the temporal activity of God should be understood more explicitly as the realization of the divine lordship in a *new* way. It is new insofar as God encounters and proleptically triumphs over sin

---

23. My indebtedness to Barth's doctrine of election as laid out in chapter 2 should also be noted here.

and the power of death in the cross and resurrection of Jesus. Until the end, when the power of death ceases to be, the being of God is at stake in history. The point to stress, however, is that through the monarchy of God's being God is ready for this history, the eschatological history of God with us set on the liberation of all things.

The concept of divine monarchy accents the divine fullness that is both prior to and which animates God's activity in time. I now turn to the Spirit as the bond of love. I have already shown how the Spirit enables God's revelatory history. In regards to the principle of the unity of deity and lordship, the role of the Spirit as the bond of love in God specifies that while God's being is at stake in history, the certainty of the triumph of God's lordship is still in God's hands. The Spirit as divine love is both the end of the Father-Son relation as the love that they have for one another as well as the power that mediates this relation. God's relation to the world is characterized through the ongoing unity of the Father-Son relation. Put another way, through the realization of the Father-Son relation in time the being of God is at stake in the world. However, the Spirit mediates this relation in a triumphant way. The prime example is Christ's victory over death. The Spirit maintains the Father-Son relation in Christ's cry of dereliction, in and through death, and as the power by which the Father raises Jesus from the dead. Death is assumed into the divine unity and thereby overcome in encounter with the trinitarian *life* of God. While the being of God hinges on the eschatological future, divine victory is grounded in God's triunity, specifically the mediating role of the Holy Spirit.

I have tried to show how the immanent Trinity is eschatological in light of the relational ends of the divine persons, particularly in view of the trinitarian construal of the divine monarchy and the Spirit's role in God as the divine love. It is important to state that this perspective does not exhaust an understanding of the divine relations. Nor are divine relations only eschatological. There is undoubtedly an eschatological thrust to the divine relations, or, as Barth puts it, "a direction which is *irreversible*."[24] However, just as long as the conception remains rooted in the revealed history of God, and accords with the divine movements of this history as its proceeds toward the eschatological end, we could also discern the protological reality and significance of the divine relations and show how it bears on both an understanding of the God-world relation and the meaning of faith. My concern above has been to fill out the truth of the statement that the immanent Trinity is eschatological and demonstrate the meaning of this claim for God's relation to us.

---

24. Barth, *CD* II/1:639. Emphasis mine.

In this section I have argued that the triune being of God grounds a proper understanding of God's living relation to history. The Trinity concept accomplishes this insofar as the eternal relations of God, based on the revelatory acts of God, are conceived in light of their historical ends. Likewise, a notion of the immanent Trinity as the eschatological Trinity, also founded on the revealed nature of the divine monarchy and the Spirit as the divine love of the Godhead, provides a way to understand the eschatological basis in God by which God acts among us in kind.

Conclusion

Following an overview of my assessments of Dorner, Barth, Pannenberg, and Jenson's theology in this study, I have taken up some of the remaining issues and further constructive possibilities for understanding the triune God's relation to history in this concluding chapter. To summarize: I have made the case for a conception of the eternal relations of God in view of their historical ends, a point which both avoids the idea an ulterior reality of God in a theory of divine correspondence and, more positively, that has a deeply scriptural dimension to it in view of God's eschatological ends. I also argued for a conception of the immanent Trinity along eschatological lines, specifically in terms of the Father's monarchy and the traditional notion of the Spirit as the bond of love in God, in order to conceive of the divine basis for God's self-enabled and living history. The intention behind each of these assessments and the constructive proposals of this work is the same: to demonstrate the fruitfulness of the doctrine of the Trinity for understanding the God-world relation. God is Father, Son, and Spirit; through the inherent vitality that permeates their relations the triune God acts among us as the living God.

Bibliography

Adiprasetya, Joas. *An Imaginative Glimpse: The Trinity and Multiple Religious Participations.* Eugene, OR: Pickwick, 2013.

Allen, Michael. "Divine Attributes." In *Christian Dogmatics: Reformed Theology for the Church Catholic,* edited by Michael Allen and Scott R. Swain, 57–77. Grand Rapids: Baker Academic, 2016.

Aquinas, Thomas. *Summa Theologica.* Translated by English Dominican Fathers. London: Burns, Oates & Washbourne, 1920.

Augustine. *Confessions.* Translated by Henry Chadwick. New York: Oxford University Press, 2008.

———. *De Trinitate.* Translated by Edmund Hill. Hyde Park, NY: New City, 2012.

Baker-Fletcher, Karen. *Dancing with God: The Trinity from a Womanist Perspective.* St. Louis: Chalice, 2006.

Balthasar, Hans Urs von. *Mysterium Paschale: The Mystery of Easter.* Translated by Aidan Nichols. San Francisco: Ignatius, 1990.

———. *Theo-Drama: Theological Dramatic Theory.* Vol. 4, *The Action.* Translated by Graham Harrison. San Francisco: Ignatius, 1994.

Barnett, William T. "'At Once Believing and Enlightening': The Systematic Theology of Robert W. Jenson as Dramatic Resolution to the Problem of Modernity." PhD diss., Princeton Theological Seminary, 2014.

Barth, Karl. *Church Dogmatics.* Translated by G. T. Thomson et al. Edinburgh: T. & T. Clark, 1936–77.

———. *The Epistle to the Romans.* Translated by Edwyn C. Hoskyns. 2nd ed. Oxford: Oxford University Press, 1972.

———. "Evangelical Theology in the 19th Century." In *The Humanity of God,* translated by Thomas Wieser and John Newton Thomas, 11–36. Richmond, VA: John Knox, 1960.

———. *Göttingen Dogmatics: Instruction in the Christian Religion,* Volume I. Edited by Hannelotte Reiffen. Translated by Geoffrey W. Bromiley. Grand Rapids: Eerdmans, 1990.

———. *Die Kirchliche Dogmatik.* Bände 1–13. Zürich: Evangelischer Verlag Zürich, 1938–67.

———. Preface to *La Prédestination* by Pierre Maury. Geneva: Labor et Fides, 1957.

———. *Protestant Theology in the Nineteenth Century: Its Background and History.* Translated by Brian Cozens and John Bowden. Grand Rapids: Eerdmans, 2002.

———. *Der Römerbrief.* Zürich: Evangelischer Verlag Zollikon-Zürich, 1940.

Beintker, Michael. *Die Dialektik in der 'dialektischen Theologie' Karl Barths*. Studien zur Entwicklung der Barthschen Theologie und zur Vorgeschichte der 'Kirchlichen Dogmatik.' Munich: Chr. Kaiser, 1987.

Blanco, Carlos. "God, the Future, and the *Fundamentum* of History in Wolfhart Pannenberg." *The Heythrop Journal* 54.2 (2013) 301–11.

Bloesch, Donald G. *Essentials of Evangelical Theology*. Vol. 1, *God, Authority, and Salvation*. San Francisco: Harper & Row, 1978.

Boethius. *The Consolation of Philosophy*. Edited by Douglas C. Langston. New York: Norton & Co., 2010.

Bonhoeffer, Dietrich. *Christ the Center*. Translated by Edwin H. Robertson. San Francisco: Harper & Row, 1978.

Brown, Robert W. "Schelling and Dorner on Divine Immutability." *The Journal of the American Academy of Religion* 53.2 (1985) 237–49.

Busch, Eberhard. *Karl Barth: His Life from Letters and Autobiographical Texts*. Translated by John Bowden. Philadelphia: Fortress, 1976.

Chalamet, Christophe. "God's 'Liveliness' in Robert W. Jenson's Trinitarian Thought." *Recent Developments in Trinitarian Theology: An International Symposium*. Edited by Christophe Chalamet and Marc Vial, 141–52. Minneapolis: Fortress, 2014.

Charry, Ellen T. *By the Renewing of Your Minds: The Pastoral Function of Christian Doctrine*. New York: Oxford University Press, 1997.

Clarke, W. Norris. *Explorations in Metaphysics: Being—God—Person*. Notre Dame: University of Notre Dame Press, 1994.

———. *Person and Being*. Milwaukee: Marquette University Press, 1993.

Clayton, Philip. "Being and One Theologian." *The Thomist* 52.4 (1988) 645–71.

Cone, James. *God of the Oppressed*. Rev. ed. Maryknoll, NY: Orbis, 1997.

Dempsey, Michael T., ed. *Trinity and Election in Contemporary Theology*. Grand Rapids: Eerdmans, 2011.

Dilthey, Wilhelm. *Selected Writings*. Edited and translated by H. P. Rickman. Cambridge: Cambridge University Press, 1976.

Dolezal, James E. "Trinity, Simplicity, and the Status of God's Personal Relations." *International Journal of Systematic Theology* 16.1 (2014) 79–98.

Dorner, Isaak August. *Divine Immutability: A Critical Reconsideration*. Translated by Robert R. Williams and Claude Welch Minneapolis: Fortress, 1994.

———. *History of the Development of the Doctrine of the Person of Christ*. Edinburgh: T. & T. Clark, 1880.

———. *A System of Christian Doctrine*: Volume I. Translated by Alred Cave and J. S. Banks. Edinburgh: T. & T. Clark, 1888.

———. "Über die richtige Fassung des dogmatischen Begriffs der Unveränderlichkeit Gottes, mit besonderer Beziehung auf das gegenseitige Verhältniss zwischen Gottes übergeschichtlichem und geschichtlichem Leben." In *Gesammelte Schriften aus dem Gebiet der systematischen Theologie*, 188–377. Berlin: Verlag Wilhelm Hertz, 1883.

Drewer, Matthew. "Dorner's Critique of Divine Immutability." *Process Studies* 31.1 (2002) 77–91.

Driel, Edwin Chr. van. "Karl Barth on the Eternal Existence of Jesus Christ." *Scottish Journal of Theology* 60.1 (2007) 45–61.

Eilers, Kent. *Faithful to Save: Pannenberg on God's Reconciling Action*. London: T. & T. Clark, 2011.

Flynn, Gabriel, and P. D. Murray, eds. *Ressourcement: A Movement for Renewal in Twentieth-Century Catholic Theology*. Oxford: Oxford University Press, 2011.

Ford, Lewis. "The Nature of the Power of the Future." In *The Theology of Wolfhart Pannenberg: Twelve American Critiques, with an Autobiographical Essay and Response*, edited by Carl E. Braaten and Philip Clayton, 75–94. Minneapolis: Augsburg, 1988.

Gockel, Matthias. *Barth and Schleiermacher on the Doctrine of Election: A Systematic-Theological Comparison*. Oxford: Oxford University Press, 2006.

———. "On the Way from Schleiermacher to Barth: A Critical Reappraisal of Isaak August Dorner's Essay on Divine Immutability." *Scottish Journal of Theology* 53.4 (2000) 490–510.

Green, Gene L., et al., eds. *The Trinity among the Nations: The Doctrine of God in the Majority World*. Grand Rapids: Eerdmans, 2015.

Gregory of Nyssa. *Ad Ablabium*. In *The Trinitarian Controversy*, edited and translated by William G. Rusch, 149–62. Philadelphia: Fortress, 1980.

———. *Against Eunomius*. In Vol. 5 of *The Nicene and Post-Nicene Fathers, Series 2*, edited by Phillip Schaff. Grand Rapids: Eerdmans, 1956.

Gunton, Colin E. *Becoming and Being: The Doctrine of God in Charles Hartshorne and Karl Barth*. 2nd ed. London: SCM, 2001.

Hector, Kevin W. "God's Triunity and Self-Determination: A Conversation with Karl Barth, Bruce McCormack, and Paul Molnar." *International Journal of Systematic Theology* 7.3 (2005) 246–61.

———. "Immutability, Necessity, and Triunity: Towards a Resolution of the Trinity and Election Controversy." *Scottish Journal of Theology* 65.1 (2012) 64–81.

Hegel, G. W. F. *Lectures on the Philosophy of Religion*. Edited by Peter C. Hodgson. Translated by R. F. Brown et al. Oxford: Clarendon, 2006.

Heppe, Heinrich. *Reformed Dogmatics*. Edited by Ernst Bizer. Translated by G. T. Thomson. Grand Rapids: Baker, 1978.

Hill, William J. *The Three-Personed God: The Trinity as the Mystery of Salvation*. Washington, DC: Catholic University of America Press, 1982.

Hunsinger, George. *Disruptive Grace: Studies in the Theology of Karl Barth*. Grand Rapids: Eerdmans, 2000.

———. "Election and Trinity: Twenty-Five Theses on the Theology of Karl Barth." *Modern Theology* 24.2 (2008) 179–98.

———. *How to Read Karl Barth: The Shape of His Theology*. Oxford: Oxford University Press, 1991.

———. "Karl Barth and Some Protestant Theologians." In *The Oxford Handbook of the Trinity*, edited by Gilles Emery and Matthew Levering, 292–313. Oxford: Oxford University Press, 2011.

———. *Reading Barth with Charity: A Hermeneutical Proposal*. Grand Rapids: Baker Academic, 2015.

———. "Robert Jenson's Systematic Theology: A Review Essay." *Scottish Journal of Theology* 55.2 (2002) 161–200.

Jennings, Willie James. *Acts*. Louisville: Westminster John Knox, 2017.

Jenson, Robert W. *Alpha and Omega: A Study in the Theology of Karl Barth*. New York: Thomas Nelson & Sons, 1963.

———. "Appeal to the Person of the Future." In *The Futurist Option*, by Carl E. Braaten and Robert W. Jenson, 147–58. New York: Newman, 1970.

————. "Choose Ye This Day Whom Ye Will Serve . . ." In *Essays on the Trinity*, edited by Lincoln Harvey, 14–19. Eugene, OR: Cascade, 2018.

————. *Christian Dogmatics*. Edited by Carl E. Braaten and Robert W. Jenson. 2 vols. Philadelphia: Fortress, 1984.

————. "A Christological Answer to the Radical Question." In *Lutheranism: The Theological Movement and Its Confessional Writings*, by Eric W. Gritsch and Robert W. Jenson, 36–44. Philadelphia: Fortress, 1976.

————. "Conceptus . . . De Spiritu Sancto." *Pro Ecclesia* 15.1 (2006) 100–107.

————. "Creator and Creature." *International Journal of Systematic Theology* 4.2 (2002) 216–21.

————. "Cur Deus Homo? The Election of Jesus Christ in the Theology of Karl Barth." PhD diss., Heidelberg University, 1959.

————. "Does God Have Time? The Doctrine of the Trinity and the Concept of Time in the Physical Sciences." *CTNS Bulletin* 11.1 (1991) 1–6.

————. *Ezekiel*. Brazos Theological Commentary on the Bible. Grand Rapids: Brazos, 2009.

————. *God after God: The God of the Past and the God of the Future, Seen in the Work of Karl Barth*. Indianapolis: Bobbs-Merrill, 1969.

————. "God, Space, and Architecture." In *Essays in Theology of Culture*, 9–15. Grand Rapids: Eerdmans, 1995.

————. "The Great Transformation." In *The Last Things: Biblical & Theological Perspectives on Eschatology*, 33–42. Edited by Carl E. Braaten and Robert W. Jenson. Grand Rapids, MI: Eerdmans, 2002.

————. "*Ipse Pater Non Est Impassibilis*." In *Divine Impassability and the Mystery of Human Suffering*, edited by James F. Keating and Thomas Joseph White, 117–26. Grand Rapids: Eerdmans, 2009.

————. "Jesus in the Trinity." *Pro Ecclesia* 8.3 (1999) 308–18.

————. "On the Doctrine of Atonement." *Princeton Seminary Bulletin* 27.2 (2006) 100–08.

————. *On the Inspiration of Scripture*. Delhi, NY: ALPB, 2012.

————. "Once More the Logos Asarkos." *International Journal of Systematic Theology* 13.2 (April 2011) 130–33.

————. *A Religion against Itself*. Richmond, VA: John Knox, 1967.

————. "A Reply." *Scottish Journal of Theology* 52.1 (1999) 132.

————. *Story and Promise: A Brief Theology of the Gospel about Jesus*. Philadelphia: Fortress, 1973.

————. *Systematic Theology*. Vol. 1, *The Triune God*. New York: Oxford University Press, 1997.

————. *Systematic Theology*. Vol. 2, *The Works of God*. New York: Oxford University Press, 1999.

————. "A Theological Autobiography, to Date." *Dialog* 46.1 (2007) 46–54.

————. *Theology as Revisionary Metaphysics: Essays on God and Creation*. Edited by Stephen John Wright. Eugene, OR: Cascade, 2014.

————. "Three Identities of One Action." *Scottish Journal of Theology* 28 (1975) 1–15.

————. *The Triune Identity: God according to the Gospel*. Philadelphia: Fortress, 1982.

————. "You Wonder Where the Spirit Went." *Pro Ecclesia* 2 (1993) 296–304.

Johnson, Elizabeth A. *Quest for the Living God: Mapping Frontiers in the Theology of God*. New York: Bloomsbury, 2007.

Jones, Paul Daffyd. *The Humanity of Christ: Christology in Karl Barth's Church Dogmatics*. London: T. & T. Clark, 2008.

———. "Obedience, Trinity, and Election." In *Trinity and Election in Contemporary Theology*, edited by Michael T. Dempsey, 138–61. Grand Rapids: Eerdmans, 2011.

Jüngel, Eberhard. *God's Being Is in Becoming: The Trinitarian Being of God in the Theology of Karl Barth: A Paraphrase*. Translated by John Webster. Eugene, OR: Wipf & Stock, 2004.

———. *Karl Barth: A Theological Legacy*. Translated by Garrett E. Paul. Philadelphia: Westminster, 1986.

———. "Das Sein Jesu Christi als Ereignis der Versöhnung Gottes mit einer gottlosen Welt: Die Hingabe des Gekrezigten." In *Entsprechungen: Gott—Wahrheit—Mensch*, 276–84. Munich: *Chr. Kaiser Verlag München*, 1980.

Kant, Immanuel. *The Conflict of the Faculties*. Translated by Mary J. Gregor. Lincoln: University of Nebraska Press, 1979.

Keating, James F., and Thomas Joseph White, eds. *Divine Impassability and the Mystery of Human Suffering*. Grand Rapids: Eerdmans, 2009.

Langdon, Adrian. *God the Eternal Contemporary: Trinity, Eternity, and Time in Karl Barth*. Eugene, OR: Wipf & Stock, 2012.

LaCugna, Catherine Mowry. *God for Us: The Trinity & Christian Life*. San Francisco: HarperCollins, 1991.

———. "The Relational God: Aquinas and Beyond." *Theological Studies* 46 (1984) 320–33.

Lee, Sang Eun. *Karl Barth und Isaak August Dorner: Eine Untersuchung zu Barths Rezeption der Theologie Dorners*. Frankfurt: Peter Lang GmbH, 2011.

Lee, Sang Hoon. *Trinitarian Ontology and Israel in Robert W. Jenson's Theology*. Eugene, OR: Pickwick, 2016.

Lewis, Alan E. *Between Cross and Resurrection: A Theology of Holy Saturday*. Grand Rapids: Eerdmans, 1994.

Mansini, Guy. "Can Humility and Obedience Be Trinitarian Realities?" In *Thomas Aquinas and Karl Barth*, edited by Bruce L. McCormack and Thomas Joseph White, 71–98. Grand Rapids: MI: Eerdmans, 2013.

McCormack, Bruce L. "The Actuality of God." In *Engaging the Doctrine of God: Contemporary Protestant Perspectives*, edited by Bruce L. McCormack, 185–244. Grand Rapids: Baker Academic, 2008.

———. "Grace and Being: The Role of God's Gracious Election in Karl Barth's Theological Ontology." In *The Cambridge Companion to Karl Barth*, edited by John Webster, 92–110. Cambridge: Cambridge University Press, 2000.

———. *Karl Barth's Critically Realistic Dialectical Theology: Its Genesis and Development, 1909–1936*. Oxford: Oxford University Press, 1995.

Molnar, Paul D. "Can the Electing God Be God without Us? Some Implications of Bruce McCormack's Understanding of Barth's Doctrine of Election for the Doctrine of the Trinity." *Neue Zeitschrift für systematische Theologie und Religionsphilosophie* 49.2 (2007) 199–222.

———. "Some Problems with Pannenberg's Solution to Barth's 'Faith Subjectivism.'" *Scottish Journal of Theology* 49 (1995) 315–39.

Moltmann, Jürgen. *The Crucified God: The Cross of Christ as the Foundation and Criticism of Christian Theology*. New York: Harper & Row, 1974.

————. *Theology of Hope: On the Ground and Implications of a Christian Eschatology.* New York: Harper & Row, 1965.

————. *The Trinity and the Kingdom: The Doctrine of God.* Minneapolis: Fortress, 1993.

Mostert, Christiaan. *God and the Future: Wolfhart Pannenberg's Eschatological Doctrine of God.* London: T. & T. Clark, 2002.

Murphy, Francesca Aran. *God Is Not a Story: Realism Revisited.* Oxford: Oxford University Press, 2007.

Nicol, Andrew W. *Exodus and Resurrection: The God of Israel in the Theology of Robert W. Jenson.* Minneapolis: Fortress, 2016.

Norgate, Jonathan. *Isaak A. Dorner: The Triune God and the Gospel of Salvation.* London: T. & T. Clark, 2009.

Oh, Peter S. *Karl Barth's Trinitarian Theology: A Study in Karl Barth's Analogical Use of the Trinitarian Relation.* London: T. & T. Clark, 2006.

Olson, Roger. "Trinity and Eschatology: The Historical Being of God in Jürgen Moltmann and Wolfhart Pannenberg." *Scottish Journal of Theology* 36.2 (1983) 213–27.

————. "Wolfhart Pannenberg's Doctrine of the Trinity." *Scottish Journal of Theology* 43 (1990) 175–206.

Pannenberg, Wolfhart. *The Apostle's Creed in the Light of Today's Questions.* Translated by Margaret Kohl. London: SCM, 1972.

————. "The Appropriation of the Philosophical Concept of God as a Dogmatic Problem of Early Christian Theology." In *Basic Questions in Theology: Volume 2*, translated by George H. Kehm, 119–83. Philadelphia: Fortress, 1971.

————. *Beiträge zur Systematischen Theologie, Band 1: Philosophie, Religion, Offenbarung.* Göttingen: Vandenhoeck & Ruprecht, 1999.

————. "Das christliche Gottesverständnis im Spannungsfeld seiner jüdischen und griechischen Wurzeln." In *Der christliche Glaube und seine jüdisch-griechische Herkunft.* 13–22. Hannover: EKD, 1986.

————. "Christologie und Theologie." *Kerygma und Dogma* 21 (1975) 159–75.

————. "Divine Economy and Eternal Trinity." In *The Theology of John Zizioulas*, edited by Douglas H. Knight, 79–86. Burlington, VT: Ashgate, 2007.

————. "Dogmatic Theses on the Doctrine of Revelation." In *Revelation as History*, edited by Wolfhart Pannenberg, translated by David Granskou, 91–114. London: Collier-MacMillan.

————. "Eternity, Time, and Space." *Zygon* 40.1 (2005) 97–106.

————. "Eternity, Time, and the Trinitarian God." In *Trinity, Time, and Church: A Response to the Theology of Robert W. Jenson*, edited by Colin E. Gunton, 62–70. Grand Rapids: Eerdmans, 2000.

————. "The God of Hope." In *Basic Questions in Theology: Volume 2*, translated by George H. Kehm, 234–49. Philadelphia: Fortress, 1971.

————. "Der Gott der Geschichte." *Kerygma und Dogma* 23 (1977) 76–92.

————. "The Great Transformation." In *The Last Things: Biblical & Theological Perspectives on Eschatology*, edited by Carl E. Braaten and Robert W. Jenson, 33–42. Grand Rapids: Eerdmans, 2002.

————. *Grundfragen systematischer Theologie.* Göttingen: Vandenhoeck & Ruprecht, 1967.

————. "Das Heilige in der modernen Kultur." *Fondamenti* 4 (1986) 105–23.

———. "Introduction." In *Revelation as History*, edited by Wolfhart Pannenberg, translated by David Granskou, 1–22. London: Collier-MacMillan.

———. *Jesus—God and Man*. Translated by Lewis L. Wilkins and Duane A. Priebe. 2nd ed. Philadelphia: Westminster, 1977.

———. *Metaphysics and the Idea of God*. Translated by Philip Clayton. Grand Rapids: Eerdmans, 1990.

———. "Der offenbarungstheologische Ansatz in der Trinitätslehre." In *Der lebendige Gott als Trinität: Jürgen Moltmann zum 80. Geburtstag*, edited by Michael Welker and Miroslav Volf, 13–22. Gütersloh: Gütersloher Verlagshaus, 2006.

———. "On Historical and Theological Hermeneutic." In *Basic Questions in Theology: Volume 1*, translated by George H. Kehm, 137–81. Philadelphia: Fortress, 1971.

———. *Problemgeschichte der neueren evangelischen Theologie in Deutschland*. Göttingen: Vandenhoeck & Ruprecht, 1997.

———. "Problems of a Trinitarian Doctrine of God." *Dialog* 26.4 (1987) 250–57.

———. "A Response to My American Friends." In *The Theology of Wolfhart Panneberg: Twelve American Critiques, with an Autobiographical Essay and Response*, edited by Carl E. Braaten and Philip Clayton, 313–36. Minneapolis: Augsburg, 1988.

———. "Redemptive Event and History." In *Basic Questions in Theology: Volume 1*, translated by George H. Kehm, 15–80. Philadelphia: Fortress, 1971.

———. "The Revelation of God in Jesus." In *Theology as History*, edited by James M. Robinson and John Cobb Jr., 101–34. New York: Harper & Row, 1967.

———. "Die Subjektivität Gottes und die Trinitätslehre: Ein Beitrag zur Beziehung zwischen Karl Barth und der Philosophie Hegels." *Kerygma und Dogma* 23 (1977) 25–40.

———. *Systematic Theology*. Translated by Geoffrey W. Bromiley. 3 vols. Grand Rapids: Eerdmans, 1991–98.

———. "Systematic Theology: Volumes 1 & 2." *First Things* 103 (2000) 49–53.

———. *Systematische Theologie*. 2 vols. Göttingen: Vandenhoeck & Ruprecht, 1988–91.

———. *Theology and the Kingdom of God*. Philadelphia: Westminster, 1971.

———. "Zeit und Ewigkeit in der religiösen Erfahrung Israels und des Christentums." In *Grundfragen systematischen Theologie: Gesammelte Aufsätze. Band 2*, 188–206. Göttingen: Vandenhoeck & Ruprecht, 1980.

Papanikolaou, Aristotle. "The Necessity for *Theologia*: Thinking the Immanent Trinity in Orthodox Theology." In *Recent Developments in Trinitarian Theology: An International Symposium*, edited by Christophe Chalamet and Marc Vial, 87–105. Minneapolis: Fortress, 2014.

Pasquariello, Ronald D. "Pannenberg's Philosophical Foundations." *The Journal of Religion* 56.4 (1976) 338–47.

Pérez, Ángel Cordovilla "The Trinitarian Concept of Person." In *Rethinking Trinitarian Theology: Disputed Questions and Contemporary Issues in Trinitarian Theology*, edited by Giulio Maspero and Robert J. Woźniak, 105–45. London: T. & T. Clark, 2012.

Peters, Ted. *God as Trinity: Relationality and Temporality in Divine Life*. Louisville: Westminster/John Knox, 1993.

———. "Trinity Talk: Part II." *Dialog* 26.2 (1987) 133–38.

Price, Robert R. *Letters of the Divine Word: The Perfections of God in Karl Barth's Church Dogmatics*. London: T. & T. Clark, 2011.

Rahner, Karl. "Der dreifaltige Gott als transzendeter Urgrund der Heilsgeschichte." In *Mysterium Salutis: Band 2*, edited by Johannes Feiner und Magnus Löhrer, 317–401. Einsiedeln: Benziger Verlag, 1967.

———. *Foundations of Christian Faith: An Introduction to the Idea of Christianity.* Translated by William V. Dych. New York: Crossroad, 1978.

———. *The Trinity.* Translated by Joseph Donceel. New York: Crossroad, 1997.

Rice, Scott P. "Timely, Transcendent, and Alive: Trinity in Robert W. Jenson's Understanding of the God-World Relation." *Pro Ecclesia* 28.3 (2019) 253–66.

———. "'Unchangeably Alive': Karl Barth's Trinitarian Doctrine of the Divine Constancy." *Canadian Theological Review* 4.2 (2015) 1–10.

Richards, Jay Wesley. *The Untamed God: A Philosophical Exploration of Divine Perfection, Simplicity, and Immutability.* Downers Grove, IL: InterVarsity, 2003.

Rothermundt, Jörg. *Personale Synthese: Isaak August Dorners dogmatische Methode.* Göttingen: Vandenheck & Ruprecht, 1968.

Ruschke, Werner W. *Entstehung und Ausführung der Diastasentheologie in Karl Barths Zweitem "Römerbrief."* Neukirchen-Vluyn: Neukirchener Verlag, 1987.

Russell, John M. "Impassibility and Pathos in Barth's Idea of God." *Anglican Theological Review* 70.3 (1988) 221–32.

Sanders, Fred. *The Image of the Immanent Trinity: Rahner's Rule and the Theological Interpretation of Scripture.* New York: Peter Lang, 2005.

Schlesinger, Eugene R. "Trinity, Incarnation, and Time: A Restatement of the Doctrine of God in Conversation with Robert Jenson." *Scottish Journal of Theology* 69.2 (2016) 189–203.

Schwöbel, Christoph. "The Eternity of the Triune God: Preliminary Considerations on the Relationship between the Trinity and the Time of Creation." *Modern Theology* 34 (2018) 345–55.

———. "Trinitätslehre: Eine Skizze." In *Gott im Gespräch*, 407–22. Tübingen: Mohr Siebeck, 2011.

Sherman, Robert. "Isaak August Dorner on Divine Immutability: A Missing Link between Schleiermacher and Barth." *The Journal of Religion* 77.3 (1997) 380–401.

Sonderegger, Katherine. *Systematic Theology.* Vol. 1, *The Doctrine of God.* Minneapolis: Fortress, 2015.

Štefan, Jan. "Gottes Vollkommenheiten nach KD II/1." In *Karl Barth im europäischen Zeitgeschehen (1935–50): Widerstand—Bewährung—Orientierung*, edited by Michael Beintker et al., 83–108. Zürich: Theologischer Verlag Zürich, 2010.

Sumner, Darren O. "Obedience and Subordination in Trinitarian Theology." In *Advancing Trinitarian Theology: Explorations in Constructive Dogmatics*, edited by Oliver D. Crisp and Fred Sanders, 130–46. Grand Rapids: Zondervan, 2014.

Swain, Scott R. "Divine Trinity." In *Christian Dogmatics: Reformed Theology for the Church Catholic*, edited by Michael Allen and Scott R. Swain, 78–106. Grand Rapids: Baker Academic, 2016.

———. *The God of the Gospel: Robert Jenson's Trinitarian Theology.* Downer Grove, IL: IVP Academic, 2013.

Tanner, Kathryn. *Christ the Key.* Cambridge: Cambridge University Press, 2010.

———. *God and Creation in Christian Theology: Tyranny or Empowerment?* New York: Blackwell, 1988.

———. *Jesus, Humanity, and the Trinity: A Brief Systematic Theology.* Minneapolis: Fortress, 2001.

Tavast, Timo. "The Identification of the Triune God: Robert W. Jenson's Approach to the Doctrine of the Trinity." *Dialog* 51.2 (2012) 155–63.

Taylor, Iain. *Pannenberg on the Triune God.* London: T. & T. Clark, 2007.

Thomasius, Gottfried. "Christ's Person and Work." In *God and Incarnation*, edited and translated by Claude Welch, 23–102. New York: Oxford University Press, 1965.

Tonstad, Linn. "'The Ultimate Consequence of His Self-Distinction from the Father . . . ': Difference and Hierarchy in Pannenberg's Trinity." *Neue Zeitschrift für Systematische Theologie und Religionsphilosophie* 51 (2009) 383–99.

Ware, Bruce A. "An Evangelical Reformulation of the Doctrine of the Immutability of God." *Journal of the Evangleical Theological Society* 29.4 (1986) 431–46.

Watson, Gordon. *The Trinity and Creation in Karl Barth.* Hindmarsh: ATF, 2008.

Webster, John. "Life in and of Himself: Reflections on God's Aseity." In *Engaging the Doctrine of God: Contemporary Protestant Perspectives*, edited by Bruce L. McCormack, 107–24. Grand Rapids: Baker Academic, 2008.

———. "Interpreting Barth." In *Cambridge Companion to Karl Barth*, edited by John Webster, 1–16. Cambridge: Cambridge University Press, 2000.

Weinandy, Thomas G. *Does God Suffer?* Edinburgh: T. & T. Clark, 2000.

———. "God and Human Suffering: His Act of Creation and His Acts in History." In *Divine Impassability and the Mystery of Human Suffering*, edited by James F. Keating and Thomas Joseph White, 99–116. Grand Rapids: Eerdmans, 2009.

Welch, Claude, ed. and trans. *God and Incarnation.* New York: Oxford University Press, 1965.

———. *In This Name: The Doctrine of the Trinity in Contemporary Theology.* New York: Scribner, 1952.

Wenz, Gunther. *Introduction to Wolfhart Pannenberg's Systematic Theology.* Translated by Philip Stewart. Göttingen: Vandenhoeck & Ruprecht, 2013.

White, Thomas Joseph. "Intra-Trinitarian Obedience and Nicene-Chalcedonian Christology." *Nova et Vetera* 6.2 (2008) 377–402.

———. "On Christian Philosophy and Divine Obedience: A Response to Keith L. Johnson." *Pro Ecclesia* 20 (2011) 283–89.

Wilkens, Ulrich. "The Understanding of Revelation within the History of Primitive Christianity." In *Revelation as History*, edited by Wolfhart Pannenberg, translated by David Granskout, 55–122. London: Collier-MacMillan.

Wright, Stephen John. *Dogmatics Aesthetics: A Theology of Beauty in Dialogue with Robert W. Jenson.* Minneapolis: Fortress, 2014.

———. "Introduction." In *Theology as Revisionary Metaphysics: Essays on God and Creation*, edited by Stephen John Wright, ix–xiii. Eugene, OR: Cascade, 2014.